D1809971

Post-Yugoslavia

Post-Yugoslavia

New Cultural and Political Perspectives

Edited by

Dino Abazović
Professor of the Sociology of Religion, Department of Political Science, University of Sarajevo

and

Mitja Velikonja
Professor of Cultural Studies, Faculty of Social Sciences, Department of Cultural Studies, University of Ljubljana

Selection and editorial matter © Dino Abazović and
Mitja Velikonja 2014
Remaining chapters © Respective authors 2014
Foreword © Reif Larsen 2014

All rights reserved. No reproduction, copy or transmission of this
publication may be made without written permission.

No portion of this publication may be reproduced, copied or transmitted
save with written permission or in accordance with the provisions of the
Copyright, Designs and Patents Act 1988, or under the terms of any licence
permitting limited copying issued by the Copyright Licensing Agency,
Saffron House, 6–10 Kirby Street, London EC1N 8TS.

Any person who does any unauthorized act in relation to this publication
may be liable to criminal prosecution and civil claims for damages.

The authors have asserted their rights to be identified as the authors of this work
in accordance with the Copyright, Designs and Patents Act 1988.

First published 2014 by
PALGRAVE MACMILLAN

Palgrave Macmillan in the UK is an imprint of Macmillan Publishers Limited,
registered in England, company number 785998, of Houndmills, Basingstoke,
Hampshire RG21 6XS.

Palgrave Macmillan in the US is a division of St Martin's Press LLC,
175 Fifth Avenue, New York, NY 10010.

Palgrave Macmillan is the global academic imprint of the above companies
and has companies and representatives throughout the world.

Palgrave® and Macmillan® are registered trademarks in the United States,
the United Kingdom, Europe and other countries

ISBN: 978–1–137–34613–1

This book is printed on paper suitable for recycling and made from fully
managed and sustained forest sources. Logging, pulping and manufacturing
processes are expected to conform to the environmental regulations of the
country of origin.

A catalogue record for this book is available from the British Library.

A catalog record for this book is available from the Library of Congress.

Contents

Foreword

In the spring of 2012, I had the good fortune of being the writer-in-residence at the Netherlands Institute of Advanced Study (NIAS) in Wassenaar, a leafy coastal suburb just north of The Hague. I was the only fiction writer present among forty or so social scientists and humanities scholars. I can remember feeling a bit like an odd duck as I sat down to craft my imaginary landscapes surrounded by these diligent members of the academy, guided by the strict rules of their disciplines.

The novel I was working on at the time was a large, sprawling affair that took place all across the globe, including a sizable section based in the Balkans during the 1990s war. I approached this subject matter with some trepidation, knowing that I was navigating sensitive territory, particularly as an American who did not speak any of the region's languages. I had read enough of the literature to see how the Yugoslav war and its aftermath had been sensationalized, mythologized and freighted with all kinds of political, religious and moral symbolism. Many writers, professional or otherwise, seemed intent on using the region to advanced their own polemic or agenda. Who was I to contribute to this cacophony of edification?

Upon arriving in The Netherlands I discovered that, completely by coincidence, one of the main working groups at NIAS was a collection of Balkan and Dutch scholars engaged in examining "The Real and Imagined in the Contemporary Balkans." I was elated at my good fortune but also fearful of what they would think of me. Their title struck at the heart of my dilemma as a fiction writer: I could create a 1000 imaginary Belgrades, but what about the real Belgrade? How could I ever know a city, a language, a people that were not my own? Would these scholars accept me as a legitimate co-investigator or cast me aside as the strange interloper I knew I was?

In truth, I had no reason to worry. Several members of the Balkan group immediately took me under their wing. They offered to read my book and provided me with the kind of precious insider's knowledge that writers long for – what would be eaten at this meal, for example, or various slang terms, common mannerisms and specific cultural references. I think part of our instant collegiality also arose because we were coming together in that rare and beautiful territory of the Advanced Institute. I had arrived at NIAS with the full intention to edit and cut down my book, to "kill my darlings," as it were, but the great gift of such an intellectual refuge is not just time and space, but a community of enquiry. Institutes like NIAS allow one to contemplate, to listen, to participate in a cross-pollination of ideas, and to make a host of surprise discoveries you did not think previously possible. This was made possible in part because every day our sole obligation was to attend a luncheon together. We would extricate ourselves from our little offices and come together to eat and discuss a wide range of topics, and then return to our offices with our heads abuzz. I found such conversations not just mind-expanding but book-expanding – literally. Instead of cutting away from my novel, I soon began adding (and adding).

The surreal setting of our academic sanctuary – a former nunnery set in the lush Dutch countryside – seemed particularly suited for the Balkan study group. They hosted a number of conferences, symposia and presentations around a wide range of cutting-edge topics reflected in their topics of study: Dino Abazović's political and religious reconciliation in post-war Bosnia, Mitja Velikonja's pro-Yugoslavnostalgism in popular Slovenian music, Dubravka Žarkov's representations of victimhood in current Balkan cinema, Vjekoslav Perica's transformation of the heroic figure in Post-Yugoslavia, Marlies Glasius's evolution of the ICTY as a theater of justice, and Maria Koinova's transnational self-identification in the Balkan diaspora. In a way, we NIAS-ites were like a collection of transnational (academic) immigrants. Hailing from various cultures, disciplines and locales, we came together in an artificial space of study and thrived precisely because of the distance between our location and our subject matter. Such dislocation, as it often does, provided a kind of clarity and perspective to the delicate work of measuring the gap between the real and the imagined.

In a certain sense, I realized that my situation was even stranger than the Balkan scholars, for at least they came from the place that they were studying. I, on the other hand, was performing a wobbly balancing act between my home, the Netherlands, and a Balkans of my imagination. And yet the parallax of such triangulation felt oddly appropriate for a novel which occupied many spaces – and no spaces – at once. I have always been a writer that thrives the further I get away from that which I am writing about.

The wonderfully appropriate disjuncture between place and subject came to a head for me one day in early spring while I was on a bicycle ride between Wassenaar to The Hague.[1]

I was weaving through the Dutch dunes, dodging bunny rabbits and flower beds, wondering about the transience of sea walls, when I happened upon a mythological looking castle – complete with turrets, ramparts, and a massive two-story gate. The castle managed, in that very particular Dutch way, to look both imposing and pastoral. I slowed, my skin prickling with recognition. What was this place? And then it hit me: this was Scheveningen Prison, home to some of the world's most notorious war criminals, including Radovan Karadžić and Ratko Mladić. The prison is sometimes referred to as "The Hilton Hague," a reference to its modern and generous facilities, which offer personal trainers, masseuses, and various cultural programming to the masterminds and facilitators of the worst genocide in Europe since World War II.

I stopped my bike and stared at the castle. The sun was shining. I could smell the sea. A group of blond Dutch children cycled past, laughing at some little witticism. I tried to understand what exactly it was I was looking at. How had a horrific war somehow culminated here, behind these picturesque ramparts, a stone's throw from our little academic enclave?

Indeed, I found myself wondering about the parallels between this prison and NIAS. Both were tucked away in the Dutch countryside, a thousand miles away from the Balkans, but whereas our studyship seemed to thrive from this distance, could the same be said for the theaters of justice? Did trying the criminal away from the scene of the crime offer some measure of critical objectivity? A salient shift in frame of reference?

I had a chance to witness firsthand several ICTY courtroom sessions from the ongoing trial of Radovan Karadžić. I was at first astonished, then bored, then astonished again by the theatrics of the procedurals on display, by the sheer volume of motions filed and sustained, by the disembodying effect of listening to simultaneous translation into and out of multiple languages, by the legions of grave barristers shuffling around in their robes and waterfall cravats, by the horrific, uncanny bureaucracy of it all.

When the courtroom proceedings for the day actually got going, I was made uneasy by the comfortable airs put on by Karadžić, who – sporting his trademark cockatoo coif of white hair – expertly slid into cross-examining the witness himself. Karadžić had exercised his legal right to act as his own counsel but something more sinister felt as if it was going on. As Marlies Glasius points out in this volume, the court had become a stage and the participants were actors in the drama. Karadžić was fully aware of his leading role in this drama as he began strutting and fretting about with apparent pleasure. The witness in the dock was head of an organization that supported victims of sexual violence back in Bosnia, and Karadžić began to skillfully give her the legal run-around, interrogating exactly what instances of rape she had seen herself and what she had only heard about. Such legal maneuvers happen all the time in the courtroom, but in this antiseptic forum, performed by the very man who stood accused of enabling such crimes to take place, Karadžić's actions turned the proceedings into a farce of itself. For me, the temporal and spatial disjunction between the tribunal and the Balkans contributed to a contextual dissonance. This courtroom felt very far away – too far – from the horrors of the battlefield. Was this, I wondered, really the best form of justice we could produce in the modern age? How was Karadžić allowed to extend the histrionic performance he had so adeptly put on during the war years into this hallowed arena of the international tribunal?

Such a surreal scene resonated with me particularly because my novel was concerned with the slippery challenge of differentiating between fact and fiction, especially during wartime, and the difficulties of laying down a definitive historical record of events. In her unpacking of the Dutch miniseries De Enclave, Dubravka Žarkov demonstrates how those attempting to reconcile the tension between fact and fiction via artistic avenues can often veer into the dangerous territory of moral relativism by glossing over the degree of responsibility among the guilty parties. Her warning sounded a chord in me and again raised that essential question: how do we represent and imagine the past without straying too far from the real? Was there even such a thing as the real?

Following my visit to the Karadžić trial, I felt some measure of defeat. Documentation, it seemed, would always be a political act, an act of aggression, of subversion – conscious or otherwise. Yet after reading the excellent scholarship in this volume, I've managed to return to a more optimistic outlook. Glasius's article on the evolving legitimacy of the ICTY helped me to understand that the seemingly endless slog of these tribunals need not be seen as a completely futile endeavor. Glasius cites Hannah Arendt, who called these kind of tribunals "certainly necessary but totally inadequate." One cannot disagree, particularly when faced with the absurd and ongoing stagecraft of Karadžić, but Glasius poses the question of whether the trial itself and not just the eventual and (no doubt inadequate) sentence can be seen as the essential crux of building a foundation of accountability. Perhaps, as is the case with NIAS, the distance between the ICTY's proceedings and its subject is not only helpful but necessary. Perhaps this great churning of bureaucracy – the motions, the paperwork, the disembodied translation, the clerks, the robes – perhaps these endless machinations of accounting are the best we could come up with not as a form of punishment but at least as a display of knowledge-making, however flawed in its execution. History is being recorded. Yes, it is an incomplete history at best (is there any other form of history?) and will never make up for the atrocities carried out during the war, but as Glasius points out, this act of recording slowly "shrinks the space for denial" and perhaps – just perhaps – sows the seeds for the kind of political and moral reconciliation that Dino Abazović outlines so well. To write is to know, is to click forward the dial of human wisdom.

The volume you now hold in your hands clicks forward the dial by more than a few notches. The Balkans will feel the tremors from the 1990s conflict for many years to come, but as the region takes stock of its future – of where it has been, where it is now, and where it imagines it wants to be – works like those in this book are critical to documenting the difficult path forwards. I could not be prouder to have participated in a semester of knowledge-making with these brilliant, generous (transnational) scholars.

Reif Larsen

Note

1. During my time in Holland, I became increasingly fascinated with how the Dutch view their country from the perfect vantage point of a bicycle seat. I found that many Netherlanders have a terrific sense of spatial awareness, informed in part, I think, by an inherent appreciation of how a large percentage of their small country has been reclaimed from the omnipresent sea. To reclaim is to reacquaint. I have a working theory that part of this geographical mindfulness arises precisely because the bicycle is the primary mode of travel in Holland. When you cycle though a landscape, you move through it just fast enough to achieve an overview of your progress but never lose touch with your surroundings, due to your self-propulsion and close proximity to the ground. In a way, you become a complicit cartographer. Such a metaphor can also be extended to the work of the scholar, who must balance momentum and relevance in a field with the minute, intimate work of close-reading their source material.

Acknowledgements

This edited volume is a result of a project that was carried out during the academic year 2011/2012 as part of a group fellowship awarded by the Netherlands Institute for Advanced Studies in Humanities and Social Sciences (NIAS), under the title "The Real and the Imagined in Contemporary Balkans." Working together for five months at NIAS, in Wassenaar, the Netherlands, the authors examined the contemporary political, cultural and symbolic realities and experiences in the former Yugoslav territories recovering from war and genocide, and the relationships between the actors and the dynamics from within these territories and those that link the region to the rest of the world. Not surprisingly, the Netherlands figures prominently in the book. A big part of this prominence comes from Dutch involvement in the history of the wars through which the former Yugoslavia disintegrated and the fact that the Netherlands has its place in the post-Yugoslav processes of transitional justice. But a good part of these links comes from the fact that half of our group has lived in this country and worked in Dutch academia, and that our collective residence at NIAS has also enabled us to interact with a number of Dutch scholars and institutions. We thank them all for this interaction.

Being at NIAS also meant being in a rich international intellectual community of scholars – and one exceptional writer – many of whom have shown genuine interest and enthusiasm for our work by attending our seminars, workshops, conferences and film screenings, and engaging in passionate debates. We thank them all, with special thanks to Reif Larsen for the Foreword. And we thank NIAS for the chance to meet them, and enjoy their friendship and intellectual input into our work.

We are also aware of the effect our "Balkans group" and our group work have had on our individual projects. We regularly set together to read and discuss each other's papers, and beyond that, made black humor jokes just about everything. So, saying that this book is a result of a "group fellowship" may be seen in quite a literal fashion.

Notes on Contributors

Dino Abazović is Professor of Sociology at the University of Sarajevo, Bosnia-Herzegovina. He also worked as Director of the Human Rights Center of the University of Sarajevo and as Academic Coordinator of the Religious Studies Program of the Center for Interdisciplinary Postgraduate Studies at University of Sarajevo.

Francesco Colona holds a BA in Sociology from La Sapienza, Rome and Research Master's in Social Science from the Graduate School of Social Science, University of Amsterdam. He spent three months in the Eastern Democratic Republic Congo doing research on drivers of violence against civilians. His research interests include civil war, peacekeeping and international criminal justice.

Marlies Glasius is Professor of International Relations at the Department of Politics, University of Amsterdam and holder of the Special Chair, Citizen Involvement in Conflict and Post-Conflict Zones, Free University Amsterdam. She was previously the managing editor of the *Global Civil Society Yearbook*, coordinator of the Study Group on European Security, and a lecturer in Global Politics at the London School of Economics and Political Science (LSE). She holds a PhD cum laude from the Netherlands School of Human Rights Research.

Maria Koinova is Associate Professor at Warwick University, UK and Director of the 5-year European Research Council Starting Grant Project "Diasporas and Contested Sovereignty." She obtained her PhD from the European University Institute (2005) and was awarded pre-doctoral and post-doctoral research fellowships from the Belfer Center for Science and International Affairs at Harvard (2002–2003), Cornell University (2007–2008), Dartmouth College (2008–2009), the Woodrow Wilson International Center for Scholars in Washington D.C. (2006, 2007), and Uppsala University (2013), among other institutions.

Reif Larsen is a novelist and NIAS writer-in-residence, New York, US. His first novel, *The Selected Works of T.S. Spivet*, was a *New York Times* best-seller and is currently being published in 29 countries. The novel was a 2010 Montana Honor book, a Border's Original Voices Finalist, and IndieBound Award Finalist and was short-listed for the Guardian First

Book award and the James Tait Black Memorial Prize. The novel is being adapted for the screen by French filmmaker Jean-Pierre Jeunet (Amélie). Larsen's essays and fiction have appeared in *Tin House*. He studied at Brown University, and has taught at Columbia University, where he received an M.F.A. in fiction. He is also a filmmaker and has made documentaries in the US, the UK and sub-Saharan Africa.

Vjekoslav Perica is Professor of History at the University of Rijeka. He holds a PhD in history from the University of Minnesota Twin Cities, US. In the late 1980s he was a journalist before moving to the US in 1991. As a US academic he has held Research Fellowships at the Woodrow Wilson International Center for Scholars and the United States Institute of Peace as well as lectured at universities in the US. In 2007 he was a US Fulbright scholar in Belgrade, Serbia and in 2012 was awarded a research fellowship at the Netherlands Institute for Advanced Studies in the Humanities and Social Sciences (NIAS).

Mitja Velikonja is Professor of Cultural Studies and Head of Research Centre for Cultural and Religious Studies at Faculty of Social Sciences, University of Ljubljana, Slovenia. He obtained his PhD from the University of Ljubljana in 1997 and since then he has been visiting professor at numerous universities including Jagiellonian University in Krakow and Columbia University as well as being a visiting Fulbright scholar at Rosemont College, US and at the Netherlands Institute for Advanced Study. He was awarded an Erasmus EuroMedia Award from the European Society for Education and Communication, ESEC in Vienna (2008).

Dubravka Žarkov is an Associate Professor in Gender, Conflict and Development at Institute of Social Sciences, The Hague/Erasmus University Rotterdam, the Netherlands. She teaches courses on feminist epistemology, conflict theories and media representations of war and violence. Her main fields of interest are gender, sexuality and ethnicity/national identity in the context of war and violence, with a focus on sexual violence on men, and its media representation.

Introduction

Dino Abazović and Dubravka Žarkov

As the war in the former Yugoslavia ended, one of the imperative needs of the newly created post-Yugoslav states – for quick recovery from war and a search for new beginnings – seems to have been at odds with the western countries' priorities of the delivery of transitional justice and of bringing these states into compliance with international legal and political norms. In the subsequent processes of negotiation between domestic and international forces of change, the post-Yugoslav nations have been redefining their collective identities. The "Balkans" has been, for a long time, a "symbolic continent" (Bakic-Hayden and Hayden, 1992) against which the regional and the European imaginary and self-imaginary were continuously redefined. The competing histories of wars and violence in the region have became interwoven with simultaneous post-socialist transformations, while social and cultural spaces have been redefined to incorporate issues of justice, democracy and participation beyond newly created state borders, or classical political domains.

At the same time, in the last two decades, scholarly attention to the region of the former Yugoslavia has largely been focused on the war and violence as the central political processes; nationalist institutions as the central actors; and ethnicity as the central identity. More recently, academic interests in the region have centered on institutional state-building and economic post-conflict reconstruction processes. However, scholars have paid rather minimal attention to either systematic considerations of the contemporary shifts in identities and interpretations of the past, or of perceptions of the future.

This book takes up this task, bringing together several thematically original and theoretically innovative ways of perceiving and understanding the region and its relations to the world. Accordingly, the work presented here is designed as an interdisciplinary, innovative scholarly

1

examination of the present-day identities and histories both inside and outside the region; their relationships with the social, political, cultural and historical "facts and fictions" that have marked the pre-war, war and post-war dynamics of different parts of the former Yugoslavia and their connections to the global world; and the actors and processes of transformation that are implicated in those relationships, within and beyond the region.

The individual contributions address the social, political and symbolic processes by which competing histories and identities are continuously re-imagined and reconstructed, whether in the offices of politicians, in spaces of religious worship, in the personal narratives of migrants, in ICTY courtrooms, or in sports, cinema and concert halls. The authors argue that, while nationalism is still a relevant force, other social dynamics and narratives about them – as generated by globalization and the re-shaping of Europe – also have a significant influence on individual countries, institutions and collectivities, the region as a whole, and its connections to the outside world.

The book examines the region through the prism of processes of change, rather than stasis. It affords special relevance to cultural dynamics which are most frequently ignored, regarding these as constitutive of social, political and symbolic processes of transformation. Going beyond simple dichotomies of socialism/post-socialism, war/ post-war, nationalism/anti-nationalism, religious/secular or historical facts/fabricated fictions, this book analyzes processes by which the old ideas, ideals, myths and practices are reshaped, transformed or discarded by different generations, groups or institutions, considering how the new ones are produced and what are the relationship between new and old ideals, myths and practices. Whether the authors look at the production of narratives in the ICTY courtroom, at the appropriation of the old socialist symbols in music by the young generations that never experienced socialism, or at the production of the new types of national and regional heroes that defy ethnicization of identities, they also systematically assume that the societies in the region are not just self-reflective and dynamic, but also very much part of contemporary European social, political and cultural processes.

The creation of international war crimes tribunals is part of those social-political processes that operate both internationally and nationally, albeit in unexpected ways. Hence the chapter by Marlies Glasius and Francesco Colona deals with the sociopolitical debates around the effectiveness of the ICTY in ending impunity, contributing to the maintenance of peace and strengthening the rule of law. This starts from a critical discussion of ICTY's own stated aims, and the shifting benchmarks for measuring the Tribunal's success and effectiveness: from grand aims of preserving peace to a minimal agenda of arresting war criminals, to furthering the case of establishing a permanent international criminal court, to social engineering. In all of those debates, the view of the "beneficiaries" from the region seems to have gained importance only recently. The authors interrogate the "effectiveness" debate, and offer methodological-epistemological reflections on how or whether we can possibly operationalize, measure, or even "know" about ICTY effectiveness, and then reflect on the number of the Tribunal's self-proclaimed (via its website) and assumed, "achievements": from holding leaders accountable, to bringing justice and giving voice to victims, to establishing the facts, to developing international humanitarian law and strengthening its rule, to deterrence and reconciliation. Critical analysis of each of those claims places a huge question mark behind them, especially when considering a discussion of the extent to which the ICTY has had the effect of sparking or on the contrary hindering debates about dealing with the past and justice, and a discussion of the ways in which engagement with the ICTY has been empowering or disempowering for victims. The authors finally turn to the concept of "theater" as useful for analysis of the ICTY actors and audiences, as well as the social, political and legal stage onto which they climb to act.

Be that as it may, the very recent ICTY rulings that released for insufficient evidence, and returned not guilty some of the accused – although not discussed in this volume – are a bitter reminder of how the new interpretation of international criminal justice can function to undermine justice, relevant not only for the region, but for international criminal justice systems in general.

As to the region, issues raised in the chapter by Glasius and Colona have specific pertinence for Bosnia-Herzegovina, being in a situation of facing its past with an underlying tension between the politics of denial and (non-)articulated oral histories. In scholarly works, unsurprisingly, this particular tension has been addressed under the "aegis" of transitional justice, including problems of truth seeking and truth telling, retribution and restoration, and finally, reconciliation. Therefore one of the most difficult dilemmas which the Bosnian-Herzegovinan society faces is its own past, which leads us to ask whether the issue of reconciliation – as restoration of right relationships – should "naturally" be considered as a matter of utmost relevance for the sake of its future? In his chapter, Dino Abazović argues that the problems of reconciliation in Bosnia-Herzegovina is above all issue of political reconciliation, creation of the citizen as a political subject, resistance to the continuous political appeals to the ethno-religious subject, seen in the context of the tension in society between retributive and restorative justice. The author explores the ambiguous role of specific actors and their (non-) influencing of the process of reconciliation. Two kinds of actors are deemed crucial: the ethno-political elites, and more importantly, the respective religious leaders. Their speeches and silences are analyzed from the perspective of the social-political dynamics of the production of ethno-religious identities and possibilities for alternative understandings of reconciliation.

The chapter by Mitja Velikonja also discusses alternatives, in the domain of music in Slovenia. For more than two decades after the dissolution of Yugoslavia, almost everything that relates to this former country has been perceived in negative terms in Slovenia. However, in recent years, in contemporary Slovenian pop and alternative music, we find an increasing number of motifs and narratives connected with the socialist Yugoslavia, its popular culture, way of life, political system and its leaders, as well as with the Partisan resistance, that appear to show the former country in a rather different light. Based on the analysis of about 150 songs and many more videos, CD covers, photos, interviews, outfits, stage appearances, symbols and so on,Velikonja asks whether this trend means continuity in, return to the old, or a completely new construction of the Yugoslav motifs. Velikonja argues that this new, a posteriori "Yugoslavist" discourse seems to be similar to the discourses of Balkanism and Orientalism: it is inherently ambiguous, positive and negative at the same time, and creates shifting hierarchies between "us" and "them," creating different kinds of distancing between contemporary Slovenia as a European state trying to erase its socialist past, on the one hand, and ex-Yugoslavia and the Balkans, on the other hand.

The examinations of the difficulties in the construction of nationhood which have affected the states emerging from the ruins of the former Yugoslavia is at the core of the chapter written by Vjekoslav Perica. Out of a number of possible key elements in the symbolic/mythical dimensions of the new nationhoods of the newly formed countries, Perica focuses on the construction of pantheons of national heroes. He argues that the wars of Yugoslav succession have been defamed and incriminated by international justice and further discredited by the world public opinion as senseless violence and crimes of genocide caused by an extremist ethnic nationalism. This fact renders it impossible to seek valid candidates for national heroic pantheons in the wars of the 1990s, even though nations would normally seek founding fathers and hero cults from such precisely nation-making wars. The solution has been found in creating national heroic cults through the belated recognition and exploitation of key prominent icons of popular culture (rock music, sport, film, literature and journalism, human rights and antiwar activists, etc.) from the late phase of Yugoslav socialism and the early wartime period. However, this development too engendered new contradictions and problems in the construction of the post-Yugoslav nationhood insofar as it required at least a partial rehabilitation of the former Yugoslavia. In addition, it is impossible to exclusively appropriate and ethnicize these old heroes of sports and popular culture. For they were products of the multiethnic, socialist nation, and constitute human capital generated by the revolution and the type of nationhood based on interethnic solidarity, modernization, secularism and urbanization. The new types of heroes should therefore be considered as part of a shared common heritage and thus exist in contradiction to the claims of singular ethnic-nationalist traditions.

The chapters by Velikonja and Perica are significant in breaking away from the widely accepted dominant scholarly focus on ethnicity and ethnic identities in the region, and especially from the inevitability of the links between ethnicity and violence. With a full understanding of the crucial role that those identities and their violent production have had in the war and in the foundational myths of the new nationstates, they nonetheless contend that now more than ever, ethnicity is just one of many phenomena around which identities are formed, and violence is not the main "mechanism of production."

It is indisputable that, next to the multiple local actors, international political, legal and military actors also played, and still play a crucial role in shaping the recent history of the region. To further this point, our book engages with hitherto neglected aspects of those roles, which have influenced not just the narratives about regional history, but also narratives and histories beyond the region. As the chapter by Glasius and Colona already showed, the entanglement of the ICTY with the understanding of regional and international history reaches far beyond its legal institutional role. The ICTY and the war crimes it has tried both appear as the sites of a struggle between competing narratives about historical truth and justice, and frame diasporic experiences of the Netherlands as a host country for migrants from Bosnia, as well as Dutch self-understanding as a moral nation. The last two chapters of the book address these two issues.

An emerging scholarship on diasporas, conflicts and post-conflict reconstruction has been preoccupied with the question of whether diasporas act as moderate or radical actors in world politics. On the basis of various cases, scholars have asserted that diasporas can be both radical and moderate actors, depending on factors such as the different groups and individuals within the diaspora, entrenchment of diasporic institutions, conflict phases in the original homeland and incentives from host-states, amongst other factors. In the European context, most such comparisons have been conducted across states, while intra-state comparisons are rare. Maria Koinova's chapter focuses on the intra-state dynamics, exploring how three diaspora groups, related to the wars of disintegration of the former Yugoslavia in the 1990s, are maintaining or shedding their conflict-generated identities and practices vis-à-vis the current post-conflict reconstruction processes in the Western Balkans. The Bosnian, Croatian, and Serbian diasporas residing in the Netherlands are the subject of this comparison. While literature on the migration and incorporation regimes tends to treat the host-state practices towards such migrants in monolithic terms because of its overarching policies, Koinova's account opens up the discussion by demonstrating shades in the host-state's attitudes towards different diaspora groups stemming from Dutch foreign policy and domestic political processes. The presence of the ICTY in the Netherlands, the involvement of Dutchbat within UN forces in Srebrenica and the raise of the right-wing, racist and xenophobic politics (and politicians) are the cases in point, that affect the lives of migrants from Bosnia in the Netherlands, interact with their conflict-generated identities and condition their transnational diasporic practices.

The Netherlands come into the picture also in the chapter by Dubravka Žarkov who analyzes a short, Dutch TV series *De Enclave*, about the Srebrenica genocide and its aftermath. The wars in the 1990s have generated a considerable cinematic production in the countries that once constituted Yugoslavia. Many of those films have received acclaim and attention in the region and internationally. Some feature films about the wars – and especially about Bosnia – have also been produced in countries that participated in peacekeeping interventions: from the US and Pakistan, to Spain, the UK and the Netherlands, with a mixed national and international reception. *De Enclave* received prestigious national awards but failed to become famous internationally, or to generate huge discussions nationally. Drawing on the insights of several theoretical fields (cinema studies, war studies, gender/masculinity studies) Žarkov analyzes *De Enclave* and its reception by looking at its representations of war violence and its perpetrators and victims. Alongside analyzing the TV series, the author also examines web-based debates, film reviews, and texts from the award-giving bodies (which set out the justification for awards). Her main concern is with the production of ontological un-recognizability of the Bosnian Other, in the context of Dutch internal and international political struggles with its role in the Srebrenica genocide. Denial of responsibility is taken over from the domain of politics into the domain of cinematic representations, by relativizing the distinctions between the victim and the perpetrator, and between the survivor and the politician who bears responsibility for (non-)intervention.

In addressing different political and cultural, social and symbolic dynamics in the contemporary post-Yugoslav region, the authors of this book argue for the shifting relevance of the violent past of the former Yugoslavia, suggesting that equal importance should be accorded to the present and future within the nationstates, as well as in relation to the process of European integration, identification and contestation. Furthermore, the authors argue that territories – in particular the newly established post-Yugoslav states – are far from being the ultimate boundaries of identity. Different social, cultural and symbolic boundaries are created through different types of attachments, through migration within the region and Europe, and through the impact of global legal, social and cultural processes. Sports, popular culture and the media offer new points of reference, which both transcend and reproduce national and regional identities and borders. It is this thorough examination of all these different entanglements of many social, political and symbolic relationships within the region and beyond, which makes, we hope, the most significant and innovative contribution of the book.

Reference

Bakic-Hayden, M. and R. Hayden (1992). "Orientalist Variations on the Theme 'Balkans': Symbolic Geography in Recent Yugoslav Cultural Politics", *Slavic Review*, 52 (1), 1–16.

1
The Yugoslavia Tribunal: The Moving Targets of a Legal Theatre

Marlies Glasius and Francesco Colona

In this chapter, we discuss the trajectory of the Yugoslavia Tribunal, not in terms of its legal output or even its political context, but primarily in terms of the perceptions and expectations people within or close to it, as well as academic observers, have had of it. We aim to describe what, according to different observers and participants, it was supposed to produce in terms of socio-political outcomes.

The factual story of precisely how the International Criminal Tribunal for the former Yugoslavia came to be established, and how it functioned in its first decade, has been described in great detail elsewhere (Scharf, 1997; Morris and Scharf, 1995; Bass, 2000; Hagan, 2003). For the purposes of this chapter we will focus on just a few elements of this story which we believe to be pertinent to our inquiry concerning expectations of the Tribunal.

In the first section, we discuss the conjunction of circumstances that enabled this novel institution to come into existence. We emphasize this point because twenty years on, in an international legal world populated with three ad hoc international criminal Tribunals (for Yugoslavia, Rwanda and Lebanon), two hybrid courts (Sierra Leone and Cambodia), and a permanent International Criminal Court (ICC) currently investigating in eight counties, the international criminal tribunal has come to appear as a commonplace institution, part of the international community's security toolkit.

But in 1993, with only the Nuremberg and Tokyo experiences and negotiations on a permanent court languishing in the UN for forty years, it was by no means an obvious response to war. This section attempts to reconstruct the legal-political imaginary that led the various actors to reach for an international criminal tribunal as a response to the atrocities being committed in the wars of the former Yugoslavia. The next session will discuss some of the founding expectations that people within and close to the institution had of it. The third and fourth parts will chart how these expectations began to move over time, first becoming more limited and focused on international effects, then to become broader again as well as more focused on the local situation. The fifth part will discuss the "benchmarks" by which the success of the Tribunal is nowadays commonly "measured," and its self-assessment and the assessments of academic authors in these respects. At the same time, it will begin to problematize the use of straightforward benchmarks of success.

Building on this, the conclusion will propose that the Tribunal was an uncontrolled experiment; its operational development was largely unforeseeable by the people most closely involved, and its effects even now only vaguely discernible, not measurable. In so far as the metaphor of "experiment," which runs throughout the text, holds, its inventors must be conceived as sorcerers' apprentices who did not know precisely what they were doing even in legal, let alone in socio-political, terms. It will end by proposing another metaphor, that of the theatre, to help us, with hindsight, conceptualize how an international criminal court relates to its socio-political environment.

What allowed the Tribunal to happen

The first call for a "Yugoslavia Tribunal" actually predates the wars. It came not from an international lawyer, but from a local journalist. On May 16, 1991, Mirko Klarin wrote an article in a local newspaper entitled "Nuremberg Now," in which he proposed that:

> Things being the way they are, would it not be better if our big and small leaders were made to sit in the dock instead of at the negotiating table? And if, with the help of world-famous experts in international laws of war, we had a Nuremberg Trial of our own, no matter how small and modest? Not when "this is all over" but instead of whatever might soon befall us. (Klarin, 1991)

This "preventive hybrid court" was not to be. But as soon as the war and its attendant atrocities got under way, the idea of a "Nuremberg-like" Tribunal was being widely circulated as an appropriate response. Three interrelated circumstances facilitated this mind-shift.

First, certain elements of the type of violence that occurred invited comparison to World War II and deployment of the concept of genocide. Previous post-war episodes of gross atrocities had either been perpetrated by white people against non-white people in the context of decolonization struggles (for instance in Algeria, Indonesia, Vietnam) or by and against non-white people (Cambodia, East Timor, Uganda). They took place in Asia and Africa, and often fit into Cold War schemata of communist/anticommunist struggles. The brutalities of the former Yugoslavia, perpetrated by and against white people in Europe, yet on the basis of ethnicity, more readily invited the "remedy of World War II," a Nuremberg-style Tribunal.

Second, the end of the Cold War facilitated the revival of the idea of a permanent International Criminal Court, after it had languished in the United Nations for more than four decades. In 1989, the International Law Commission had been authorized by the UN General Assembly to begin drafting a Statute. The motion had been proposed by Trinidadian Prime Minister Arthur Robinson (initially under the guise of a means to pursue drug traffickers), but drafted with the help of former Nuremberg prosecutor Ben Ferencz and Egyptian law professor Cherif Bassiouni (Glasius, 2006, 10–11).

Third, the wars of Yugoslavia coincided with revolutionary changes in the global media landscape and in the cost and availability of visual recording devices (Cushman and Mestrovic, 1996). Forced expulsion, destruction of religious sites, and mass rape in Bosnia all became known to the world very rapidly, often with graphic images attached. Both the ubiquitous availability of images of brutality and the association of a few of those images with the Holocaust contributed to a public outcry in Western Europe and the United States. As Chuter points out, while the most lethal Nazi extermination camps such as Belzec, Sobibor and Treblinka have not left us with acute visual images, "the iconography of the camp, with its photographs of skeletal survivors, is overwhelmingly from the Auschwitz model... So when the Serbs began to collect Croats and Muslims in 1992 and put them into camps a historical nerve was suddenly touched" (Chuter, 2003, 106).

In August 1992, days after footage of Omarska camp had been tele-vised, the London Conference on Yugoslavia adopted a proposal by the French and German foreign ministers to consider the creation of an ad hoc criminal court (Specific Decisions, 1992). In October 1992, a Security Council resolution authorized the establishment of a commis-sion of inquiry. However, this Commission was left with very few funds or cooperation from states, allegedly because both UN officials and the British and French governments felt that an overly zealous response to war crimes would scupper chances of a peace settlement. The first chairman resigned in protest, and the Commission was taken over by the energetic Cherif Bassiouni, who quickly found 50 volunteers and $800,000 from the Soros and the MacArthur foundations, and set up a database on violations at DePaul University in Chicago. The Commission also held on-site investigations and exhumations, and one of its members assembled a 40 strong all-female team of lawyers, mental health specialists and interpreters to interview more than 200 victims and witnesses of rape (Scharf, 1997, 44–48; Bassiouni, 1996, 61–122). Meanwhile, the Security Council adopted a resolution in February 1993 authorizing the establishment of an ad hoc Tribunal. Once authorized by the Security Council, Bassiouni's effort morphed into the evidence *and* the personnel base for the new Tribunal – although he was not allowed to be its prosecutor.

Diverse founding expectations

The Security Council Resolution bringing the ICTY into existence expressed the following expectations of the Tribunal:

> Determined to put an end to such crimes and to take effective measures to bring to justice the persons responsible for them; Convinced that in the particular circumstance of the former Yugoslavia the establishment of an international Tribunal would enable this aim to be achieved and would contribute to the restoration and maintenance of peace ... decides that an international Tribunal shall be established. (UN Security Council Resolution 808, 1993)

In other words, the Security Council deemed the Tribunal to be good for arrest and trial in itself, for particular and perhaps also "semi-general" deterrence (i.e., beyond existing perpetrators, but within the region) of war crimes, and for the advent and maintenance of peace. It could be questioned, of course, how serious and sincere the drafters of the Resolution were about these aims. On the one hand, a link with the restoration of peace (after having identified a threat to it) is more or less necessary to give the UNSC authority to take measures, on the other hand the Tribunal has been widely seen as a concession to the call to "do something" when states were not willing to engage in peace enforcement. Nonetheless, these particular aims were articulated rather than others, and should be considered as giving some guidance as to what the official founders had in mind.

With others, the establishment of the Tribunal evoked very different expectations. The Bassiouni report sought in its final report to "emphasize the high expectations of justice conveyed by the parties to the conflict, as well as by victims, intergovernmental organizations, nongovernmental organizations, the media and world public opinion" (Final Report, 320, reproduced in Bassiouni, 1996, 122). This assessment probably does reflect the expectations of NGOs, certain media, and at least some victims; although it must clearly be taken with a large grain of salt for the warring parties and intergovernmental organizations.

Judging precisely from the latter perspective, Bass concludes that the establishment of the Tribunal was "an act of tokenism by the world community, which was largely unwilling to intervene in ex-Yugoslavia but did not mind creating an institution that would give the *appearance* of moral concern... The Tribunal was built to flounder" (2000, 207).

From within, the perspective was yet different. The first President of the Tribunal, Antonio Cassese, acknowledged with a sense of understatement that "We faced quite a few problems. The most obvious were that we had no budget, and little support from states," but he "strongly opposed giving up. I argued that we could not kill what Claude Jorda from France and I often called 'une magnifique aventure morale et juridique'" (Verrijn Stuart and Simons, 2009b, 47).

While debates on the Tribunal in the US administration have been minutely registered, academic authors writing in English on the establishment of the Yugoslavia Tribunal in the 1990s pay little or no attention to its initial reception in the region. A rare exception is Dušan Cotič, a "Yugoslav" lawyer invited to provide a "local" perspective to an early edited volume (Clark and Sann, 1996). He already concludes that regional media bias as well as the early framing of the Tribunal in international media in terms of "Serb crimes" "undoubtedly rallied Serbian public opinion against the proposed court" (Cotič, 1996, 10–12).

So, on inception, the Tribunal was a magnificent adventure, officially supposed to contribute to the restoration and maintenance of peace, believed by its supporters to raise high expectations of justice, believed by others to be built to flounder, and opposed by Serbian public opinion.

Adjustment: lowering and internationalizing criteria

In the early years, the people who signed up for the legal experiment that was the Yugoslavia Tribunal (prosecutors, judges, registry) found themselves in an empty laboratory, understaffed, tinkering with basic equipment, carrying out pilot tests with the trials of some low-level thugs. They waited in vain for their vital ingredient: high-level defendants.

The experiment looked set to fail. Gary Bass follows up his above-quoted opinion that the Tribunal was built to flounder as follows:

> At first, it did not disappoint. It staggered from one crisis to another: lack of funding; lack of intelligence cooperation from the great powers; lack of staff; threats of amnesties; inability to do investigations; inability to deter war criminals. (2000, 207)

> The lack of any effort on the part of major western powers to deliver either a working budget or defendants has been well-documented (Forsythe, 1996; Bass, 2000, 206–275; Maogoto, 2004, 143–178). What has been less emphasized is how the Tribunal was kept alive by the dogged persistence of a handful of lawyers, exemplified for instance by Graham Blewitt, the acting deputy prosecutor who kept working when he failed to get paid – or supervised – for many months (Hagan, 2003, 59).

Two influential volumes of the mid-1990s (Morris and Scharf, 1995; Clark and Sann, 1996) demonstrate how after the Tribunal's shaky start, the measure of its success was largely reduced to one single question: can any big fish be caught? Peter Burns saw this as depending on political and financial support, and held that "the signs are not encouraging" (Burns, 1996, 158). David Forsythe hoped that a few convictions could be secured with procedural fairness, but the "equivalents of Goering and Eichmann, much less Hitler, will not be tried" (Forsythe, 1996, 203). Christian Tomuschat even imagined how the Tribunal might "founder, without being able to conclude proceedings in even a single case" (Tomuschat, 1996, 26). Forsythe concluded that "perhaps in an armed conflict around 2050, there might be an international war crimes tribunal that functioned better than this one" (Forsythe, 1996, 203).

With hindsight, these reflections have turned out to be too pessimistic. The Tribunal's low point was the "hear no evil, see no evil" attitude that marked both the Dayton agreement itself and the troop deployment in its aftermath. As has been described elsewhere, the tide began to turn in mid-1997 and both the Tribunal's budget and its access to suspects gradually began to improve (Bass, 2000; Maogoto, 2004). The Tribunal's "teeth" became undeniable with the transfer of Slobodan Milošević. Those of the big fish that did not cheat the Tribunal by death (see below) were eventually all brought to The Hague.

But what is more striking than the pessimism of the pronouncements cited above, is what they held to be at stake with the successful catching of Yugoslav suspects. Morris and Scharf, both intimately involved in the foundation of the Tribunal from within the United Nations and the US State Department respectively, argued in 1995 that its success ought to be measured in terms of three questions: Will it be procedurally fair? Will it be effective in bringing perpetrators to justice? And finally, will it pave the way for other tribunals, or impede them? (1995, 331). They concluded by discussing seven other situations in the world to which, if the Yugoslavia Tribunal were to become at least a qualified success, the "Tribunal solution" could be applied. Tomuschat also cast his fear of the failure of the Tribunal in the light of the negotiations for a permanent court: "a most unfortunate precedent may be set. In particular, it would become almost impossible, and in any event useless, to pursue further the efforts ... toward creating a treaty-based international criminal court" (Tomuschat, 1996, 26). Burns did believe at the time of writing that the Tribunal might become a "prototype" for a permanent court (Burns, 1996, 164); Forsythe on the contrary held that such a court was impossible for the same reason the Yugoslavia Tribunal was failing: lack of political will (Forsythe, 1996, 203). But they all used the same benchmark for success: furthering the development of international law in the form of more tribunals. On the judges' bench, the view of the ultimate purpose of the Yugoslavia Tribunal appears to have been the same. Judge Cassese articulated his refusal to give up his legal and moral adventure by explaining "I said if we go home now, then we will never establish this precedent, and we will never know if we can apply international criminal justice ... we could not fail, because through us, the whole international community would fail. I strongly felt that our failure would also mark the end of any international criminal justice." (Verrijn Stuart and Simons, 2009b, 47–48).

The effects of the Tribunal *on and in the region*, including in the terms of the Security Council resolution, deterrence and restoration and maintenance of peace, faded into the background at this point. The manifest failure of deterrence receives cursory attention in some of these discussions; what ordinary people in the warring territories know about or make of the Tribunal, none at all. Later findings, to be discussed below, that the record of the Tribunal has been deeply problematic in terms of its reception and effects in the region, should be considered in this light: if the international legal community was not casting its expectations of the Tribunal in terms of benefits to the region, the failure of such benefits to materialize becomes less surprising.

Adjustment: widening and localizing criteria

In the latter half of 1997, 14 new arrests were made, bringing the number of suspects up to 22, and going up to the chain of command (Maogoto,

2004, 160). Now that suspects were in place, the legal machinery kicked into action. Now that the wars appeared to be over (in reality, Kosovo was yet to come), the successor states were primarily perceived by the Tribunal as a simultaneous source of, and obstacle to, the vital ingredients: suspects and witnesses. As international troops and successor states changed their attitude regarding the apprehension of suspects, views on what would constitute a successful Tribunal also began to shift: from "the Tribunal must have some high-level defendants" to "it must have Tudjman and Milošević in The Hague" to "it won't be enough while Karadžić and Mladić are at large" to a different set of criteria altogether.

As the Tribunal became more seriously engaged in the business of arresting and putting on trial important players in the Yugoslav wars, and as Bosnia in particular was NGO-ized in the aftermath of Dayton, international voices began to pay attention to local views. Thus, Coliver, who spent the years 1996–1998 in Bosnia writes that '(m)ost Croats and Serbs viewed the Tribunal as utterly biased against their communities," and that "large segments of the Bosniak community were disappointed" in the Tribunal in 1997, and that these sentiments only grew in 1998 (Coliver, 2000 20–21). These refrains have continued to be heard over the next decade and a half. She also calls for outreach activities, and for translation of relevant documents in local languages, neither of which had happened at that time. (Coliver, 2000, 28–29). A decade later, outreach activities were still found to be woefully inadequate (Clark, 2009b; Orentlicher, 2010).

The academic literature also becomes more reflective, and begins to widen the scope of criteria by which the Tribunal should be judged. In 2000, Gary Bass published *Stay the Hand of Vengeance*, one of the first full-length studies of international criminal justice, approaching the topic from a more philosophical perspective. He argues that "the Nuremberg experience suggests war crimes Tribunals are not a quick fix, but part of a much more ambitious and time-consuming project of social engineering" (Bass, 2000, 296). He then proceeds to critically assess the record of international criminal tribunals, including the Yugoslavia Tribunal, against what he claims are the five main liberal arguments in their favor: purging threatening leaders; deterring war criminals; rehabilitating renegade states; putting the blame on individuals, not ethnic groups; and establishing the truth (Bass, 2000, 287–304). Whilst casting doubts on all these, he ends up defending the Tribunal experience on the basis of moral rightness, and on an argument – as contestable as the "liberal claims" he challenges – that it mitigates impulses to take revenge.

When Slobodan Milošević is finally brought to trial, august critical legal scholar Marti Koskenniemi publishes a long article discussing the

Milošević case (Koskenniemi, 2002). He critically compares it to the Nazi trials of Eichmann, Papon, Touvier and Barbie. His argument is that in such political cases, motives beyond establishing guilt or innocence in the particular case, such as healing traumatized societies, deterrence, didactic purposes, or establishing a record of historical truth and contributing to the constitution of a collective memory are not only difficult or impossible to meet, they may actually interfere with the fairness of the trial (Koskenniemi, 2002).

Subsequently, well-known American criminologist John Hagan began what came to be a decade-long research interest in the Tribunal with a book on its inner workings and tensions (Hagan, 2003). He points at the engagement with victims as an important driver of the "sense of purpose" of the Tribunal's staff, but – unlike in his later work on the Tribunal – he does so from the inside out, relating the staff's vision of what they are doing for victims, rather than the victims' own perceptions. In the final chapter the book widens out to consider the realpolitikal landscape in which the Tribunal operates, and speculates how international criminal justice in its ICC form, "without the Americans," will develop.

The current benchmarks

Ten years later again, the Tribunal is now approaching the end of its mission. Above, we discussed how the goal posts for assessing "success" or "effectiveness" of the Tribunal shifted over time from being diverse and nebulous, to a minimal focus on arrests and on somehow furthering the establishment of a permanent international criminal court, to a wider, political-theoretical assessment against various "social engineering" purposes. We will now discuss the most common criteria it is currently being assessed on, how it assesses itself against these criteria, and what the academic literature makes of them.

We make use here of a relatively new development since the middle of the last decade, which reflects yet another shift in the focus of academic interest: the publication of a plethora of empirical studies, in English, focusing on perceptions and effects of the Tribunal in the region. We take as our point of departure the six "achievements" the Tribunal lists on its own website, and add to these two other oft-discussed aims: deterrence and reconciliation.

Holding leaders accountable

"Holding leaders accountable" is the first of the list of "achievements" the Tribunal displays on its website. On July 20, 2011, the Tribunal took custody of the last of its indictees: Goran Hadžić. All living indictees have now been tried or otherwise "processed." Given the Tribunal's shaky start, this is an achievement worth acknowledging. Nonetheless one may wonder whether, with the shift to a focus on "leaders," the Tribunal has fulfilled its UN mandate to "bring to justice *the* persons responsible for them." (italics mine) According to a strict reading of the Security Council Resolution, everyone who committed a crime should be held accountable. The 161 accused by the Court constitute far from the totality of the offenders. It is contested even whether it includes all of those most responsible at the highest level: Ramet (2012, 5) lists six top-level politicians and military men who escaped indictment, including most egregiously Borisav Jović, who clearly incriminated himself in his memoirs.

Moreover, important indictees have "cheated the Tribunal by death" in many different ways. Some, including Tudjman and Izetbegovic, died of natural causes before the political climate had shifted enough to facilitate their arrest. Others, including most famously Milošević, but also Kovačević and suicide Milan Babić, died during trial. Still others died while resisting arrest (Drljača) or were assassinated so as not to incriminate others (Ražnatovic aka Arkan). While it does not seem entirely rational to rate these untimely deaths, natural or otherwise, as mitigating the Tribunal's success at holding leaders accountable, it is nevertheless sometimes perceived as such in the region.

Thirdly, some of the most recent verdicts, including the case of Haradinaj and the appeal verdicts of Gotovina and Perišić, raise the question whether a leader tried and acquitted has been held accountable. Populations affected by the crimes these three leaders had been charged with are largely convinced of their moral and political guilt. But the causal link between violent acts on the ground and high level defendants is often difficult to prove. Liberal trials depend on the idea that when the evidence is insufficient, a not guilty verdict must be returned, otherwise they are just show trials. But the not guilty verdicts are difficult to explain to those most affected, and typically interfere with some of the social aims of international criminal justice. The letter by Judge Harhoff which became public in the summer of 2013, accusing a fellow judge of politically motivated acquittals, while not backed up by evidence nor taken very seriously by fellow lawyers, further interferes with the perception of accountability. Finally, there has been the questionable practice of plea-bargaining, most famously epitomized by the insincere confession and early release of Biljana Plavšić (Subotić, 2012).

But even if we focus on those accused who were found guilty and sentenced, we must ask what "holding someone accountable" actually means in this context. The Tribunal and most of the literature appears to take accountability to refer to punishment: "the Tribunal has dismantled the tradition of impunity for war crimes," it says on its website. In Bosnia, however, the Tribunal is often accused of meting out sentences too mild in comparison to the gravity and atrocity the indictees committed. Ivković and Hagan note how their interviewees in Sarajevo were urging the judges to "please go ahead and not feel sorry for the criminals, especially because of the example it sets for many nationalists in the former Yugoslavia and across the world. Be harsher in sentencing!" (2006, 394).

Beyond relative severity, however, crimes against humanity inevitably raise the issue pointed out by Hannah Arendt in relation to the trial of Hermann Goering that punishment is "certainly necessary but totally inadequate" (quoted in Koskenniemi, 2002, 2). In the eyes of those, like Ivković and Hagan's interviewees, who went through the war and lost people, the liberal retributive justice of the Tribunal may indeed be experienced as an inadequate degree of being held accountable.

Another interpretation of accountability is to focus less on punishment and more on the trial itself. According to the Oxford American Dictionaries, someone is accountable when "required or expected to justify actions or decisions." Indeed, war crimes trials could be seen as one long interrogation of the accused about the nature of their decisions and actions. However, this public reckoning purpose is disrupted precisely when defendants begin to "justify" themselves on criteria that differ from the standards applied by the Tribunal (see Meijers and Glasius, 2013, on the problem of charismatic defendants like Karadžić).

Connected to this, a final aspect of accountability is the often expressed aspiration of international criminal justice to "individualise guilt" (see for instance Amann, 2000, 2003; Drumbl, 2007), so as to rewrite war history from a Schmittian account of group enmity into a Kantian account of individual wrong. It is questionable whether this is a tenable approach to mass atrocities from a historical perspective (see also Subotić, 2012), and whether the implicit exculpation of everyone who was not indicted is "just." Beyond this, it is doubtful whether and in whose eyes the Tribunal has succeeded in individualizing guilt. Many of the top defendants built their defense entirely around the opposite position: that they acted solely as representatives of their nation. The extensive recent empirical literature suggests that many people in the region follow the defendants in interpreting guilt and innocence in collective terms. Serbs complain about the predominance of Serbians prosecuted (Clark, 2012); Croats freely claim that "nobody has been prosecuted in The Hague for the various crimes, including rape, torture and murder, committed in [some] Serb-run camps" (Clark, 2012, 407), and complain about the release of military leaders that committed crimes against Croats (Clark, 2012, 408); and Bosniaks "could not understand, and still cannot understand, how their soldiers and officers could be accused of war crimes, because they believe that their nation was the victim of genocide perpetrated by Serb and Croat forces" (Saxon, 2005, 563–564).

Bringing justice to the victims

The Tribunal claims two achievements relating to victims: "bringing justice to victims" and "giving victims a voice." In relation to the first, it claims that "(b)y holding senior individuals responsible for the crimes committed in the former Yugoslavia, the Tribunal is ensuring that the victims can see that the individuals who are responsible for their suffering are convicted by an international criminal court and sent to prison." For the Tribunal, then, trial and punishment equals bringing justice to victims, so that this achievement is actually none other than the previous. This equation has been challenged by academics and by the victims themselves.

Clark challenges the argument of Antonio Cassese, who purports that "justice dissipates the call for revenge, because when the Court metes out to the perpetrator his just desserts, then the victims' calls for retribution are met" (Cassese, 1998b). In Clark's opinion, "[f]rom the perspective of victims, their calls for retribution are not being adequately met and war criminals are not being given their just deserts" (Clark, 2009b, 471). And as suggested above, it is even less possible to imagine that victims would consider the release of defendants against whom the judges found that there was insufficient evidence as "just deserts." Finally, Stover describes how Srebrenica survivors in particular, have often rejected any justice from a "UN court" because the UN was the very organization that failed to save their loved ones (Stover, 2007, x–xi).

Naturally, one cannot generalize, and some victims may have felt the trials to be a form of justice. Their feelings about what constitutes justice may also change over time, and the passage of very much time between crime and punishment has been a feature of the Tribunal. But it must be recognized that Koskenniemi's view appears to be closer to the experience of most victims than Cassese's:

> When trials are conducted by a foreign prosecutor, and before foreign judges, no moral community is being affirmed beyond the self-congratulatory "international community." Every failure to prosecute

is a scandal, every judgement too little to restore the dignity of the victims, and no symbolism persuasive enough to justify the drawing of the thick line between the past and the future (Koskenniemi, 2002, 11).

Giving victims a voice

The Tribunal sees itself as having given voice to victims, since it "has provided thousands of victims the opportunity to be heard and to speak about their suffering... As of early 2011, more than 4,000 witnesses had told their stories in court." Technically speaking, these voices have indeed been heard, and recorded in court transcripts.

According to Eric Stover, who interviewed 87 witnesses before the Tribunal, some victims are well aware of and entirely comfortable with the nature of the "voice" they are given: they have a compelling need to tell their story, and see themselves as making a deal whereby they give the Tribunal factual truths, and the Tribunal helps them give meaning to what has happened. Their actual experience of witnessing varies tremendously. One of the Stover's interviewees reports: "(p)ower flowed back from the accused to me," while another felt "profoundly humili- ated" (Stover, 2007, 71). Stover concludes that witnessing has both good and ill effects, and much depends on the manner in which the witness is both prepared and debriefed, and subsequently followed up after return. He reflects a very mixed Tribunal record in this respect: while the Victims and Witnesses Unit acted very professionally, the more important conduct of the prosecution varied from careful preparation, debriefing and staying in touch to lack of preparation and subsequent neglect of vulnerable witnesses.

Even if the Tribunal had consistently acted according to best practices, and victims had overwhelmingly enjoyed the witness box experience, we may question whether this constitutes "giving victims a voice." The hearing of witnesses in a trial is not done in order to give them a voice, it is a means to an end: getting the defendant convicted or released. Hence, only those victims who are both useful to the prosecution or defense and willing to testify have a voice, and they may only talk about that which is deemed legally relevant.

Establishing the facts

The next achievement the Tribunal puts forward is to have established the facts. It says: "[t]he Tribunal has established beyond a reasonable doubt crucial facts related to crimes committed in the former Yugoslavia." It also highlights how its work is creating a historical record that contributes to combating denial and preventing attempts of revisionism. Building a historical record has long been part of what the court sees itself as doing. Even in 1998 presiding judge Cassese wrote: "[t]he proceedings of an international criminal tribunal build an impartial and objective record of events" (Cassese, 1998b). However, the Tribunal's webpage does not extensively argue how trial proceedings establish a historical record. It lists a series of "facts" instead. It seems that through this list the facts are established – in the Tribunal's own eyes – beyond a reasonable doubt. Scholars have to some extent affirmed the Tribunal's self-assessment regarding the establishment of a historical record (Wilson, 2011; Armatta, 2012).

But this begs the question: beyond whose reasonable doubt? The protagonists of the facts themselves have challenged the facts the Tribunal establishes, in court and out of it, day in, day out. Facts that may be beyond the reasonable doubt of the judges may be considered very doubtful by people in the region. There are strong variations in the approval ratings of the Tribunal between successor states, between ethnic groups, and over time (see for instance, Ivković and Hagan, 2006; Klarin, 2009; Ivković and Hagan, 2013). Nonetheless, reading the work of Clark (2012), Orentlicher (2010), Rangelov (2006), Spoerri and Freyberg-Inan (2008), and Saxon (2005), among many others, the consistency with which people of all ethnic groups consider the Court as biased against their own group is striking.

Clark criticizes the claim that a historical record is being built from a different perspective, related to the focus on leaders discussed above: "[i]f only a tiny percentage of potential war criminals are brought to justice, this will create an incomplete record of guilt and responsibility that will always be open to abuse and manipulation" (Clark, 2009b, 473). Indeed, a *full* historic record could only begin to be served by an initiative such as the RECOM, which proposes a regional truth commission.

Nonetheless, Diane Orentlicher has in her report *Shrinking the Space for Denial: the Impact of ICTY in Serbia* (2008) put forward the argument that the work of the Tribunal is shrinking the "historic" and public space that could be used for denial or revisionism. At the same time she acknowledges that "public opinion polls undertaken in recent years suggest that most Serbian citizens either have not yet been persuaded that Serbs committed a majority of war crimes during the 1990s conflicts or are unwilling to acknowledge what they know" (Orentlicher, 2008, 86). Lara Nettelfield makes a similar claim about the impact of the Ćelebići trial in Bosnia: whilst there continues to be some contestation, it has created an important new master-narrative (2010, 200–202.) The shrinking of the space for denial in turn manifests itself again in the trial chamber: defendant Radovan Karadžić, whilst trying to argue that some or all of the Srebrenica victims were in fact fighters, no longer literally denies that the massacres took place (Meijers and Glasius, 2013).

One very particular form of establishing the facts that the Tribunal can justifiably claim is in the cases of missing persons, where their fate has been revealed by indictees, usually after a guilty plea. For instance, as cited from a court transcript on the Tribunal's website, Dragan Nikolić helped localize a mother's two sons in a mass grave in Debelo Brdo: "And it was in this group of people that Enis and Bernis, this lady's sons, were. I knew them well. And from what I heard, they were liquidated – they were liquidated on that site…And if I remember her sons well, one of her sons was wearing a denim jacket and trousers. And should there be an exhumation, perhaps he could be recognized by his clothes. And if an exhumation takes place, I believe that's where her sons would be found." However, it is again problematic to claim this as a primary benefit of the Tribunal. Just as a truth committee would better serve the compilation of a more complete record, the International Commission for Missing Persons (ICMP) and other initiatives are more appropriate for identifying the missing.

Perhaps the most profound problem with the Tribunal's claim to establishing the facts has been identified by Koskenniemi. It is not just that the people in the region do not (yet, fully) believe the judges' version of the facts, but that the Tribunal itself, whilst pretending to stand outside history, is inevitably part of it, and that defendants like Milošević will not fail to contest it on this terrain: "The engagement of a court with 'truth' and 'memory' is thus always an engagement with political antagonism, and nowhere more so than in dealing with events of wide-ranging international and moral significance…This is not a disinterested enquiry by a group of external observers but part of the history it seeks to interpret" (Koskenniemi, 2002, 25).

While Koskenniemi fails to spell out exactly how the Yugoslavia Tribunal is part of the history it seeks to interpret, focusing instead on historical analogies like the Eichmann, Touvier and Papon trials, it is easy to fill in the blanks. In Bosnia in particular, the Yugoslavia Tribunal after Dayton could be seen, as one commentator had it, as a "kind of Nuremberg experience after Poland and half of the Ukraine had been ceded to the Nazis." The Tribunal cannot escape from having been set up instead of an intervention that could have prevented or halted ethnic cleansing.

The prosecutor's handling of the war in Kosovo draws the Tribunal even more directly "into history," casting doubt on its carefully cultivated image of evenhandedness. While before it could point at the mix of indictments to substantiate its claim that "all sides must face justice for war crimes," afterwards even its cosmopolitan supporters must acknowledge that it is all sides but one: alleged crimes associated with NATO activities are not to be investigated.

A final consideration regarding the Tribunal's capability to "establish the facts" concerns the time frame. Short-term popularity polls may not be a good guide to the long-term cognitive impact of a Tribunal. German approval ratings of Nuremberg went from 78 percent in 1946 to 38 percent four years later to just 10 percent by 1952 (Koskenniemi, 2002, 5–6). Nonetheless, and despite their focus on aggression more than genocide, within a larger time frame they are typically perceived as a resounding success in terms of establishing the facts of the Holocaust, both with Germans and with the world at large (Karstedt, 1998; Bass, 2000, 296). With sufficient hindsight, we are capable of judging Nuremberg as simultaneously an instance of victor's justice and an excellent first stab at establishing a historical record.

Developing international law

As seen above, in the early years of the Tribunal, academics saw the institution largely in terms of its ability to further international criminal law, in the form of more tribunals as well as a permanent international criminal court. The existence of the Tribunal, and more specifically the presence of its prosecutors at the ICC negotiations, did indeed strengthen the case for an ICC (Glasius, 2006, 51–53). And in cases where there was a political obstacle to ICC involvement, such as Cambodia or Sierra Leone, the idea of an ad hoc tribunal became a normal tool for the international community where before the Yugoslavia Tribunal it would not have been considered.

So the Tribunal justifiably lists as an achievement that "[s]ince its establishment more than a decade ago, the Tribunal has consistently and systematically developed international humanitarian law. The Tribunal's work and achievements have inspired the creation of other international criminal courts, including the International Criminal Tribunal for Rwanda, the Special Court for Sierra Leone and the International Criminal Court" as well as developing the substantive and procedural law for these other courts.

Strangely, this achievement appears to be largely overlooked in the more recent academic literature, which with the normalization of international criminal justice, has also instituted a normalization of criticizing international criminal justice. This may be because it is simply beyond us to compare our current dispensation to an alternative version of history, in which international criminal courts would not have come into existence.

Strengthening the rule of law

In the Tribunal's output-oriented description of its achievement in terms of "strengthening the rule of law," the website reports that "[t]he Tribunal has encouraged judiciaries in the former Yugoslavia to reform and to continue its work of trying those responsible for war crimes committed there during the 1990s. The Tribunal works in partnership with domestic courts in the region – transferring its evidence, knowledge and jurisprudence." Furthermore it highlights how the Tribunal "has also served as an incentive to authorities in the former Yugoslavia to reform their judiciaries, and has been a catalyst for the creation of specialised war crimes courts."

Most of the academic literature concerned with the state of the rule of law in the region, and the Tribunal's possible impact on it, focuses on Bosnia and Serbia. It diverges widely in its opinions. Orentlicher suggests that "[t]he Tribunal has played a distinctive role in spurring and shaping a major transition within Bosnia's domestic system for prosecuting wartime atrocities" and that the fact that "an effective war crimes process was established in Bosnia also ranks among the ICTY's most important legacies" in the strengthening of the local institution (Orentlicher, 2010, 107). She notes that the OSCE has, as a result, gone from seriously doubting whether the judicial system in Bosnia was in compliance with the rule of law (Orentlicher, 2010, 109) to judging it as having delivered "efficient, fair, and human rights compliant proceedings" (OSCE, 2011, 7).

Nettelfield finds that the Tribunal has not only spurred local trials, but also provided a base of evidence for associations of survivors to pursue justice elsewhere: thus the Tribunal's jurisprudence has facilitated civil suits by Srebrenica survivors against the Netherlands. She also finds that war veterans believed trials to be the best way of dealing with crimes committed during the Bosnian war, and most would like to see more local trials (Nettelfield, 2010, 232).

When it comes to the population's trust in the judiciary, Ivkovich and Hagan argue that, as support for the Tribunal declined, support for local trials improved: "Sarajevans became less concerned that their local judges might be politically biased" (Ivković and Hagan, 2006, 402). Moreover, "[j]ust more than half of the Serbs living in Sarajevo and more than half of the Croats living in Sarajevo and Vukovar approve of trying cases in these jurisdictions." However, "in sharp contrast, more than a two-thirds majority of the Serbs (68.5 percent) interviewed in Belgrade believed that the appropriate jurisdiction was in the local courts of the offender's country" (ibid.). Moreover, a recent UNDP Special Report gives a different perspective on Bosnian perceptions of their local courts more generally. The report opens by saying that "[t]he lack of confidence in the judiciary in BiH is a common determinant that permeates throughout this report" (UNDP, 2011, 10).

Spoerri and Freyberg-Inan, in a study of Serbia, are even more skeptical, finding that "negative perceptions of the Tribunal are associated with shifts in the domestic balance of power away from 'pro-reform' and toward 'anti-reform' forces" (2008, 351) and that "the ICTY's discursive linkage not to norms of reconciliation and justice but, rather, to the experience of conditionality and the threat of international isolation provides the permissive contextual backdrop to these power shifts" (Spoerri and Freyberg-Inan, 351). Far from considering the Tribunal to have strengthened the rule of law, they hold that "in conjunction with their instrumentalization in domestic politics, [the Tribunal] might have made an already tenuous transition even more difficult" (355), or in any case "that perceptions of the ICTY have probably intensified the trends that keep Serbia's democratic trajectory precarious to this day" (Spoerri and Freyberg-Inan, 355).

In sum, there has been a discernible influence of the Tribunal on the development of national transitional justice institutions in the form of domestic war crimes trials, but to frame this as a contribution to "strengthening the rule of law" is too big and nebulous a claim to lend itself to substantiation, and is deeply contested.

Deterrence

As seen above, deterrence was one of the ostensible aims of the Security Council in setting up the Tribunal. Strangely enough, while the more general emerging literature on international criminal justice likes to speculate about its deterrent effect, the literature focusing on the region has little to say about it.

In terms of its short-term record, the conclusion can only be that the Tribunal has spectacularly failed to deter. At the margin, the Tribunal's existence may have mitigated some war crimes. According to American diplomat Galbraith and prosecutor Goldstone, for instance, Croat leaders in Bosnia and the Krajina respectively were somewhat cowed by the idea of prosecution for war crimes, and modified their behavior accordingly (Bass, 2000, 294). But the worst atrocity of the Bosnian war, the Srebrenica massacre, occurred after the Tribunal had become operational, and the war in Kosovo took place at a time when the Tribunal already had dozens of suspects in custody. For whatever reasons, fear of prosecution was neither preventing war nor deterring the commission of war crimes.

Reflections about long-term deterrent effects are necessarily speculative. As seen above, judge Cassese believes that trials deter fresh violence because they mitigate victims' thirst for revenge; Gary Bass also holds this to be one of the few saving graces of trial justice (Bass, 2000, 304–310). Nuremberg prosecutor Ben Ferencz constructs the connection between trials and deterrence in a different way: "[y]ou can only point to the horrors of this type of criminal behavior and where it leads. You can hope that by showing the suffering, there will be some deterrent effect" (Verrijn Stuart and Simons,, 2009a, 28). Koskenniemi on the other hand holds that "fitting crimes against humanity or other massive human rights violations into the deterrence frame requires some rather implausible psychological generalisations" (2002, 8), and Amann has it that "the numbers are too small to make a rational wrong-doer hesitate" (2000, 174).

These speculations notwithstanding, the question of long-term deterrence in the region and beyond, remains evidently unanswerable. We now live in a world where the possibility of being tried for war crimes and crimes against humanity will be increasingly known to potential perpetrators, although the chances of actually being caught remain slim. Whether and to what extent this deters remains almost impossible to determine.

Reconciliation

Antonio Cassese has consistently claimed that the activities of the Tribunal foster reconciliation: "[t]he role of the Tribunal cannot be overemphasized. Far from being a vehicle for revenge, it is a tool for promoting reconciliation and restoring true peace" (ICTY, 1994, §16).

The empirical literature tends to disagree with Cassese's view. Clark for instance links it to the "establishment of the facts": "[t]he crucial point is that the truth cannot have a positive effect unless it is acknowledged. A truth which is contested will promote divisions and antagonism rather than reconciliation and healing" (2009a, 426). Amann, while much more favorably disposed towards the truth-telling function of the Tribunal, nonetheless finds Cassese's claim regarding reconciliation "somewhat breathtaking" (2000, 175).

An exception to the generally skeptical literature on reconciliation is Sandra Coliver, writing in 2000, who discerns three "processes of reconciliation" to which she sees the Tribunal contributing: the neutral-ization of war criminals in local politics, the return of refugees, and the compilation of a historical record (Coliver, 2000 26–27). This highly creative interpretation of what constitutes reconciliation, and how the Tribunal contributes to it, calls to mind Clark's observation that "[t]here is a vast literature on reconciliation, but very little consensus on how to define the concept" (2009a, 421, note 32). According to a maximal interpretation, insisting that victims throughout the regions have forgiven perpetrators and general populations have acknowledged wrongdoing, the region, and the Tribunal's role in it, falls woefully short. A minimal conception on the other hand could interpret the fact that severe inter-ethnic violence has been rare in the region over the last decade – with the 2004 riots in Mitrovice as the main exception – as a sign of "reconciliation."

Conclusion

Our intent in the review above has not been to echo the chorus of literature that criticizes the Tribunal for its failure to meet a number of ambitious socio-political "targets," although we do hold at least some of these criticisms to be well-deserved. Rather, we have tried to show, first, that the Tribunal started its work without there being a clear consensus on what, sociologically speaking, its aims were, and second, that many of the "benchmarks" that have subsequently emerged fall into the realms of the immeasurable, for three general reasons that we will summarize below.

First, as Gary Bass has it, to the question "(d)o war crimes Tribunals work? The only serious answer is: compared to what?" (2000, 310). We cannot systematically observe non-crimes, nor can we systematically compare the severity of crimes committed against the backdrop of a past or present Tribunal to crimes committed in its absence. Moreover, there has not been and there cannot be a "control group" that went through the Yugoslav wars without the experience of a Tribunal, to which we could compare post-conflict processes of justice to victims, establish-ment of facts, local and global rule of law, deterrence or reconciliation.

Second, even if we could better operationalize these broad and nebu-lous benchmarks, we do not know whether to judge the failings and accomplishments of the Tribunal within a time frame of five or twenty or fifty years. The Nuremberg experience would suggest that the hind-sight reputation of a Tribunal may improve spectacularly, whilst the ability to trace attribution becomes even more problematic.

Finally, we must recognize that the kinds of crimes that were committed in the former Yugoslavia are to some extent beyond repair by any "transitional justice institution." As Ferencz has put it, the suffering of victims can be "beyond the reach of specification, comprehension, or compensation" (Verrijn Stuart and Simons, 2009a, 134), and as Arendt has made clear, trial and punishment after the fact are necessarily inadequate.

We can discern, and still have profound scholarly disagreements on, certain effects of the Tribunal, but this does not allow for anything but educated guesses on the "performance" of the Tribunal in the sense of effectiveness. This does not mean that interactions between Tribunals and their socio-political environment are beyond social science analysis. Instead of subjecting international criminal tribunals to "impact assessments," we propose an alternative model that allows us, if not to measure, at least to conceptualize how we may think of effects of tribunals on their environments (and vice versa).

In order to do so, we take inspiration from the legal theory of expressivism applied by Amann and Drumbl to international criminal justice. According to Amann "[t]heories of expressivism analyse the message of a governmental act, such as a prosecution or a sentence to punishment" (2003, 176). Mark Drumbl gives us a very normative and aspirational account of how trials may disseminate messages to audiences:

> Trials can educate the public through the spectacle of theatre – there is, after all, pedagogical value to performance and communicative value to dramaturgy. This performance is made all the more weighty by the reality that, coincident with the closing act, comes the infliction of shame, sanction and stigma upon the antagonists (Drunbl, 2007, 175).

Amann, however, has in another piece argued that "[t]he message understood, rather than the message intended, is critical" (2000, 238). This leads us to a broader, more ambiguous conception of the international criminal trial as theatre: yes, trials can educate publics, but they can also cause audiences to respond in very different ways. From the foundations laid by Drumbl and Amann, we freely convert expressivism from a normative theory justifying international trial and punishment into an empirical theory which allows for an investigation of the messages sent by such trials, and the messages as received by target populations. The theatre metaphor allows us to conceptualize these processes in terms of stage, actors and audiences (see also Meijers and Glasius, 2013). While this model of analysis obviously requires further elaboration, and further empirical research, we will begin to sketch here how the experience (or indeed, as we have suggested throughout, the experiment) of the Yugoslavia Tribunal might be conceptualized in these terms.

The stage

International criminal courts are not institutions that can take their legitimacy for granted. If we recast the insight by Koskenniemi cited above, that war crimes trials cannot stand outside the history they tell, in terms of our theatrical metaphor, then the stage on which the performance is produced co-determines the nature of the production, and its reception. The Yugoslavia Tribunal moved from being a rather desperate and pathetic civil society-led side-show to a mainstream state-supported production. This affected the nature of the production in different ways, allowing on the one hand for the appearance of much more significant actors, but also constraining what could be performed in particular ways (no NATO indictees, for instance).

The production was staged, first in the context of ongoing wars, later in the context of peace imposed on the terms of the international community, leading to some more, and some less independent successor states. Some would argue that the individual trials and convictions remained a relative sideshow in relation to events and resolution of the wars themselves.

As we have repeatedly seen in the Yugoslavia Tribunal's trials, prominent defendants can – and will – use the stage the Tribunal offers them to challenge the nature of the production itself. Milošević, Karadžić and Šešelj have all challenged the legitimacy of the Tribunal in court. If the defendant succeeds in delegitimizing the Tribunal in the eyes of (some of) the audiences, messages will certainly still be sent and received, but expressivism will not work in the way envisaged by Drumbl.

The actors

The main actors in the legal theatre are, of course, the prosecution, the defendant and his lawyers (sometimes joined together in one super-role, where defendants have chosen to represent themselves), and the judges. While the extent to which the judges, before the final verdict, actively intervene in hearings may differ from case to case, the former two roles take centre-stage. Witnesses may make brief but impressive appearances, but they are literally "supporting roles" created to bolster either the prosecution or the defense's narrative. In many cases before the Tribunal, prosecution and defense have fundamentally disagreed on what story, what moral, they want to convey to the public. Defendants are not always content with the part implicitly assigned to them by the expressivists, bowing their head in shame and silently awaiting judgment for several years.

Instead, they may disturb and contest the representation of what happened during the wars, the individualization of guilt and the legitimacy of the proceedings itself. Moreover, the complaints of defendants about the legitimacy of the court and the biased nature of the case have often gone largely unchallenged by the prosecution – both inside the courtroom and outside of it. The prosecution only plays the antagonistic game on one of the levels the defendants challenge them: the matter of their legal responsibility for the crimes. Defendants like Milošević, Gotovina, Karadžić and Šešelj on the other hand paint on a larger canvass: they are concerned with the history of "their people" and their own place in it.

Radovan Karadžić, for instance, delves deeply into history to contextualize his actions in war-time Bosnia. He starts off by explaining that in "Turkish times we were a docile people, suffering and trying to preserve their [sic] culture through 500 years of unbearable conditions." As the war starts, there was a "vast disproportion in manpower": the Serbs were "outnumbered" by the Muslim army which was "three times stronger." Moreover, "they received weapons from Iran (with the knowledge of the United States) continuously through Croatian territory." Karadžić also portrays himself not so much a political leader but as a Christlike figure for the Serbian people: "They said Karadžić was the ultimate leader. If they knew the Serbian people properly, they would have said that Karadžić was the ultimate servant of his people, and this is what you can find in – in the Gospels" (see Meijers and Glasius, 2013, for a more extensive discussion of defense and prosecution discourses in the Karadžić case). It is unlikely that any of these allusions are intended to sway the judges in terms of his guilt or innocence in relation to the crimes charged. Karadžić must have current or perhaps even future audiences in the region in mind.

The competition of different narratives is to be expected (and perhaps essential) in a criminal trial, both defending another version of reality. Koskenniemi sees this as a catch-22:

> to convey an unambiguous historical "truth" to an audience, the trial will have to silence the accused. But in such a case, it ends up as a show trial. In order for the trial to be legitimate, the accused must be entitled to speak. But in that case, he will be able to challenge the version of truth represented by the prosecutor and relativise the guilt that is thrust upon him upon the powers on whose strength the Tribunal stands. (Koskenniemi, 2002, 421)

We believe Koskenniemi's assessment to be too deterministic. Unambiguous historical truths aside, the narratives of defendants and prosecutors will have different plausibility, and hold different lessons, for different audiences at different points in time. The Tribunal's experience does suggest that prosecutors and judges may be lacking self-awareness as "actors," or be caught in the limitations of being a legal actor, playing down the political aspects that make this theatre of such great interest to audiences in the first place. Often, defendants have understood their presence in a stage-like environment, and their audiences, all too well. Nonetheless, whether defendants become more martyred or more discredited in the course of the trial, and for whom, remains contingent.

The audiences

As crucial as the authors sending the message, are those who are the subject of the expressivist potential of trials: the audiences. As we have shown above, academic understandings over who the most important audience for the Tribunal was have shifted over time. In the first five years, they were primarily interested in the impact of the Tribunal on the establishment of the ICC and other such initiatives, presumably via the impression the Tribunal made on diplomats and political leaders. What "the locals" made of the Tribunal was not considered particularly relevant. In recent years on the other hand, local reception has become the most prominent focus of academic studies. But local audiences, even more than international ones, do not come to these performances as blank sheets. They live in – sometimes divided, sometimes artificially homogenized – societies which are constantly reasserting their foundation myths, closely related to the narratives told in the courtroom. Since there is no single message being sent out of court, but different and often diametrically opposed ones, different stories will resonate with different groups. Different audiences pay different levels of attention, to different aspects, but above all they will interpret performances differently. Victims may only be interested in the aspects of cases that most closely touch on their personal histories, whereas nationalists will "hoover up everything" to fit into their foundational framings.

In the context of polarized post-conflict publics, the antagonistic nature of criminal trials may be mirrored in a rather perverse form of expressivism. Yet audiences too are not timeless, and will continue to reinterpret the performances of the soon to be closed down production company "Yugoslavia Tribunal."

References

Amann, D. (2003). "Assessing International Criminal Adjudication of Human Rights Atrocities", *Third World Legal Studies*, 16, 19–181.

Amann, D. (2000). "Message as Medium in Sierra Leone", *ILSA Journal of International and Comparative Law*, 7, 237–245.

Armatta, J. (2012). "Historical Revelations from the Milošević Trial", *Southeastern Europe*, 36, 10–38.

Bass, G. (2000). *Stay the Hand of Vengeance: The Politics of War Crimes Tribunals*, Princeton: Princeton University Press.

Bassiouni, M. C. (1996). "The Commission of Experts Established pursuant to Security Council Resolution 780: Investigation Violations of International Humanitarian Law in the Former Yugoslavia", in R. Clark and M. Sann (eds), *The Prosecution of International Crimes*, New Brunswick: Transaction Publishers, 61–122.

Burns, P. (1996). "An International Criminal Tribunal: The Difficult Union of Principle and Politics", in R. Clark and M. Sann (eds), *The Prosecution of International Crimes*, New Brunswick: Transaction Publishers, 125–164.

Cassese A. (1998a). "Reflections on International Criminal Justice", *The Modern Law Review*, 61, 1–10.

Cassese, A. (1998b). "On the Current Trends Towards Criminal Prosecution and Punishment of Breaches of International Humanitarian Law", *European Journal of International Law*, 9, 2–17.

Chuter, D. (2003). *War Crimes: Confronting Atrocity in the Modern World*, Boulder: Lynne Rienner.

Clark, J. N. (2009a). "Plea Bargaining at the ICTY: Guilty Pleas and Reconciliation", *European Journal of International Law*, 20 (2), 415–436.

Clark, J. N. (2009b). "The Limits of Retributive Justice: Findings of an Empirical Study in Bosnia and Hercegovina", *Journal of International Criminal Justice*, 7, 463–487.

Clark, J. N. (2012). "The ICTY and Reconciliation in Croatia: A Case Study of Vukovar", *Journal of International Criminal Justice*, 10, 397–422.

Clark, R. and M. Sann, eds (1996). *The Prosecution of International Crimes*, New Brunswick: Transaction Publishers.

Coliver, S. (2000). "The Contribution of the International Criminal Tribunal for the Former Yugoslavia to Reconciliation in Bosnia and Herzegovina", in D. Shelton (ed.), *International Crimes, Peace, and Human Rights: The Role of the International Criminal Court*, Ardsley, NY: Transnational Publishers.

Cotič, D. (1996). "Introduction", in R. Clark and M. Sann (eds), *The Prosecution of International Crimes*, New Brunswick: Transaction Publishers, 3–16.

Cushman, T. and S. Mestrovic (1996). *This Time We Knew: Western Responses to Genocide in Bosnia*, New York: New York University Press.

Drumbl, M. (2007). *Atrocity, Punishment and International Law*, Cambridge: Cambridge University Press.

Forsythe, D. (1996). "Politics and the International Tribunal for the Former Yugoslavia", in R. Clark and M. Sann (eds), *The Prosecution of International Crimes*, New Brunswick: Transaction Publishers, 185–206.

Glasius, M. (2006). *The International Criminal Court: A Global Civil Society Achievement*, London: Routledge.

Hagan, J. (2003). *Justice in the Balkans: Prosecuting War Crimes in the Hague Tribunal*, Chicago: University of Chicago Press.

Ivković, S. K. and J. Hagan (2006). "The Politics of Punishment and the Siege of Sarajevo: Toward a Conflict Theory of Perceived International (In)Justice", *Law & Society Review*, 40 (2), 369–410.

Ivković, S. K. and J. Hagan (2013). "Images of International Criminal Justice in the Former Yugoslavia", in Chrisje Brants, Antoine Hol, Dina Siegel (eds), *Transitional Justice: Images and Memories*, London: Ashgate, 181–202.

Karstedt, S. (1998). "Coming to Terms with the Past in Germany after 1945 and 1989: Public Judgments on Procedures and Justice", *Law and Policy*, 20, 15–56.

Klarin, M. (1991). "Nuremberg Now!" *Borba*, May 16. Reproduced (translated) in *International Tribunal for the Prosecution of Persons Responsible for Serious Violations of International Humanitarian Law Committed in the Territory of the Former Yugoslavia since 1991, The Path to The Hague: Selected Documents on the Origins of the ICTY* (1996), 35–37.

Klarin, M. (2009). "The Impact of the ICTY Trials on Public Opinion in the Former Yugoslavia", *Journal of International Criminal Justice*, 7, 89–96.

Koskenniemi, M. (2002). "Between Impunity and Show Trials", *Max Planck Yearbook of United Nations Law*, 6, 1–35.

Maogoto, J. (2004). *War crimes and Realpolitik; International Justice from World War I to the 21st Century*, Boulder: Lynne Rienner.

Meijers, T. and M. Glasius (2013). "Discursive Politics in the Theatre of Justice: the Karadžić Case", *Human Rights Quarterly*, 35, 720–752.

Morris, V. and M. Scharf (1995). *An Insider's Guide to the International Criminal Tribunal for the former Yugoslavia: a documentary history and analysis*, Irvington: Transnational Publishers.

Nettelfield, L. (2010). *Courting Democracy in Bosnia and Herzegovina: The Hague Tribunal's Impact in a Postwar State*. Cambridge: Cambridge University Press.

Orentlicher, D. F. (2008). *Shrinking the Space for Denial: The Impact of ICTY in Serbia*, New York: Open Society Justice Initiative.

Orentlicher, D. F. (2010). *That Someone Guilty Be Punished: The Impact of the ICTY in Bosnia*, New York: Open Society Justice Initiative.

Organization for Security and Cooperation in Europe Mission to Bosnia and Herzegovina (OSCE) (2011). *Delivering Justice in Bosnia and Herzegovina: An Overview of War Crimes Processing from 2005 to 2010*, OSCE: Sarajevo.

Ramet, S. R. (2012). "The ICTY – Controversies, Successes, Failures, Lessons", *Southeastern Europe*, 36, 1–9.

Rangelov, I. (2006). "International Law and Local Ideology in Serbia", *Peace Review: A Journal of Social Justice*, 16, 331–337.

Saxon, D. (2005). "Exporting Justice: Perceptions of the ICTY Among the Serbian, Croatian, and Muslim Communities in the Former Yugoslavia", *Journal of Human Rights*, 4, 559–572.

Scharf, M. (1997). *Balkan Justice: the Story Behind the First International War Crimes Trial since Nuremberg*, Durham, N.C.: Carolina Academic Press.

Specific Decisions by the London Conference (1992). 27 August. Reproduced in *International Tribunal for the Prosecution of Persons Responsible for Serious Violations of International Humanitarian Law Committed in the Territory of the Former Yugoslavia since 1991, The Path to The Hague: Selected Documents on the Origins of the ICTY*, 1996, 49–51.

Spoerri, M. and A. Freyberg-Inan. (2008). "From Prosecution to Persecution: Perceptions of the International Criminal Tribunal for the former Yugoslavia (ICTY) in Serbian Domestic Politics", *Journal of International Relations and Development*, 11, 350–384.

Stover, E. (2007). *The Witnesses: War Crimes and the Promise of Justice in The Hague*, Philadelphia: Pennsylvania Studies in Human Rights.

Subotić, J. (2012). "The Cruelty of False Remorse: Biljana Plavšić at The Hague", *Southeastern Europe*, 36, 39–59.

Tomuschat, C. (1996). "International Criminal Prosecution: The Precedent of Nuremberg Confirmed", in R. Clark and M. Sann (eds), *The Prosecution of International Crimes*, New Brunswick: Transaction Publishers, 17–27.

United Nations Development Program in Bosnia and Herzegovina (UNDP) (2011). *Facing the Past and Access to Justice from a Public Perspective*, Special Report, UNDP Sarajevo.

UN Security Council Resolution 808, (1993).

Verrijn Stuart, H. and M. Simons (2009a). "The Prosecutor: Interview with Benjamin Ferencz", in Heikelina Verrijn Stuart and Marlise Simons (eds), *The Prosecutor and the Judge; Benjamin Ferencz and Antonio Cassese, Interviews and Writings*, Amsterdam: Amsterdam University Press, 13–46.

Verrijn Stuart, H. and M. Simons (2009b). "The Judge: Interview with Antonio Cassese", in Heikelina Verrijn Stuart and Marlise Simons (eds), *The Prosecutor and the Judge; Benjamin Ferencz and Antonio Cassese, Interviews and Writings*, Amsterdam: Amsterdam University Press, 46–89.

Wilson, R. (2011). *Writing History in International Criminal Tribunals*, Cambridge: Cambridge University Press.

2
Reconciliation, Ethnopolitics and Religion in Bosnia-Herzegovina

Dino Abazović

Introduction

So much has been written about Bosnia-Herzegovina that almost every aspect of its very recent past has been discussed from various perspectives and in different disciplinary approaches. At the moment, it is important to note that the political system of Bosnia-Herzegovina is highly complex institutionally. This is one of the results of the political negotiations that led to the Dayton Peace Accords (DPA, 1995), which endorsed consociational mechanisms of power-sharing that trade individual human rights and liberties for nominal equality among (ethnic) groups.[1] The state is underperforming economically, there is a perpetual political crisis and progress toward membership in the European Union (EU) – so often understood as the final destination of the "transitional journey" – is almost non-existent. The key findings of the EU 2011 Progress Report on Bosnia-Herzegovina emphasize, although in a diplomatic manner, that the overall pace of reforms has been very limited.[2] The majority of efforts by international and domestic actors to mitigate the consequences of the war at the level of social relations have been insufficient, largely because many of the roots of the conflict still prevail, in a variety of new and old forms. Consequently, a predominant *ethnicization* of all aspects of social and political life is one of the crucial issues that have not yet been adequately addressed.

More than 16 years since the war ended, Bosnian-Herzegovinan society is still struggling to find a means of reconstruction that would result in a solid base and prospect for a better life. As time goes by it becomes ever clearer that the political and institutional design of Dayton-tailored Bosnia-Herzegovina do not contribute to the vital processes society needs, such as the mending of broken social relationships and the rebuilding of interethnic confidence. As McMahon some time ago observed:

> these solutions cannot create the country envisioned by the peace agreement because the existing institutional framework prevents them from doing so. Nation-building efforts in Bosnia, as currently conceived, cannot reintegrate the country or transform its society because such strategies are, in fact, at odds with the country's governing structure. (2004–2005, 583)

The very Peace Agreement was also "a masterful diplomatic creation precisely because of its imprecision, allowing all sides, including the international community, to claim some kind of victory" (Pajić, 2001, 49). At its core, it relies on fundamental contradictions. Declaring a unified state of Bosnia-Herzegovina while recognizing two antagonistic entities, proclaiming democracy while entrenching ethnically based institutional structures and reaffirming individual rights while legitimizing ethnic majoritarianism, from the outset raised serious concerns as to which political concept in Bosnia-Herzegovina would prevail.

The condition at the level of the state is such that the concept of power-sharing does not function within the restrictions of (*proportional*) ethnic representation – as it has not for many years. Instead of a positive consensus on cooperation in order to rebuild institutions, there is a negative consensus, which is manifested through the systemic blockage on the implementation of decisions necessary for restoration, social reconstruction, and political reconciliation. The situation for the last 16 years or so has been better defined as "absence of war" than by "peace" itself. Bosnia-Herzegovina as constructed by DPA[3] has revealed itself to be an ineffective creation based on the constant re-generation of crisis that encourages the accumulation of political power by ethno-nationalist elites.

All in all, its own past and present is one of the most difficult dilemmas society in Bosnia-Herzegovina has faced. So the questions arise: is the issue of reconciliation something that is "naturally" of the utmost relevance to the society's future? And what reconciliation means, what kind of reconciliation the Bosnian-Herzegovinan population, its leadership and state institution envisage?

In this chapter, I argue that reconciliation in Bosnia-Herzegovina needs to be approached as *political reconciliation* of the society that struggles with issues of justice in the aftermath of war crimes. Secondly, I explore the ambiguous role of two crucial sets of actors who do (or do not) influence the process of reconciliation: the ethno-political elites and respective religious leaders.

The notion of reconciliation I am advocating is both descriptive, and to a certain extent, normative. Following Colleen Murphy,[4]"at its most general level, the goal of processes of political reconciliation is to cultivate a political relationships" (2010, 28) which can express reciprocity and respect for moral agency, or reciprocal agency. Therefore, by accepting Murphy's main argument, I concur that the focus should be on society-wide political reconciliation, since this is considered critical for the successful consolidation of new democracies and for sustaining peace generally. Accordingly:

> the rebuilding of political relationships through processes of reconciliation cultivates forms of interaction premised on the equal respect for individuals and their agency; a commitment to the reciprocal sharing of the benefits and burdens of social cooperation; and an institutional structure is based on rule of law and on political, economic, and social institutions in which all individuals have a genuine opportunity to participate. (Murphy, 2010, 34)

To tackle the problem of social reconstruction and reconciliation in Bosnia-Herzegovina, I argue that one must attend to the political and social context induced and maintained by ethnic and religious symbiosis, as well as to the nexus that has arisen between ethno-political elites and religious actors in the past two decades. Further, "a primary concern of policies of political reconciliation should be ending injustice and oppression, and addressing the conditions that facilitate and support injustice and oppression" (Murphy, 2010, 11).

The legacy of war and ethno-religious politics in Bosnia-Herzegovina

The proliferation of ethno-politics has been spurred on not only by the legal reasoning of the Dayton Peace Accords and the Constitution of Bosnia-Herzegovina (Annex IV of DPA), but also by processes that began in the late 1980s, when the Socialist Federated Republic of Yugoslavia (the former Yugoslavia) was on the brink of dissolution.

As socialist Yugoslavia dissolved, the mobilizing discourse of the emerging nations was articulated in ethno-religious, rather than democratic-political, terms. At the same time, religious communities were seen as the guardians of national heritage and values. Together, these two processes provided institutional, ideological and symbolic support to new ethno-political entrepreneurs. Genevieve Zubrzycki has analyzed the mechanisms by which religious symbols become sacralized and has argued that such symbols garner consensual support only in specific politico-structural contexts. To a much larger degree than in the Polish case, where "it was not political institutions and symbols that were sacralized and became the object of religious devotion ... but religious symbols that were first secularized and then *resacralized as national*"(2006, 219), in the former Yugoslavia, and particularly in Bosnia-Herzegovina, religion has become a hard political fact.[5]

During the socialist period, when the multi-confessional societies of the former Yugoslavia were under the influence of principal politics (the Communist Party of Yugoslavia, i.e., the League of Communist of Yugoslavia), the place and role of religion in socio-political matters was understood dichotomously. Ideologically, religion was perceived as a traditionalistic, anachronous, and retrograde phenomenon incompatible with the new progressive "thought of the epoch," and the religious leadership was seen almost exclusively as anti-revolutionary. At the same time, religion was understood culturally and historically, in relation to the national beings and feelings of the South Slavic peoples.

But, as I have argued elsewhere (Abazović, 2010), the early post-socialist period in Bosnia-Herzegovina has been characterized by two powerful and related processes: a *"nationalization of the sacral"* and a *"sacralization of the national."* In other words, ethno-national political ideologies have demanded (and have been granted) the support of organized religious doctrines in order to legitimize new establishments. There have been no exceptions within the three major religious communities (the Islamic Community, the Roman Catholic Church, and the Serbian Orthodox Church). Various reasons have made such a development viable, but two reasons have been ideologically and historically essential. First, during the so-called communist period of 1946–1990, the religious communities were self-represented as the only considerable-size source of counterculture that had significant effect to every social stratum. The second has to do with the process of ethno-national differentiation among the domicile Bosnian-Herzegovinan population. That is, religions and confessions have become a crucial *differentia specifica*, and the majority of peoples consider religion and confession as the marker of the ultimate Self-Other dichotomy,[6] as well as for the structuring of individual and collective consciousness.

Religion in Bosnia-Herzegovina is not confined to religious leaders or official expressions, but is also manifested in local traditions and customs, family rituals, practical rites, private narratives and personal affiliations to (religious) community, with or without specific doctrinal knowledge.[7] Nonetheless, religion is always a social phenomenon, and it manifests at different levels: on the individual level – as a spirituality of life, a matter of personal identity and worldview; on the collective level – as a faith-based community, with its doctrinal teachings, moral norms, symbols, rituals, practices; and on the level of institutions – as relevant bodies that include leadership and specific types of hierarchy.

After the collapse of socialism religion was revitalized, as it came to be understood as a political fact – religion was politicized through ethnicization. As this occurred, the "understanding" of religion has, unfortunately, narrowed: religion has been oriented and reduced to ethnicity, rather than to its immanent universal characteristics, features and mission, thus, ethnic and religious identities collapsed into each other. As a result, confessional (collective) identities have been encouraged and religion also has become the means for the political legitimization of the new order. On the level of everyday life, this has been possible because, as R. Scott Appleby has argued:

> the seeds of Serbian, Croatian, and Bosnian religiosity were not stamped out under communist rule, even among so-called secularized masses; but neither were they nurtured. Scattered and left untended, they were eventually planted in the crude soil of ethnonationalism. (2002, 71)

During the war, politicized and ethnicized, religion becomes a powerful tool for mobilization against "ethnic enemies." Although many scholars who have worked on the armed conflicts in the former Yugoslavia do not consider them religious conflicts,[8] collapsing religious and ethnic identities and involvement of religious institutions and its leadership in the war made religious sites targets of actual and symbolic violence. Paul Mojzes (1998) argues that during the Bosnian war the generalized charge of fundamentalism was being used fairly indiscriminately to describe the position of rival faiths, which is an appropriate designation of some extremism in each group, but it's not a truthful presentation of the overall community. Indeed, there are a number of examples that religious leaders at all levels of hierarchy, as well as various other religious actors on numerous occasions, condemned the violence and requested peace. But these voices have been silenced!

The consequences of the war in Bosnia-Herzegovina were devastating – as an outcome of massive ethnic cleansing during the armed conflict, nearly one and a half million Bosnians and Herzegovinans have been recorded as refugees and internally displaced persons. Today the death toll after the war in Bosnia-Herzegovina (1991–1995) is generally esti-mated at around 102,000[9] persons: around 55,000 of those killed were civilians,[10] while just over 47,000 were soldiers.

Presently, the everyday lives of the majority of Bosnia-Herzegovina citi-zens are overwhelmed by "ethnic modes," their worldview channelled in ethnic terms. Despite a level of the individual attachment to their ethnic group – and certainly many do not define themselves in exclusively ethnic terms – the institutional and political milieu makes every indi-vidual fully aware of the real effects of being ethnically marked by their social surroundings.[11] Ethnic issues enter citizens' homes, and persistently follow each and every communication, even the most benign, among members of the population. One can conclude that the post-warethno-political order in Bosnia-Herzegovina is based on the political production and maintenance of an entire network of differences. There is no room for a citizen in such a network, especially not for his or her individual rights and freedoms. This is true to such a shattering degree that the lack of individual freedoms and rights almost cannot be posed as a problem. Somewhere along the way towards ethno-political supremacy the indi-vidual citizen got lost, and this is no longer even considered a problem. Even if something does not announce itself as a problem, however, this does not mean it is not, in fact, a problem. In this case, I would argue with Amy Gutmann, "the political authority of a group ... does not justify the oppression of individuals within the group" (2003, 53–54).

Consequently, in Bosnia-Herzegovina ethno-politics should be under-stood as the result of ethno-religious nationalism, its political narratives and practices that are used as a tool to justify ethnicallybased social constructions and institutions.[12] The ethno-politics in the case of Bosnia-Herzegovina is a set of political circumstances and praxis in which each person's citizenship is predetermined by his or her kinship, which is to say by his or her belonging to a specific community of supposedly shared origin. The subversive mechanism of ethno-politics consists in enacting *ethnos* as *demos* and substantiating, to paraphrase Etienne Balibar (2003), an imaginary community of membership and filiations that is the collective subject of representation, decision-making and rights. As a result, the functions of representation and decision-making, as well as the establishment of the legal framework, are permeated by discrimination on the basis of kinship.

The issues of transitional justice

Thus, to understand the current socio-political dynamics of Bosnia-Herzegovina, it is not enough to see it as a war-torn, post-conflict, disoriented society entrapped in so-called transition. Its specific societal processes must be attended to, in particular the pervasive social tensions around different ways of dealing with the past, where denial, silence/silencing and drive to confront it are among the prominent ones. Unsurprisingly, in recent scholarly works this tension has been addressed mainly under the "aegis" of transitional justice. The concept of transitional justice for Bosnia-Herzegovina is commonly approached as it is in the analysis of many other war-torn societies, post-dictatorships, "new democracies," and "regimes in transitions." In this context, it has been analyzed in relation to problems of truthseeking, truthtelling, retribution, restoration, and, finally, reconciliation.

Here, as it is elsewhere, transitional justice is connected to a slew of other major issues, including problems of injustice, gross human rights violations, and (war) crimes committed in the past. In this case, however, discussions about what models of transitional justice are appropriate must take into account the deep divisions that still exist in the society of Bosnia-Herzegovina, where peoples are alienated from state institutions and in particular from institutions of justice. According to the relevant literature, there are at least seven different options open to new democracies:

> amnesia or inaction; pardons; full amnesty; prosecution and trials (either domestic or international); lustration (disqualifying collaborators from public office); publicity (the opening of the Stasi files in Germany is the key example here); conditional amnesty or truth commissions. (Allen, 2004, 4)

In Bosnia-Herzegovina, public opinion about these different models appears, at first glance, to be highly polarized, for intense debates about the worthiness and applicability of various models regularly appear in the print media.[13] What is striking about this case, however, is that this polarization is not actually widespread. This is because, although there is notable divergence of opinion among experts, the vast majority of the population seems to be chronically unwilling to engage publically in discussion about reconciliation. In a way, the public discourse about transitional justice in Bosnia-Herzegovina is affected by the fact that, as a society, Bosnia-Herzegovina:

> Suffer[s] from a deficit of truth – factual knowledge about past atrocities is lacking, officials resist acknowledging the existence of such events (even when this is a matter of widespread knowledge), and victims seek acknowledgment of their suffering. (Allen, 2004, 5)

Although one should not lose sight of the needs and perspectives of the victims in any discourse about reconciliation, the process of political reconciliation itself is not solely victim-oriented, for it encompasses other societal actors and agents in post-conflict societies and societies recovering from repressive rule. The victim-centered concepts of reconciliation can be subsumed under the theories of reconciliation as forgiveness, a legitimate – and quite common – theoretical approach. In this context, Mark R. Amstutz conceives political forgiveness:

> as an interactive process in which the burdens of past wrongdoings are repaired, resulting in the healing of human relationships. To be successful, forgiveness depends upon a number of core elements, including consensus about wrongdoing, remorse and repentance, renunciation of vengeance, cultivation of empathy and mitigation or cancellation of deserved penalty. (2006, 157)

But unlike theory, practice is much more problematic. Regrettably enough, none of the abovementioned core elements of reconciliation sufficiently come to life in the Bosnia-Herzegovina society. And as time goes by, the politics of denial precludes the possibility of consensus building about wrongdoings. Remorse and repentance have been understood as weakness, the renunciation of vengeance as (not necessarily authentic) politically correct speech, and the cultivation of empathy as meaninglessly abstract to those in need. The mitigation or cancellation of penalties being considered "just," meanwhile, is perceived as being out of the question.

Taken as a whole, the official discourse of the ruling ethno-political elites is, thus, in service to the maintenance of what Dubravka Ugrešić (2012) addresses as the "confiscation of memories," or the practice of the manipulation of the past[14]– either by a blatant politics of denial, or by a one-sided victimization. And for the victims, it is not solely about the factual truth; it is a problem of societal acknowledgement of the truth, acknowledgement as a need for human dignity. To cite Giorgio Agamben, it is about the testimony that "guarantees not the factual truth of the statement safeguarded in the archive, but rather its unarchivability, its exteriority with respect to the archive – that is, the necessity by which, as the existence of language, it escapes both memory and forgetting." (1999, 158)

The feelings among the victims of having been humiliated are intensified not merely when faced with the rejection of recognition about what has happened, but typically when the interpretation of the already established facts have been deliberately distorted to achieve political goals and rationalize injustices. Therefore, Alan J. Torrance is right when he insists that:

> in contexts such as Rwanda and Bosnia (let alone in the aftermath of the Holocaust)...one cannot help but ask about the propriety of the word *reconciliation*, let alone the language of "forgiveness" in the political realm. Given the unthinkable atrocities, the scenes of mass murder, rape, and gratuitous violence, and the sustained pillaging of burning of homes, one must ask whether talk of forgiveness and reconciliation does not border on the grotesque where survivors are stalked by events that are unthinkable for us, unforgettable for them. (2006, 59)

In discussing issues of restorative justice, political forgiveness and the possibility for reconciliation Amstutz contrasted backward-looking retributive justice, which focuses on the legal prosecution and punishment of offenders, with restorative justice, an approach that emphasizes truth telling, moral accountability and reconciliation.

> Although retribution, the prevalent state practice in confronting collective wrongdoing, is an effective strategy for implementing legal justice, it does not necessarily contribute to the healing of victims, the restoration of community life, and most importantly, the consolidation of right-based democracy. (2006, 152–153)

The discussion about retributive justice is to a certain extent relevant for the Bosnian-Herzegovinan social context. The International Court of Justice (ICJ) rulings from February 2007 effectively determined the character of war to be international, and yet, "despite the evidence of widespread killings, rape and torture elsewhere during the Bosnian war, especially in detention centres, the judges ruled that the criteria for genocide were met only in Srebrenica."[15]

Already in 1993 the International Criminal Tribunal for the former Yugoslavia (ICTY) was established by the United Nations in response to mass atrocities then taking place in Croatia and Bosnia-Herzegovina.[16] Beyond a reasonable doubt, the ICTY has established crucial facts related to crimes committed in the former Yugoslavia, and its judgments could contribute to create a historical record, to combat denial and prevent attempts at revisionism. As a part of the "completion strategy," ICTY has transferred cases against intermediate and lower-level accused to

Bosnian-Herzegovinan, Serbian and Croatian national jurisdictions. In addition, domestic prosecutors and courts have also initiated cases, with or without involvement by the ICTY.[17]

The continued importance of the ICTY and its work, as well as the work of domestic/national courts, should not, however, preclude a reassessment of the notion that retributive justice lessens the needs of victims. In broader social and political terms, war crimes trials have not made a visible contribution to launching a process that would normalize relations among different ethnic groups. The findings of the United Nations Development Program (UNDP) in the Bosnia-Herzegovina Special Report *Facing the Past and Access to Justice from a Public Perspective*[18] (2011) shows that nearly all NGOs and victims' associations from all over the country have expressed their dissatisfaction with the outcomes of the trials, claiming that the victims' needs were not sufficiently met through formal court proceedings. The research also shows that the burden of the past most often arises from an imprecise and incomplete knowledge about the past, since the majority of the respondents consider that it is still necessary to shed light on all the facts of the 1992–1995 war, which remain vague ever since the war ended. A prevailing public opinion is that the level and scope of attention and support, which the government institutions and the society as a whole have been giving to victims, are insufficient and uncoordinated.[19] Despite of the ongoing court cases, a number of nongovernmental organizations have expressed concern in their numerous public statements and reports that the victims of crimes committed during the 1992–1995 war and their relatives are still being denied access to truth, justice and reparation.[20]

Obviously there is a specific ambiguity in place since the overwhelming majority of citizens also demand a solution through the criminal justice system, and at the same time, public confidence is low in any of the criminal justice mechanisms in place.[21] Already in late 2005, a decade after the war ended, the UNDP in Bosnia-Herzegovina published its Early Warning System Special Report entitled *Justice and Truth in BiH: Public Perception*. The report has been part of the UNDP's contribution to the debate about transitional justice in Bosnia-Herzegovina. Demands for criminal justice and law public confidence in courts is one of Report's central conclusions.

Accordingly, Boris Buden (2012), speaking about the regional notion of justice, contends:

> This does in no way imply that I do not support the Hague Tribunal. On the contrary! The very existence and actions of that Court are the best evidence that our nations are, in a political and even more

so in a moral sense, phantoms of a sort. By demonstrating themselves incompetent to prosecute their own war criminals, they have lost, in my opinion, their historical justification. What good is nation without justice? What do I have in common with the people who view notorious criminals as heroes?[22]

Many – if not all – mechanisms of transitional justice, based on attributing individual guilt, have been "reinterpreted within and folded into dominant ethno-political narratives about collective guilt and innocence" (Eastmond, 2010, 8) by dominant ethno-political entrepreneurs. In addition, there is a very low level of social trust in Bosnia-Herzegovina, a highly fragmented social sphere and a high level of social exclusion. Therefore:

> societal exclusion or discrimination on the basis of social identity is of fundamental concern because of how such exclusion or discrimination restricts what individuals are free to do or become in their relations with others. That is, the fundamental normative concern in the context of reconciliation is not with misrecognition or the absence of recognition itself; rather, it is with the ramification of such exclusion or misrecognition. (Murphy, 2010, 35)

How, then, to balance the desire to rebuild society by restoring proper social relations (*ergo* political reconciliation) against the widespread belief that "reconciliation-as-forgiveness" is ethically unacceptable, since it leaves the majority of perpetuators unpunished, and at the same time victims needs are not sufficiently met?

The first step is to unconditionally, truthfully, and straightforwardly argue that forgiveness can be and should be distinguishable from justification and excuse. The next is to comprehend, as Murphy has claimed, that reconciliation-as-forgiveness is just one out of several different conceptions about reconciliation. Others are reconciliation as creation and stabilization of normative expectation and trust; reconciliation as a political value; and reconciliation as the constituting of a political community.

In that respect, the crucial question for the future of Bosnia-Herzegovina is how to reconstitute Bosnia-Herzegovina as a political community rather than as ethno-religious communities. In other words, how to re-assert the right of its citizens not to be discriminated against in public and political life on the basis of ethno-religious principles? How to break out of the imposed context of "ethnic equality" and demand an "ethic equality"[23] in which everyone is endowed with the same human dignity and freedom of choice concerning matters of public and private interest, self-development, and group affiliation? Or not to be affiliate with a group at all? Individuals have every right to make religious or ethnic affiliation the cornerstone of their personal identities and to align themselves with communities defined in these terms, but this does not mean that this is the only legitimate view of identity or that it should be imposed on others, especially in the political realm. Finally, as Marita Eastmond pointed out:

> [The] key point made is that, given the everyday problems of people in post-war settings, reconciliation with former enemies may not be seen as a primary concern. The theme permeating post-war life in BiH was rather the striving for a sense of normality – not so much by consciously engaging in inter-ethnic reconciliation, as by invoking and practicing widely shared norms such as those of economic security and neighborhood sociality. (2010, 12)

So, what's religion got to do with it?

Ugo Vlaisavljević has rightly observed that, "if a religious doctrine, its norms and values, way of understanding and behavior is the soil in which the ethnic Self is imbedded, then religion appears as the main source of legitimization in politics." This is certainly the case for Bosnia-Herzegovina, with the result that "religion, in which all the capital of ethnic symbols and meanings has been invested, plays an important role in politics in the period of ethnic renewal, regardless of whether ecclesial authorities have agreed to it or not." (2003, 102)

Yet another issue that comes into play in the case of Bosnia-Herzegovina is the definition of "the nation." Jürgen Habermas's critique of Karl Schmitt is theoretically relevant here. Habermas argues that the problem with Schmitt (and others) is that the constituent power of the nation is understood to be a concrete and organic collectivity, rather than a legal framework.[24] Habermas writes:

> This existentialist version [of Karl Schmitt] continues to share essential features with the traditional concept of "the political." Certainly, the collective identity of the people is no longer defined in the legal terms of a sovereign state, but in the ethnonational concepts of political romanticism instead. However, the shared features of descent, tradition, and language cannot ensure the social cohesion of the collective by their supposed organic nature alone. Rather, the political

leadership must continually mobilize the nation against external or internal enemies. (2011, 31)

Although the armed violence has ended, the conflict is not over in Bosnia-Herzegovina. Nevertheless, a number of options are available for its management and settlement, including those that consider religion a potentially valuable, but critically underutilized peace-building tool. Still, in spite of numerous efforts by "Western" governmental and nongovernmental organizations engaged in conflict resolution and peace-building – including interreligious dialogue that encompass expatriate and domestic religious communities and faith-based organizations – the overall results and achievements have been very limited thus far.

Indeed, when it comes to the value of religious communities and truth commissions for transitional justice, Bosnia-Herzegovina seems to constitute a negative case. In this respect, according to Daniel Philpott (2007), the experience of Bosnia-Herzegovina is akin to that of Ireland and Poland and contrasts sharply with that of Guatemala, Brazil, Chile, South Africa, Sierra Leone, Timor-Leste, Peru and Germany, where religious leaders and communities have exercised an important influence on transitional justice.[25] He gives two reasons for the success of the religious communities in these countries:

> First, they shaped the decision for truth commissions through speaking out publicly, lobbying and sometimes even organizing efforts to investigate past injustices themselves. Second, they shaped the actual functioning of truth commissions by influencing the selection of commissioners, sometimes actually serving as commissioners, providing logistical support for organizing and conducting hearings, locating and supporting victims and witnesses and providing counseling in the wake of hearings. (2007, 101)

Bosnia-Herzegovina's position as a negative case could be due to religious leaders' ambivalent role during the war, or the insufficient ecumenical and interreligious structures that conspired to limit the organized religious potential for peacemaking. Whether for these or other reasons, Bosnia-Herzegovina's organized religions have so far chosen the course of "eloquent silence," responding to significant speech acts with silence. Let me briefly address this with three illustrative examples.

Three years ago, two publishers from Croatia and Bosnia-Herzegovina (*Ex Libris* and *Synopsis*) jointly printed a translation of the book *Ethics*, an important work by Dietrich Bonhoeffer and a text highly relevant for the entire region. The foreword to the book, entitled "Ethical Concreteness of Revelation: the Incentive for Contextual Reading of the Ethics," was written by the young Bosnian-Herzegovinan theologian AlenKristić. Although Kristić openly and directly appeals for intra-religious dialogue about the contemporary political situation, he also writes that:

> after the nationalistic insanity of 1990s, ... if Vukovar, Srebrenica and Sarajevo could happen to us ... who, after all of that, ... can be so narcissistic, so devilishly supercilious, to dare to call himself a Christian? (2009, 1)

Although Kristić's comments were quite provocative, there were no reactions to his argument at all. Silence sometimes speaks more than words, and in this case the silence that followed was quite eloquent indeed.

The second example is a text delivered by a high ranking cleric from Eastern Christianity, which is to say from the "Eastern lung," to quote Pope John Paul II. In a speech opening an international conference on interreligious understanding, Bishop Grigorije of the Serbian Orthodox Church (Zamusko-Hercegovačka and Primorska Bishopric) said:

> ... some members of religious communities, on all sides, did not find the strength to oppose the general insanity of hatred and war during the crucial moments of religious and ethnical polarization. In order to prevent similar occurrences in the future, we should speak about this and analyze all the aspects of the problem in depth, not avoid it as a subject of conversation, because if we remain silent we will encourage the evil people on all sides to continue using religion and the name of God for hatred and crime. The [religious] community, which shows more honesty and accountability in doing so, will display that is the closest to God.[26]

Although this statement called for response and discussion, there was no significant reaction to it, just an eloquent silence.

Finally, a year ago Adnan Silajdžić, Professor at the Faculty of Islamic Studies Sarajevo, send the open letter to the Islamic community's official newspaper *Preporod* as a response to the editorial comment written about at that time to a seminar on *The Islamic Discourses in Bosnia-Herzegovina*. According to Silajdžić:

> ... it is a time for undertaking some serious research on the quality and status of Bosniaks' religious consciousness at the end of the

last millennium and the beginning of the new one ... [D]uring the seminar I said, without excluding myself, that the false and hypocritical communication between professors and [the Islamic] community officeholders paradigmatically marks the absence of personal, lively and intellectually mediated [religious] belief.[27]

Outside of some editorial comments about this Silajdžić statement and a few anonymous posts on the *Preporod* website forum, all in all the response was, again, an eloquent silence.

What do these examples tell us? The institutional capacity (or lack of it) as well as a symbolic capital of the narrator in specific context and about "sensitive" issues does not inevitably influence the hearing. The silence does not necessarily have to mean denial, but can be seen as a practical strategy in confronting the actual problems, or those emerging from the past. However, if a majority of members of religious communities are struggling on a daily basis with past and present injustices, their respective religious leaders have a moral obligation to respond to eloquent – and at times even sinister – silence, and to provide the ambience and space for the witnesses involved to testify. Since, as Giorgio Agamben has noted, "the authority of the witness consists of his [sic] capacity to speak solely in the name of an incapacity to speak – that is, in his or her being a subject," (1999, 158) the religious leaders could help to facilitate the processes of dialogue and help to give witnesses the authority and subjectivity they deserve.

Instead of artificial and fruitless public debates about whether Bosnian-Herzegovinan society is becoming too militantly atheistic or too clerical, which is mostly a case in discussion about the place of religion in contemporary Bosnia-Herzegovina, the emphasis should be on the role organized religion plays in social reconstruction. As Philpott has argued:

> If right relationship is at the core of the meaning of reconciliation, and if justice means comprehensive right relationship, as it arguably does in the Abrahamic religious traditions, then it follows that reconciliation is indeed itself a conception of justice.... (2007, 98)[28]

Accordingly, from doctrinal religious sources a distinctive course of action could ensue. Ultimately, it could be argued that this entire debate is about religious authenticity. But then we are left with the underlining question: what does "religious authenticity" mean? Certainly it does not mean the "political religiosity" that often ends in idolatry – or theologically speaking, the worship of false gods like nation and ethnicity, which is surely against the fundamental teachings of the dominant religions in

Bosnia-Herzegovina. Overemphasizing the potential role of religion is just as precarious as underemphasizing it. Between *"yes"* and *"no"* there are myriad versions of *"possibly."*

It is therefore plausible to think about the role of religion in social reconstruction and reconciliation, as well as of religious authenticity, in terms that

> religious reasons does not only depend on cognitive beliefs and their semantic nexus with other beliefs, but on existential beliefs that are rooted in the social dimension of membership, socialization, and prescribed practices. (Habermas, 2011, 62)

The relevant religious communities of Bosnia-Herzegovina might deploy all of their resources – including not only their ritual sites, sacred spaces, educational institutions, faith-based association and organizations, community centers and so on, but also their symbolic capital – in the creation of a forum for the public articulation of needs, a forum that can serve both members of the "in" group of the religious communities and non-members. The more bottom level for such activities – the more beneficial! When it comes to facing the past, intergroup and intragroup dialogues should be fostered in parallel.

Concluding remarks

Bosnia-Herzegovina is faced with a diverse set of issues, but the underlining paradox is that the institutional framework established through the Dayton Peace Accords favors the political options that are the least supportive of its implementation. The design of its political institutions does not encourage cross-ethnic cooperation; rather, it institutionalizes ethnic discrimination. For a new political system to be effective in a society with a sinister past, for it to encourage public deliberation, participatory democracy and representative government, the society must confront that past. This process of confrontation is of the utmost importance, as the introduction of a new regime does not erase the past. This is not to say, however, that "facing the past" should be understood in terms of blame or the assignation of guilt. As Nenad Dimitrijević has argued:

> the principal point of justification should not be condemnation, ascription of guilt, paving the way for official apologies, or even reconciliation. It should rather be understood as the reconstruction of the motivational patterns of a behavior that in the recent past led to

a massive violation of human rights and universal moral values. The practical-political objective of such a reflection would be to enable the citizens to regain their recently and severely damaged capacity to distinguish between right and wrong, just and unjust. (2006, 374)

In terms of fostering a process of reconciliation as the restoration of the just political relationship, the religious actors could be some of the crucial actors, given their historical and contextual position within society. Stephen R. Goodwin's asserts that social reconciliation generally lies beyond the structural realm and does not respond to the mechanical manipulation of institutions. He writes, "because reconciliation is a pre-eminently human endeavour involving the moral and ethical will of individuals and communities alike, it is most naturally situated in the locus of the personal and relational, not the structural and institutional" (2003, 174). At the individual level, hence as a matter of personal religiosity, this might be true.

But in the face of failures, limits, and retrenchments of the political institutions (state), some sort of establishments should fill the gap. The organized religions in Bosnia-Herzegovina, by doing so, can (re-)define their place and role within the wider civil society and recognize that:

> Modern religions have within their power the capacity to resist deadly violence and to do so in the name of the holy. ...communities of faith in which the historical argument about the proper ethical interpretation of the sacred remains vigorous and is sustained through many formal and informal channels, moves its adherents away from narrowly conceived ethnic, nationalistic, and tribal self-definition and toward a more tolerant and nonviolent social presence. (Appleby, 2002, 79)

Significantly enough, there is no better way for religious actors – at the level of institutions and communities – to experience *metanoia*: dealing with their own negative past as reorientation, as a fundamental transformation of outlook and as a redefinition of their (public) position. In particular, since the very relevant critique of the ethnopolitical nature of the current political order and the ethnicization of the society – which is highly discriminatory and leads to regular human rights violations – can inherently come only from those who helped such a scenario come to life. And accordingly only they can be effective in halting the current negative tendencies in Bosnia-Herzegovina. Therefore, the political reconciliation encompasses the reconstruction of both individual and communal identities in Bosnia-Herzegovina.

Notes

1. It is worth noting that a related debate about consociational representation was triggered by the ruling of the European Court of Human Rights in the case of Dervo Sejdić and Jakob Finci v. Bosnia-Herzegovina from 2011 (Applications No. 27996/06 and 34836/06 of December 22, 2009). In brief, as Hodžić and Stojanović have noted, "the judgment ... established that there is systemic constitutional discrimination of all persons not belonging to the constituent peoples on account of their inability to stand as candidates for positions in the Presidency of BiH and the House of Peoples of the BiH Parliamentary Assembly, has posed a veritable challenge not only to Bosnia's constitutional system, but also to the theory and practice of constitutional engineering in divided societies." (2011, 15)

2. The full text of the EU 2011 Progress Report on Bosnia-Herzegovina can be accessed at http://ec.europa.eu/enlargement/pdf/key_documents/2011/package/ba_rapport_2011_En.pdf

3. The politico-institutional structure of Bosnia-Herzegovina presently is that of a state comprised of two entities (the Federation of Bosnia-Herzegovina and Republika Srpska), each with a very high level of autonomy. In itself, the Federation of Bosnia-Herzegovina comprises 10 cantons. The town of Brčko, which was the subject of international arbitration, now has the status of a district and is still under direct supervision of a special international envoy.

4. The conception of political reconciliation I am using here and after is largely based on work of Colleen Murphy (2010, 28).

5. See Vrcan (2001); Velikonja (2003); Perica (2004); Abazović (2006).

6. Like in Dubravka Žarkov's analysis of gender and ethnicity, I also "perceive ethnicity in a similar way ... as a relation and category of *power*, always concerned with living individuals or communities, but, never *reducible to them*" (2007, 12).

7. Belief, knowledge, experience, practice and consequences are helpful in determining the types of religiosity for different cases, and certainly these differ from one individual to other, but no matter how exactly religion is practiced, its effect is always real.

8. Milan Vukomanović underlines a basic fact that only those wars which are fought over religious problems and issues should be considered as religious ones; still, the war has had a certain religious dimension, for it was waged not only among people, but also against sacred spaces, houses of worship, cemeteries and other religious sites, many of which were completely destroyed. All of the parties in the war employed religious symbols in their ethno-national/political mobilization and military efforts. One study (Grbo, 1996) that encompassed just a third of the Bosnian-Herzegovinan territory showed that 705 sacred objects were demolished and damaged during the conflict. Out of that number, 435 were Islamic, 146 Catholic, 117 Serb-Orthodox and 7 Jewish.

9. See more in Tabeau and Bijak (2005).

10. In one of his essays Marko-Atila Hoare suggests that the most striking fact to emerge from the study of the Research and Documentation Centre Sarajevois that 83 percent of civilian deaths in the Bosnian war were Muslims (Bosniaks). He notes the fact that Muslims were only one of the three principal Bosnian

nationalities that suffered higher civilian than military casualties. But the point Hoare would like to emphasize is that he "make[s] these observations by way of a preliminary, in response to those who enjoy playing the numbers game with regard to the Bosnian genocide. Whether 100,000 or 200,000 died in the Bosnian war should have no bearing on our recognition that this was a terrible crime, or on whether we consider what happened to have been genocide. But if numbers cannot be used to confirm or deny a genocide, they can tell us a lot about when, where and how most of the killing occurred, who were the principal perpetrators and who were the principal victims." For detailed discussion see more in Marko-Atila Hoare (2008).

11. For an anthropological perspective on this see Stefansson (2010).

12. For a better overview of ethno-politics in Bosnia-Herzegovina see Mujkić (2007).

13. It is important to notice that one model of transitional justice does not necessarily exclude others. In other words, two or more models are often implemented at the same time in a given situation, just like it is a case in Bosnia-Herzegovina.

14. "The authorities in our post-Yugoslav countries abundantly manipulate the past. The past usually only serves for a manipulation. Those in power deal with exhuming and burying corpses, every minute they drag one out when it is needed and every minute they bury another one if it is needed. The most frightening is that the intelligentsia, that should be both the filter and the arbiter, most often puts itself into service of the authorities resulting in the blossoming of the practice of erecting memorials and demolishing them; a practice of publishing slurred textbooks (where in one environment there is one valid historical truth and in another environment a different one)" (from an interview with Dubravka Ugrešić, "Neko će morati da ukloni ruševine," available at http://pescanik.net/2012/01/neko-ce-morati-da-ukloni-rusevine/).

15. Max Arthur, "Court: Serbia Failed to Prevent Genocide," San Francisco Chronicle, Monday, February 26, 2007.

16. In official documents, the ICTY lists the following achievements, among others: holding leaders accountable, bringing justice to victims, giving victims a voice and establishing the facts. Up to this point, the ICTY has indicted 161 persons for serious violations of international humanitarian law committed on the territory of the former Yugoslavia and has concluded proceedings for 126 defendants. The proceedings for 35 more accused persons are ongoing. As of early last year, 4,000 witnesses had told their stories in court. See more at http://www.icty.org

17. Based on the National War Crimes Prosecution Strategy, adopted in late 2008 by the Council of Ministers of Bosnia-Herzegovina, currently there are more than 1200 ongoing cases before the courts in Bosnia-Herzegovina (the Court of BiH, 10 Cantonal Courts in Federation of BiH, 5 District Courts in Republika Srpska, and the Basic Court of Brcko District of BiH). The basic objective of the Strategy is to prosecute the most complex and top priority cases within the seven years and other war crime cases within 15 years of the time of the adoption of the Strategy. For more info see http://www.sudbih.gov.ba/?jezik=e

18. United Nation Development Program in Bosnia-Herzegovina (UNDP in BiH): "Facing the Past and Access to Justice from Public Perspective: Special

Report," Sarajevo (2011); the Report represents a comprehensive analysis of the findings of the public opinion poll; the full text of report is available athttp://www.undp.ba/upload/publications/Facing%20the%20Past%20 and%20Access%20to%20Justice.pdf

19. UNDP Report "Facing with the Past ... " (2011, 12).

20. One of the very recent reports by the Amnesty International, from March 2012 focuses on the survivors of wartime rape. The Reports' conclusion is: "Successive governments in BiH have failed to acknowledge the rights of civilian victims of wartime sexual violence and provide them with access to justice, truth and reparation. Consequently, those local authorities responsible for providing services, even to a limited extent, are woefully under-resourced and ill-equipped to address these women's needs...Almost two decades after the end of the conflict, Amnesty International finds itself once again having to call on the state and entity authorities in BiH to fulfill their international legal obligations to address the survivors' suffering and guarantee them access to swift justice and full reparation." Amnesty International, "Bosnia-Herzegovina: old crimes, same suffering: no justice for survivors of wartime rape in North-East Bosnia-Herzegovina," p. 12. The full text of report is available athttp://www.amnesty.org/en/library/asset/EUR63/002/2012/en/ f688b1c8–1fa2–46ba-ae26–0b6ec344401f/eur630022012en.pdf

21. UNDP Report (2005); the full text is available athttp://www.undp.ba/upload/ publications/Justice&Truth%20in%20BH%20English.pdf

22. Interview with Boris Buden available at http://pescanik.net/2012/04/intervju-sa-borisom-budenom/

23. For more on this, see Mujkić, Abazović and Seizović (2008).

24. For Karl Schmitt, according to Habermas, "national membership is determined by common race, belief, common destiny, and tradition – in other words, by ascriptive features." Thus, Habermas continues, "Schmitt shares a collective and plebiscitary conception of democracy that is directed against the egalitarian conception of human rights and against a deliberative conception of politics" (2011, 31).

25. I will not go into an in-depth discussion about the countries mentioned here, but this list begs the question of whether these activities were all successful because they were carried out by Christian churches. Then again, the cases from Poland and Ireland tell a quite different story. Still, the theological understanding of issues such as justice and forgiveness differs in the Jewish, Christian and Islamic traditions, and this should be taken into account when addressing the respective perspectives on reconciliation.

26. International Conference has been held on December 8–9, 2006 in Trebinje, Bosnia-Herzegovina, organized by IKV Pax Christi, the Netherlands and Forum gradjana Tuzla, Bosnia-Herzegovina. Shorthand from the conference is available at http://www.forumtz.com/publikacije/stenogramBOS.pdf

27. See Preporod, No. 3/917, year XL.

28. "Jewish perspectives, reconciliation mirrors God's covenant with Israel, to which God is faithful and willing to restore, even after repeated strayings. Christian theologians root reconciliation in God's own reconciliation with humanity through Jesus Christ. In Islamic writings, reconciliation flows from the mercy of Allah (the greatest of Allah's ninety-nine names), his willingness to forgive the repentant and Qur'anic injunctions to reconcile" (Philpott, 2007, 97–98).

References

Abazović, Dino (2006). *Za naciju i Boga: sociološko odredjenje religijskog nacional-izma*, Sarajevo: Magistrat.

Abazović, Dino (2010). "Rethinking Ethnicity, Religion and Politics: The Case of Bosnia and Herzegovina", *European Yearbook of Minority Issues*, 7, 2007/08, Koninklijke Brill NV, 317–326.

Agamben, Giorgio (1999). *Remnants of Auschwitz: The Witness and the Archive*, D. Heller-Roazen (trans.), New York: Zone Books.

Allen, Jonathan (2004). "Memory and Politics: Three Theories of Justice in Regime Transitions", presented as part of the Transitional Seminar Series. Friday November 5, available at http://www.ideals.illinois.edu/bitstream/handle/2142/3510/TSPaAllen.pdf?sequence=2

Amstutz, Mark R. (2006). "Restorative Justice, Political Forgiveness, and Possibility of Political Reconciliation", in Daniel Philpott (ed.), *The Politics of Past Evil: Religion, Reconciliation, and the Dilemmas of Transitional Justice*, University of Notre Dame Press.

Appleby, Scott R. (2002). *The Ambivalence of the Sacred: Religion, Violence, and Reconciliation*, New York: Rowman & Littlefield Publishers, Inc.

Arthur, Max (2007). "Court: Serbia Failed to Prevent Genocide", *San Francisco Chronicle*, Monday, February 26.

Balibar, Etjen (2003). *Mi, gradjani Evrope*, Beograd: Beogradski krug.

Buden, Boris (2012). "Intervju", available at http://pescanik.net/2012/04/intervju-sa-borisom-budenom/Dennett, Daniel C. (2006).*Breaking the Spell: Religion as Natural Phenomenon*, New York: Penguin Group.

Dimitrijević, Nenad (2006). "Justice beyond Blame: Moral Justification of (the Idea of) Truth Commission", *Journal of Conflict Resolution*, 50 (3), 368–382.

Eastmond, Marita (2010). "Introduction: Reconciliation, Reconstruction, and Everyday Life in War-torn Societies", in Marita Eastmond and Anders H. Stefansson (eds), *Special Section: Beyond Reconciliation: Social Reconstruction after the Bosnian War, Focaal European Journal of Anthropology*, 57 (14), Summer, 3–16.

Goodwin, Stephen R. (2003). "From UN Safe Havens to Sacred Spaces: Contribution of Religious Sodalities to Peace Building and Reconciliation in Post-War Bosnia-Herzegovina", *Studies in World Christianity*, 9, October, 171–188.

Grbo, Ismet (1996). *Ogledalo nasilja*, Sarajevo: SDA – Centrala Sarajevo.

Gutmann, Amy (2003). *Identity in Democracy*, Princeton: Princeton University Press.

Habermas, Jürgen (2011). "'The Political': The Rational Meaning of a Questionable Inheritance of Political Theology", in E. Mendieta and J. Vanantwerpen (eds), *The Power of Religion in the Public Sphere*, New York: Columbia University Press.

Hoare, Marko-Atila (2008). "What Do the Figures for the Bosnian War-dead Tell Us?" at http://greatersurbiton.wordpress.com/2008/01/04/what-do-the-figures-for-the-bosnian-war-dead-tell-us/, accessed on April 22, 2012.

Hodžić, Edin and Nenad Stojanović (2011). *New/Old Constitutional Engineering? Challenges and Implications of the European Court of Human Rights Decision in the Case of Sejdić and Finci v. BiH*, Sarajevo: Analitika – Center for Social Research.

Kristić, Alen (2009). "Foreword", in Bonhoeffer, Dietrich, *Etika*, Rijeka, Sarajevo: Ex Libris and Synopsis.

McMahon, Patrice C.(2004–2005). "Rebuilding Bosnia: A Model to Emulate or to Avoid?" *Political Science Quarterly*, 119 (4), 569–593.

Mojzes, Paul (1998). "The Camouflaged Role of Religion in the War in B&H", in P. Mojzes (ed.), *Religion and the War in Bosnia*, Atlanta, Georgia: The American Academy of Religion, Scholars Press.

Mujkić, Asim (2007). "We, the Citizens of Ethnopolis", *Constellation*, 14 (1), 112–128.

Mujkić, Asim, Dino Abazović and Zarije Seizović (2008). "The Role of Human and Minority Rights in the Process of Reconstruction and Reconciliation for State and Nation-Building: Bosnia-Herzegovina", at http://www.eurac.edu/en/research/institutes/imr/Documents/20_BiH.pdf

Murphy, Colleen (2010). *A Moral Theory of Political Reconciliation*, Cambridge University Press.

Pajić, Zoran (2001). "The Role of Institutions in Peace Building", in Žarko Papić (ed.), *International Support Policies to South-East European Countries, Lessons (Not) Learned in B-H*, Sarajevo: Müler.

Perica, Vjekoslav (2004). *Balkan Idols: Religion and Nationalism in Yugoslav States*, Oxford University Press.

Philpott, Daniel (2007). "What Religion Brings to the Politics of Transitional Justice", Journal *of International Affairs*, Fall/Winter, 61 (1), 93–110.

Stefansson, Anders H. (2010). "Coffee after Cleansing? Co-existence, Co-operation, and Communication in Post-conflict Bosnia-Herzegovina", in Marita Eastmond and Anders H. Stefansson (eds), "Special section: Beyond Reconciliation: Social Reconstruction after the Bosnian War", *Focaal European Journal of Anthropology*, 57 (15), Summer, 62–76.

Tabeau, Ewa and Jakub Bijak (2005). "War-related Deaths in the 1992–1995 Armed Conflicts in Bosnia-Herzegovina: A Critique of Previous Estimates and Recent Results", *European Journal of Population/ Revue Europenne de Demographie*, 21 (2–3), 187–215.

Taylor, Charles (2007). *A Secular Age*, Harvard University Press.

Torrance, Alan J. (2006). "The Theological Grounds for Advocating Forgiveness", in Daniel Philpott (ed.), *The Politics of Past Evil: Religion, Reconciliation, and the Dilemmas of Transitional Justice*, University of Notre Dame Press.

Ugrešić Dubravka. (2012). "Neko će morati da ukloni ruševine", available at http://pescanik.net/2012/01/neko-ce-morati-da-ukloni-rusevine/

Velikonja, Mitja (2003). *Religious Separation and Political Intolerance in Bosnia-Herzegovina*, Texas A&M University Press.

Vlaisavljević, Ugo (2003). "Ethno-politics and the Divine Good", *Transeuropeennes*, 23, 91–106.

Vrcan, Srdjan (2001). *Vjera u vrtlozima tranzicije*, Split: Dalmatinska akcija.

Vukomanović, Milan (2012). "Religijska dimenzija jugoslovenskih sukoba", athttp://veraznanjemir.bos.rs/index.php?page=tekstovI_analize&lang=srp&su baction=showfull&id=1248353218&archive=&start_from=&ucat=12&lang=srp &page=tekstovI_analize, (accessed May 14).

Žarkov, Dubravka (2007). *The Body of War: Media, Ethnicity and Gender in Break-up of Yugoslavia*, Durham: Duke University Press.

Zubrzycki, Genevieve (2006). *The Crosses of Auschwitz: Nationalism and Religion in Post-Communist and Religion in Post-Communist Poland*, Chicago: University of Chicago Press.

3
New Yugoslavism in Contemporary Popular Music in Slovenia

Mitja Velikonja
(Translated from Slovenian by Olga Vuković)

Introduction – imaginary Yugoslavia

To speak about socialist Yugoslavia in the present-day Slovenia governed by nationalist and neo-liberal ideologies is controversial because of both terms, *socialist* and *Yugoslavia*. Judging exclusively by dominant discourses and from afar, one could get the impression that everything about Slovenia's transition is clear, binary and evolutionary: Slovenia eventually gained independence and escaped the *Balkan quagmire*; it turned its *thousand-year-old dream* into reality by becoming part of *Europe* – where it always belonged.[1] By contrast, the former political system was simply a *bloody dictatorship*, Yugoslavia was *exploiting the Slovenes*, its leaders were *tyrants*, the Partisan fighters' struggle during World War II was nothing less than the *Bolshevik revolution*, and other south Slavic nations are seen through the prism of the stock Balkan stereotypes. Put briefly, it seems that everything related to the term "Yugo" suggests an unstoppable civilizational decline and moral disaster. These obstinate ideological constructs could lead one to conclude that the less the Slovenes have to do with their Yugoslav and socialist past, the better for them. And yet, a closer look suggests a much more complex situation.

In certain discourses in Slovenia – for example, yugonostalgic discourse, or one related to what has come to be known as the Balkan scene, or even consumer and popular culture discourses – the "frozen" image of socialist Yugoslavia perpetuates old connotations but also carries new, positive ones. Although still marginal, these pro-Yugoslav discourses pointing to the brighter sides of the late federation have recently been increasingly present among the broader public as well.

In this study I use a cultural studies approach to research the discrepancy between the predominantly negative image of the former country in dominant political discourses (the top-down approach) and its positive image in Slovenian popular music. In analyzing Slovenian Yugoslavist discourse, I use the inductive method, concentrating exclusively on music that refers to socialist Yugoslavia and Partisan resistance during World War II. Therefore, the framework of this study is the positive image of Yugoslavia in the ideological imaginary of popular music today, 23 years after the dissolution of the former country. Even a cursory glance at this music shows that it contains no negative Yugoslavism and that Yugoslavia, Tito, Partisan fighters, and *those times* are invariably portrayed in a positive light.

Put differently, the negative Yugoslavism in dominant political discourse is countered by the positive Yugoslavism in popular music. I will be interested in the musical basis of the positive side of the "invented Yugoslav tradition," meaning only the "sunny side" of the ambivalent and sometimes antagonistic discourse of the lost Yugoslav world – or in other words, the positive aspects of its "imagined authenticity." My attention will be focused on the cultural meanings of the rock 'n' roll versions of socialist melodies, the uniforms once worn by Partisan fighters and Tito's pioneers and now sported at concerts, the red stars on album covers, the appeals to join the fight for a more just world, and old proletarian slogans revamped in the era of *democracy, Europe* and *the new world order.*

The main research question I will try to answer is whether this pro-Yugoslav music supports or refutes, legitimizes or subverts dominant political discourses in Slovenia that are still predominantly anti-Yugoslav. Are the composers and performers serious in their intentions, or primarily interested in entertainment? I approached this topic from the cultural studies perspective, meaning that two levels of analysis are inevitably involved: the horizontal and the vertical. In other words, my research on the cultural production is coupled with ideology criticism. The horizontal level is that of cultural variety, while the vertical level reveals its ideological and specifically political dimension. The findings of the research are presented in the last part where I raise the question of the ideological and political dimensions and the consequences of this retrospective and positive construction of the former Yugoslavia in Slovenian popular music. Therefore, rather than using the common approach, that is, rather than analyzing individual musical groups or performers, songs or videos, I have identified and researched the most frequent themes, content and emphasis, and their implicit and explicit meanings.

Let me first explain the meaning of the concept of the new Yugoslavism in Slovenia as I use it in this study. Taking as the point of departure critical approaches to discursive compositions of different *Easts* – Orientalism and Balkanism – I believe that a similar approach may be used in studying the narrative heritage of socialist Yugoslavia and a posteriori constructs about it. That is to say, in this study I do not look at Yugoslavia as a political entity that began to disintegrate in 1991 through a series of destructive wars, but concentrate on its current ideological representations. I research the "imaginary Yugoslavia" that materialized only after its physical counterpart had been destroyed. This is the Yugoslavia that can be found in yugonostalgic elegies, among cyber communities and on dedicated web sites, in retro-marketing, in first-hand memories of the generations that lived in Yugoslavia and in second-hand images created by the post-Yugoslav generation, and last but not least, in music that speaks about *those times*.

I call this ideological discourse "new Yugoslavism." In contrast to the old unifying discourse that emerged in the first half of the nineteenth century and took on various forms, new Yugoslavism is an ideological image of socialist Yugoslavia viewed from both an insider and an outsider perspective, that is, from the insider perspective of the former Yugoslav republics, and from their outsider perspective after 1991 when they became independent states. Yugoslavist discourse in Slovenia arises from the specific situation of the country: Slovenia had been part of Yugoslavia for almost seven decades; it was the first to secede, and at the moment it is the only successor state that has joined the two main trends of European integration. According to all indicators – geographical location, historical heritage, political tradition, cultural context and ethnic structure – it is a Central-European, Balkan and Mediterranean country. During the turbulent twentieth century, it was part of several countries in succession, governed by different political and economic systems, ideological determinants, foreign relations strategies, social stratification and cultural preferences.

It is also necessary to say a few words about the overlapping ideologies of Balkanism and Yugoslavism in Slovenia, as well as the differences between the two. The notions of Yugoslavia and the Balkans are often interchanged and used as synonyms, in such a way that the Balkans refers to Yugoslavia only rather than other Balkan countries too. It is precisely this geographical, historical, cultural and political proximity of Yugoslavia and the Balkans that adds Balkan nuances to Yugoslavism. As a consequence, it often happens that talk about Yugoslavia inevitably veers into Balkanism, in both the positive and negative sense. However, there is a clear distinction between Balkanism and Yugoslavism: the Balkan Other is associated more with the post-Yugoslav Other of the past two decades or so. It is characterized by nationalism, backwardness, rural mentality, patriarchy and turbofolk, and inevitably, with excessive hedonism. The Yugoslav Other seems to be more modern, more progressive, more urban and multicultural and – an apparent contradiction given that Yugoslavia was a socialist state – more pro-western. Metaphorically speaking, the difference between the Balkan and the Yugoslav Other is a difference between brass bands and rock 'n' roll groups, and, in terms of ideologies, between ethno-nationalism and socialism. Balkan otherness is exotic cultural otherness, while Yugoslav otherness is the exotic political counterpart of contemporary Slovenia. There is yet another important difference between the two: the Balkan Other is an external Other, while the Yugoslav Other is an internal Other to contemporary Slovenianness; it is its predecessor. As a matter of fact, not even the ideological constructs of the most intransigent Slovenian nationalists can simply overlook several decades of Slovenia's Yugoslav past.

To sum up, in my understanding, new Yugoslavism is a complex, multilayered, internally split and contradictory ideology that has been developing both inside and outside the borders of the former country. It is present in both mainstream and alternative popular culture, with the latter either unobtrusively sneaking into the mainstream (more popular performers) or decisively opposing it (and therefore remaining on the margins). In both cases, the phenomenon consists of an a posteriori construction of images relating to the Yugoslav political system, social order, cultural production, everyday life and, inevitably, the Partisan fighters' resistance. Much like ideological discourses on the Orient and the Balkans, this discourse, too, is internally contradictory in its interconnecting of apparently incompatible notions. To use Weber's terminology, new Yugoslavism as "an ideal type" comprises both negative evaluations, accusations and systematic demonization of the former common state (primarily found in dominant discourses), as well as positive ones including the glorification of Yugoslavia and respect for it (in various pro-Yugoslav discourses, initially marginal but recently increasingly present in mainstream pop culture). Much like Balkanism and Orientalism, contemporary Slovenian Yugoslavism is not a homogeneous ideology: the negative images of the Other appearing in dominant discourses (a Balkan person, an Oriental person, in this case a Yugoslav "aboriginal")[2] are always countered by positive images in marginal and alternative discourses. While the Orient is the opposite of the self-image of the West, and the Balkans is the opposite of Europe, in the case of

Slovenia this antipode is Yugoslavia. In the second phase, ideological binarism is upgraded through identity transformation: we have transformed from *former Yugoslavs* into *contemporary Slovenes.*

Methodological approach and theoretical background

My epistemological starting point is that every message has ideological meanings and political consequences regardless of whether or not the authors, the protagonists and the audience are aware of these, and whether or not this is their intention. Much like any other cultural production, contemporary popular music, which is no longer reserved for the younger generation only, is an ideological battlefield where various power structures intersect along with their mechanisms for coding and decoding, connoting and denoting, privileged and alternative readings of meanings, and various goals. It comprises various musical trends, ranging from those that seek alternatives and new possibilities of expression and seek to promote new cultural patterns and ideological values, through the ones that subvert existing trends, to those that adhere to conservatism, regress, and adapt to dominant ideological discourses and values, strengthening them in the process. The very fact that the songs I explore in this essay refer, either directly or indirectly, to the former common state, which has been systematically denigrated in dominant discourses ever since the end of the 1980s, represents a unique political statement, much assigning about the *beauties of our homeland Slovenia, its hardworking people* and *peaceful country life* constitutes a political statement.

In exploring the ideological depth of the multifarious cultural production or, put differently, in establishing the where, how and why of positive Yugoslavism in Slovenian music, I used a number of methods. The principal one was textual analysis of lyrics, interviews, public statements, articles and the entire spectrum of visuals. I sought to identify the most frequent themes and analyze the pattern of their use. I collected clips from print and electronic media and the Internet, posters and flyers. I also conducted interviews with some of the performers. The next method was observation through participation in various events and concerts. I should add here that I always had a keen interest in music, during the era of Yugoslavia as well as in contemporary Slovenia.

I approached the research historically and comparatively, or, in Levi-Strauss's terminology, diachronically and synchronically. I placed the contemporary musical production along a timeline, looking for its (dis)continuity; I tried to establish how Slovenian popular music developed within the Yugoslav context and outside it. At the same time, I placed it into a synchronic, "non-historical" analytical framework, that is, the "here and now" framework. I compared pro-Yugoslav popular music in Slovenia with similar/different music elsewhere in the world, but primarily with that in Yugoslavia's other successor states. Finally, I approached the subject in a top-down manner: I analyzed discourses, that is, various forms of cultural production and ideological messages, rather than the public perceptions and receptions of these. This research approach then determined the methodological approaches mentioned above and the theoretical starting points discussed below.

Theoretically, I used two starting points in researching the subject. On the one hand, I was interested in retro as a cultural phenomenon that I view as a pragmatic and instrumental playing with the elements of the past in order to achieve certain goals. There are no content differences between retro and nostalgia – both are oriented towards the past and fascinated by recent history (history that is still close and alive), and both endeavor to re-actualize it in the present. However, although related, the two are not the same. While nostalgia is loaded with sentimentality, has a recognizable "warm" emotional tone and carries emancipatory and restitutive potential, retro is colder, deliberately alienated (to avoid possible accusations of showing excessive sympathy towards the past or lamenting a lost past), "purposive" (instrumental) and even "sacrilegious" (because it indifferently touches upon certain "sacred" themes and makes fun of these). While nostalgia is much more mimetic and serious, retro can be amusing and unburdened; it creates and maintains an ironic distance and, in ideal circumstances, remains open to novelties, hybridization and perturbations of meaning. Nostalgia offers solace and seeks solutions in the past for current problems, but retro delights in the past "for the sake of the past itself," or because of its pragmatic usefulness in the present.

Guffey says that retro is "half-ironic, half-longing," has "non-serious and subversive instincts" and "does not seek out proud examples of the past; it shuffles instead through history's unopened closets and unlit corners" (2006, 10, 11, 14). Reynolds (2011, xii) writes that retro "refers to a self-conscious fetish for a period stylization (in music, clothes, design) expressed creatively through pastiche and citation." Brown distinguishes between repro, retro and repro-retro:

> Repro pertains to reproducing the old pretty much as it was, albeit meanings may have changed in the meantime. Retro refers to combining the old with the new, usually in the form of old-style styling with hi-tech technology. Repro-retro, on the other hand,

involves second helpings of the past, insofar as it revives or reproduces something that traded on nostalgia to start with. (1999, 365)

I agree with Bennett (2003, 161) who says that

> post-war generations are able to hold on to their perceptions of
> youth and to engage in nostalgic representations with the help of the
> popular culture industries which continue to market music, styles
> and various forms of memorabilia to ageing babyboomer audience.

However, when researching the retro production in the West as opposed
to that in the East, it is necessary to take into account an essential difference – the West did not experience such a radical political, social, cultural
and economic change as the East did. There was no such fundamental
turn in mentality or narrative discontinuity in the western memory.
Retro "implies rupture," says Guffey justifiably (2006, 160, 161), and
"does not allow historical epochs to grow old gracefully." Therefore,
while retro production in the West can be perceived primarily in relation to mass and consumer culture, in the post-Yugoslav case it always
carries an explicitly political tone. In other words, it is not retro for the
sake of retro: a return to the recent past does not restrict itself to the area
of culture, but every glance back into the past in pop culture necessarily
has more or less explicit political connotations.

Accordingly, when analyzing these phenomena, it is necessary to
approach them from the perspective of ideology criticism. In my
understanding, the cultural polyphony I address here – and *polyphony*
can be understood in its literal meaning, since I write about music –
involves a dual struggle: to harmonize with the tunes played by the
power structures in society and to out-voice them. In other words, not
all tones are equally loud. Critical social sciences, from Marxism and
(post)structuralism to the Birmingham School, insist that there is no
ideologically neutral cultural content. For example, Barthes writes (2003,
11) that, "from the moment it is voiced, even if in the intimacy of the
subject, language is in the service of power." For this reason, I cannot
treat Yugoslav subjects in contemporary Slovenian music as being only
another variegated, playful form of the *postmodern condition*; it is much
more than that. Yugoslavia and the Partisan fighters' war are still hot
political topics in all parts of the former country, and every reference to
them in any area carries political meaning.

In this study I pursue two theoretical lines. The first is that ideology
always has a material existence as well. When an individual is concerned,

"the existence of the ideas of his belief is material in that *his ideas are his material actions inserted into material practices governed by material rituals which are themselves defined by the material ideological apparatus from which derive the ideas of that subject*" (Althusser, 1980, 71). In other words: ideology is always "realized" in practice, and it always has material effects. For this reason, the music I address in this chapter is not ideologically neutral, innocent, or "non-ideological" as many of its authors and listeners believe. The process of representation "always involves power relations and it is mediated through historically changing institutions, class structures, taken-for-granted historical accounts and scientific assumptions," says Duncan (1993, 53).

The other important theoretical deliberation that guided me throughout this research was the inherent ambivalence of every ideological discourse. Every ideological discourse is split in itself, and each one combines its opposing, or to be more precise, antagonistic positions. The contradictory nature of ideology manifests itself in the fact that the constructions of both Us and Them are not unequivocal: both have "good and bad aspects," and understandably, the good sides prevail in Us and the bad sides prevail in Them. Let us take as an example Orientalism and Balkanism: it is possible to find in both positive, pleasant, attractive characteristics. However, dichotomy as such is not neutral; it is not a comparison of equals, nor a fifty-fifty relation – the hierarchy is always established; Us is above Them (and, in counter-hegemonic readings, Them is above Us). What is primary and what secondary, or how this is evaluated, positively or negatively, is a matter of the constellation of power structures. The "solution" offered by dominant ideologies is a transition from Them to Us, that is, the "civilizing" of Them, who thus make an evolutionary step forward. Naturally, the ideological trap lies in the fact that Them can never really (or in large numbers) become Us, regardless of how hard they try. Bhabha explains this (1994, 122) with the ambivalence of "colonial mimicry." They are "almost the same, but not quite."[3] With this, Us subordinate Them effectively and for good; although They are supposed to become Us at some point in the future, it is an almost impossible endeavor.

Duncan (1993, 44) argues that "the concept of the Other, being relational, is dependent upon two sites": ambivalence within the group "is necessarily projected into their attitude towards the Other." The binary opposition between Us and Them, "serves the dual purpose of reinforcing and defining group identity while simultaneously ordering complex difference into a simpler, homogeneous entity which is more easily appropriated." The more we resemble someone and the closer we are, the bigger the ideological difference that must be established to "prove" how different we are. Proximity – spatial or temporal – is the most keen of all to generate otherness: within the ideology of constructing the Other, small differences become huge and insurmountable otherness. "The narcissism of small differences" manifests itself in terms of space and time: one that is the Other in relation to our culture can be our close companion from the past or our contemporary somewhere else. I speak here about the temporalization and spatialization of the Other, but the essence is the same: both Others are the constitutive opposition of Us. In other words, without a temporal/spatial Other, the identity of Us cannot become shaped.

Judging by dominant discourses, Slovenia has two Others: a spatial one and a temporal one. Generally speaking, Slovenia's closest Other in terms of space, its current ideological binary opposite, is the Balkans – and this is why we supposedly have nothing in common with it. In Slovenian dominant discourse – that is, the statements of politicians and nationalist intellectuals – it is possible to find a multitude of negative Balkanisms. Slovenia's closest Other in terms of time, or the Other in its history, is SFRY – and with it, too, we supposedly have nothing more in common. In this ideological discourse, the opposite of Slovenia's self-image is the image of Yugoslavia, and the opposite of the self-image of a contemporary Slovene is the image of the former Yugoslav. The closer we are, the more we need to differ; the smaller the difference, the more it needs to be inflated. In this way, similarities between identities are repeatedly destroyed – binarized and then hierarchized. The heterogeneity of Our and Their identities is homogenized in an ideological process that first separates and then subordinates/superordinates.

The Other is therefore the inverse image of the Self. The ideological construction of the Yugoslav in contemporary Slovenian Yugoslavism, both positive and negative, that is in the *pro et contra* perspectives on Yugoslavia, can be explained through the prism of different approaches through which the West creates the images of the Orient, as proposed by Appadurai (1988, 41). These are essentialization (Otherness is in them), exoticizing (they are completely different from us), and totalizing (they are all the same). This is the basis on which the "completely different" Yugoslav Other is evaluated. It is essentialized, exoticized and totalized as something bad in dominant discourses, and as something good in marginal albeit increasingly propulsive discourses. I would like to repeat once more: every explanation of cultural practices necessarily hits upon the issue of social power structure. What is involved is not a simple circulation of meanings, or horizontal relations among differences, or their instability and fluidity, but primarily their hierarchization. Differences in ideological constructions always indicate the subordination or super-ordination in social reality, in people's interrelations and their social situations – and vice versa. Smith (1993, 89) says that "symbolic mean-ings, then, are held in place by power, and it is only by challenging a definition that we can discover where this power lies," and "how this power operates." My approach to the analysis in this concrete case is also based on this principle.

Object of research

Initially, I collected materials for this study randomly and sporadically (I picked everything that caught my ear or eye), but during the last four or five years I approached the task more systematically. I was inter-ested in music, performances, videos, album covers, images, language, symbols and lyrics within practically all genres of contemporary music in Slovenia that referred to *those* times: street punk, alter hip hop, nu-metal, pop rock, pop, turbofolk as well as singer-songwriters and choirs. This study contains only a selection of the hundreds of items I heard or watched. I should also add that the performers (more than 50 of them), their songs and the various genres of popular music I studied almost never appeared together at concerts, or on compilations or in broadcasts. Practically each performer has his/her/their target audience and venues. These range from the picnics of the Yugoslav generations to student parties, from the rallies of angry trade unionists to village fairs, and from competitions for Eurosong contests to Partisan celebra-tions; the audience is equally diverse, ranging from alternative circles to weekend nostalgics.

In making a selection, I looked for performers who drew on, or at least made references to anything related to the socialist Yugoslavia, or to the present, insofar as it is related to the Yugoslav era. Therefore, the keywords or images I used were as follows: *Yugoslavia, socialism, commu-nism, Tito, Partisan fighters, the red star, Tito's pioneers, the Yugoslav flag,* slogans such as *brotherhood and unity*, and topics, archive footage, music and expressions characteristic of the cultural, political and everyday life of Yugoslavia. Performers greatly differ in how they use these subjects: with some, their whole work is suffused with themes and images related to Yugoslavia, while others use it only sporadically, or the reference is contained in their name or image. The reasons why they refer to Yugoslavia also vary, ranging from sentimentality, populist flattery of *the voice of the people*, marketing motives and pleasure, to criticism of the present times or even an appeal for change. Naturally, most of them are motivated by more than just one of these reasons. As to the albums, photos, statements, records and videos – I bought some of these, I found others on web sites, on YouTube or in the media, and I obtained still others in personal interviews with performers.

I sorted the collected items by performers, adding a note on the musical genre and dividing them into four groups: (1) performers whose (almost) entire repertoire involves Yugoslav motifs; (2) performers who use such motifs in only a few songs or video spots; (3) performers who made only one musical "excursion" to this area, and (4) those who use this kind of content in their video spots, graphic image or names. I am well aware of the pitfalls of every attempt at categorization, and I know that in this case, too, most performers could be placed in more than one group. Below is a short introduction to these performers by the categories mentioned above.

1. *The garage (female) choir Kombinat,* who want to *inscribe the heritage of resistance in red chalk,* was established in 2008. Their repertoire consists of rearranged revolutionary, Partisan and proletarian songs from around the world. The same symbolism is also found on their posters and flyers: the color red, avant-garde images of women workers, Che Guevara-style women guerrillas, the hammer and sickle, and slogans like *towards the Sun. Zaklonišče prepeva,* whose slogan is *New times – old dilemmas,* have released six albums since the mid 1990s. They play typical Yugorock and mainly sing in Serbo-Croatian, rather than Slovene. Their lyrics, videos and performances criticize nationalism and post-Yugoslav reality, praise *old time* values and the contemporary Balkan "trip," and all of this is peppered with a good deal of humor. *Rock Partyzani's* slogan is *For our Fatherland – marching with Rock Partyzani!* which they took over from their predecessor, Agropop. They have released two albums and several songs accompanied by attractive videos. Their self-definition is *A party band using Partisan iconography,* with an additional remark that *no one does the same.*[4]
2. The second group comprises performers who refer to topics such as Yugoslavia, socialism and Partisanship only in certain songs. The female choir *Carmina Slovenica* reworked several Partisan songs for their album *Na juriš in the Mood!*[5] subtitled *From a March to Swing;* the album cover features a red star. *Lepi Dasa* combines Slovenian and Serbian turbofolk in an ironic manner, and through his image of the macho *Balkan man* summarizes and subversively parodies all the stereotypical images of *Southerners* and Yugoslavia perpetuated by

Slovenian nationalism. The pop eclectic, *Magnifico*, made only a few songs that deal with these topics using simple but elaborate lyrics, but "Yugoslavianness" and "Balkanness" are implicit in most of his other works too. *Mi2* is a rock band that places special emphasis on lyrics. The singer and songwriter *Iztok Mlakar* ironically delineates *those times* in two of his songs (certainly critically, albeit with sympathy and in an agreeable manner), while he is a more relentless critic of the present times. Strong criticism of the present situation can be found in rapper *Paj's* album entitled *Po Jusu*. *Zoran Predin*, a frontman of the now defunct Lačni Franz group, has been lately appearing as a chansonnier. In addition to two revolutionary songs, he now also sings in Croatian, unlike in the past. *Roy de Roy* is a *Carinthian-Yugoslav-Partisan-folk-ensemble* whose members are Slovenes living in Vienna. Their slogan is *Polka Punk beats Balkan Ska,* and among other things they sing satirically about the past times of the Yugoslav era.

3. Many groups and individual performers of various musical genres who have made only one song of this kind appear on the compilation *Tistega lepega dne…* (*On that Beautiful Day*, 1996) featuring remakes of Partisan and proletarian songs (e.g., "Heavy Less Wanted," "Gojc & Basisti," "Jerca Mrzel," "Dicky B. Hardy," "Jani Kovačič," "Barbara Pešut," "Lolita," the former Borghesia's singer *Darij IV* and others.). In a slow blues song, the Istrian folk-singer *Franci Blašković* and his colleague *Marko Brecelj* criticize, through a description of Tito's court proceedings, capitalist society in general. The Balkan ethno band *Leni Kravac* included in its song "Zajednica 2" parts of Tito's speech, while their on-line announcement of the release featured the Yugoslav coat-of-arms. The entertainer *Brendi* made a song called "Delavska (Worker's Song)," in which, in his characteristic lumpenproleteriat style, he sings about food, firefighters and his love affairs. On his album *Borec v meni* (*A Fighter in Me*), released on the day of Victory, May 9, 2011, *Mirko*, a rapper from Novo Mesto, critically addresses current political and social issues, with the album cover and his image also reflecting this. In his song accompanied by the electric guitar only, *Damir Avdić*, who has been living in Slovenia lately, goes even further and in addition to condemning the present state of affairs, also rejects uncritical, sentimental nostalgia for Yugoslavia. The street-punk group *GUB* and the punk group *Scuffy Dogs* also refer to Yugoslavia and those times; the latter ironically state in one refrain that they want to *serve in the Yugoslav People's Army*. *Ičo Lumbago, Samo Boris and Valterap* strongly attack social injustice, the domination of patriarchy, revisionism, chauvinism and clericalism

in contemporary Slovenia. The mainstream rappers *Klemen Klemen*, *Murat and Jose* and *Zlatko* mention these subjects only in passing, as do *Slon in Sadež* in their unique and witty manner. *Črna mačka* is a typical *something-for-everybody* group or, in their words – *a group for every occasion*. Their repertoire ranges from the usual folk melodies to turbofolk pieces. Five very dissimilar performers have rearranged old songs: *Pankrti* continue to perform their "Bandiera Rossa" at their frequent reunions; pop punkers *Zablujena generacija* reworked the Partisan song "Šivala je deklica zvezdo" ("The Girl Stitched the Red Star"), the chamber jazz/fado band *Bossa de Novo* performs the popular "Pesem XIV Divizije" (a song of the well known World War II division), and *Rok'n'bend* and *Stayerc production* sing "Hej brigade" ("Hey Brigades") – the latter recorded a video spot for this song at Osankarica, the location of the last battle of the Pohorski bataljon, a famous Wolrd War II partisan unit.

4. The fourth group includes performers who use these motifs only in their videos, names, images and, outfits, or on posters and album covers: *Ali En*, the ad hoc pop bend *Tris*, the transvestite trio*Sestre* (video), *Red Five Point Star*, *Tito in ekšn*, *Štefan Kovač Marko Banda*, *Drago Mislej Mef in Narodnoosvobodilni bend (Mef and the People's Liberation Band)*, *Cancel*, *Dario Seraval* and *Zablujena generacija*. Some performers chose ironic derivations for their names: for example the ska band Skartisan, DJ Tito or the title of the second album of Pasji kartel rappers, Kartel's Theory (alluding to the surname of Edvard Kardelj, the ideologist of socialist Yugoslavia). At concerts and for promotional photos, The Drinkers, Kill Kenny and Niet wear T-shirts featuring Tito or other symbols of socialist Yugoslavia. *Dan D*, who play sophisticated alter rock, used documentary footage of Tito's funeral for their reworking of Niet's song "Lep dan za smrt" ("A Nice Day to Die"), which placed the original lyrics in quite a different context.

Laibach is a special example, and a very interesting one viewed from the perspective of this text. On the one hand, their music substantially changed over time, moving from Wagnerian industrial to affable techno, as did their social status – from being almost an enemy of the state that caused moral panic and resulting prohibitions, they turned into one of the most respected export items of Slovenian art. On the other hand, their aesthetics – and that of the entire NSK (Neue Slowenische Kunst) – did not change much over time; it involves an imaginative rotation of visual representations of various powerful modern and postmodern (meta)narratives. The more controversial these are, the more willing they are to use them. These range from left-wing and right-wing totalitarianism of the twentieth century to Christianity, Alpine culture and nationalism, and from old, cold war ideologies to new, NATO militarism and consumerism. Their retrograde or retro-modern iconography – as one of the specific forms of postmodern art – had in fact announced early on aesthetic escapades into recent history and its reinterpretation, including the Yugoslav past. Their videos also contain Partisan imagery, then motifs from the Soviet and Yugoslav revolution and the era of socialism building, the industrial aesthetics from socialist times and more.

Horizontal approach: the analysis of cultural dimensions of this music

In brief: *Yugo rocks!* In this chapter I will try to answer the questions of *how* and *why*. I am interested in the cultural sweep of the phenomenon, that is, its manifestations. Within the cultural approach, both levels, the horizontal and the vertical, should be addressed in relation to each other. In this chapter, the study material is classified by sub-sections and accompanied by short reflections. I look into the three main aspects of this music: its form, content and finally its ambitions.

Form

I was interested in the (re-)production of this music, meaning that I sought to establish *whether it predominantly consisted of new songs or rearranged old songs*; or, drawing on Brown (1999), whether it consists mostly of repro, retro, or repro-retro. Retro is prevalent: most bands produce new songs taking the old times as a point of departure. The rearrangements by the Kombinat and Carmina Slovenica choirs and the pieces appearing on the compilation *Tistega lepega dne* (*On That Beautiful Day*, 1996) would qualify as repro, while Rock Partyzani's work could be described as repro-retro, since they partly write new songs and partly compile nostalgic sequences from old Slovenian pop, rock and punk songs of the past three decades, including those by their predecessor, Agropop.

Therefore, there are more new, retro works that include old ideological phrases (*comrades, brotherhood and unity, Death to Fascism – Freedom to the People, from the Vardar River to Mt. Triglav*, etc.). My conclusion is that, while this music indeed relates to *those times*, it does this in new ways. This is not a simple reproduction of the old that would be close to the hearts of the older pro-Yugoslav generations, but mainly new songs intended for younger people.

The choice of language is an issue in its own right. Disregarding six albums by Zaklonišče prepeva with lyrics in Serbo-Croatian, Slovene is predominant. This is especially interesting in the light of the fact that the dominant language of Yugoslav pop and rock performers was precisely Serbo-Croatian, the language now dubbed *naški* (ours). However, the lyrics in Slovene include many Serbo-Croatian interjections, or even a mixture of several languages, for example a line or two in Serbo-Croatian, English, German and so on. On the other hand, revolutionary songs from around the world are preserved quite intact in the original languages. Magnifico uses a strong Serbo-Croatian accent when singing, or writing, in either Slovene or English. Given that Slovenia is characterized by strong linguistic nationalism, the very use of *čefurščina*[6] in this music, much like the use of Serbo-Croatian, represents a rather subversive act lending to this music an unambiguous political flavor. Both languages are also used in the criticism of Slovenian nationalism in other sub-cultural practices (in graffiti and street art, comic books, etc.).

I further sought to establish if there were more *new or old messages* in these songs. There are many remakes of old songs that carry old messages into new times. These messages acquire quite a different character in the new context and point to the ways in which problems were solved in the past. Many problems are similar to the ones encountered today: social injustice, exclusion, intolerance or domination by the powerful. However, new songs carrying old messages that are still topical today are much more suggestive: they criticize the present time and glorify the supposedly better past. Still other songs have become so popular over time that they are now reproduced as if they were ordinary evergreens.

This brings us to a broader consideration arising from the fundamental cultural studies' premise about the circulation of meanings across various discursive practices. Practically all messages in these songs are new because the context is new, and different from those of 30, 50 or 70 years ago. The same lyrics and the same melodies can therefore acquire quite a different meaning in new circumstances. But not necessarily, so interpretation is mainly left to the listener. To be more concrete, to which *fatherland* does the song "It's nice to be young in our fatherland" refer? To the former Yugoslavia, or to present-day Slovenia? Who has been expelling us and from which *fatherland*, as the old Partisan song Bilećanka says? For which *libertà* did *partigiano* from the "Bella ciao" die? Whose army are the brigades from "Hej brigade" and "XIV division," and for whom does the little girl *stitch the red star* now? The message remains semiologically open: it can be appropriated by the advocates of different, even diametrically opposite ideological positions.

In the group of new and rearranged songs (and accompanying visuals) the prevalent *themes* are Partisans and references to mass culture and everyday life in *those times*, followed by proletarian and socialist themes and those speaking about Yugoslavia as a country. Some songs come from other revolutionary movements. The dominance of Partisan themes, that is, themes from the *heroic period*, is in a way logical: nostalgia always refers to the period that had a future, looked forward and dreamed about better times. On the other hand, the neo-liberal ideology of present-day consumer society is expressly presentistic: the end of history, no future, everything is here and now, accessible, on sale (but, to be a bit sarcastic, only for those who have a valid credit card). In addition to Partisanship, the second most important thematic area is the "golden age" of socialist Yugoslavia (the 1970s and the early 1980s, in the eyes of the majority of Yugoslavs). This is evident from references to pop culture (music, movies, sport, fashion, design and commercials) and the lifestyle of that time.

Next, I sought to answer whether the pro-Yugoslavism of this music implies a specific *musical genre*, a genre that was popular in *old times*. One would expect to see the domination of Yugorock, but this is not true – practically the entire spectrum of contemporary popular music is present. Classical Yugorock – that is to say, hard and blues rock of the 1970s and the early 1980s, interspersed with Balkan ethnic elements, which also chronologically coincides with the golden era of Yugoslav rock 'n' roll – is played only by Zaklonišče prepeva and partly by Rock Partyzani. In terms of music exclusively, this is "new old" music, a conservative leap back into the time of 35 years ago, but equipped with fresh, critical content (including pop-leftism, anti-NATO and anti-capitalist messages). The flavor of previous times is also introduced by the Kombinat and Carmina Slovenica choirs. All other performers belong to other genres, ranging from folk-singers to hip-hoppers and from punks to pop singers. The deficit of "real" Yugorock is obviously compensated through the thematic Yu-Rock and Balkan parties, compilations and frequent performances by Yugorock musicians who are still touring.[7]

The celebration of socialism and Yugoslavia in independent Slovenia began on the alternative scene, which had formerly been in disfavor with the Yugoslav ruling elite (particularly the punk scene). Some see this as a contradiction: to a member of the punk band GUB, the preference for those times in contemporary punk is somehow incomprehensible, since under the previous system the punks were not exactly on friendly terms with the ruling elite, but now they praise it as the best of the best. In my understanding, this reveals the continuity of alternative music's opposition to both the past and the present political system and mainstream culture. At that time, it was left-wing criticism of the aging socialist system; now it is left-wing criticism once again, but this time of the neo-liberal and nationalist system, and part of it is the exposition of the positive dimensions of the socialist system and of Yugoslavia as a state.

Content

The next set of questions relates to the content of these songs. What is the image of Yugoslavia presented in these songs? How is it related to other layers of culture? Is this a revival of an old image or the shaping of a new one? One symptomatic trait is that Yugoslavia is frequently depicted with humor: the Yugoslav times on the whole appear congenial and funny. "Each parody is a version of the whole system in miniature," says Hariman (2008, 258).

I also sought to establish *which elements of the past prevail* and are celebrated: everyday life, the political system, personalities or the political past. I will present these step by step. An important place is occupied by personal nostalgia for lost loves or careless youth. Although these are placed within the wider signifying networks of the time, they do not carry direct political connotations. Then, the *trademarks* of socialist Yugoslavia that were part of everyday life frequently find their way into these songs, for example, *brotherhood and unity*. Many pieces are in fact a real "Yu-collection" of former pop culture signifiers and elements of everyday life, which were once wittily described by the Mandić (1976): the best such example is the Yugo song by Rock Partyzani. Naturally, the country's leader of the time is unavoidable. *We swore oaths (all sorts of them) in front of His picture, we listened to the myths, but all their endless prayers were useless,* sing Zaklonišče prepeva. Blašković and Brecelj start their song with Tito's famous speech at the court proceedings in 1928, and continue in pristine Istrian dialect: *'cause I'm comrade mechanic metal worker, a real proletarian, an exemplary communist and a hardcore atheist, God is my witness.* Another excerpt from Tito's famous speech, *we spilt a sea of blood for the brotherhood and unity of our nations, and we will not allow anyone to touch it or undermine it from the inside,* can be found in Laibach's Država (The State).

The sexualized images of Tito's young female pioneers appear in many videos. Other similar stereotypical *Yugoslavs* are a blue-collar worker, an inevitable Partisan fighter, and a sportsman in the track suit of the Yugoslav national team or some other popular football team.[8] The red star and the socialist and political party flags and emblems appear on album covers, posters and flyers, in videos and at the concerts of many performers mentioned above.

Additionally, Yugoslavia as a state is also celebrated. *There was a land, a land of champions, a land called Yugoslavia,* says Magnifico. The Partisan fighters' resistance and their wide support base among people are also shown in the best light, while collaboration with the Fascist enemy is uncompromisingly condemned. The following is how Zaklonišče prepeva delineates it: now it seems like *the Partisans under Mount Triglav were on the wrong side, the traitor has been proclaimed a saint, the idiotic judge has decided so.* Historical revisionism is frequently criticized using the language of the revisionists themselves, that is, the language of the anti-Partisan and anti-Yugoslav camps. In the song "Dežela" ("Country"), the ad hoc trio Ičo Lumbago, Samo Boris and Valterap sarcastically declare that *Partisans are rats, and domobranci should be honored.*

The red thread running through all these songs is the rehabilitation of Slovenia's socialist and Yugoslav past. Much like the dominant discourses that take this subject to the other extreme, these lyrics also exaggerate. The ridicule of the former state in the discourses of Yugoslavia's opponents is countered by ingenious portraits of that same country. The Yugoslav past appears idyllic and cozy, cleansed of all negative elements and episodes. Naturally, the authoritative nature of the socialist system is never mentioned, nor is the persecution of opponents or the traumatic post-war events.[9] Every positive, even if parodic evaluation of the past and/or the different is also an implicit attack on the present day situation, which, as a rule, promptly turns into explicit critique and – as we shall see later in the text – into appeals for radical change.

At this point, I would like to mention another observation. Through the excessive use of *we, we are, and our* rhetoric, of the kind "we are this and we are that," the Yugoslav Other who lived in the community and for the community is totalized. The collectivism and communitarianism of the socialist era are contrasted to present-day individualism and atomization. The performers speak from the position of the Yugoslav (not the Slovenian) *we.* For them, the Yugoslav is the Self and the Slovene is the Other, and this is the position from which they criticize the latter. In their view, the past (Yugoslavia, socialism, the spirit of resistance) is better than the present (Slovenia, capitalism, torpid conformism).

I also looked at *cultural hybridization* within this music, or the connecting of new content and forms with older cultural and ideological layers. Hybridization (in music) is a global cultural phenomenon, and such mixtures can be encountered all around the world. In our case, images from the past are grafted onto rock 'n' roll and other pop music genres, most frequently in a satirical and ironic manner.[10] The rebellion of rock music is connected with Partisan resistance, in both words and images. Zaklonišče prepeva say that, like their fathers who carried guns, they too want to *take their electric Gibsons and storm across the Balkans and beyond.* It's not only rock 'n' rollers carrying Partisan uniforms, but also Partisans carrying guitars. Rock Partyzani's slogan could be *Guitars instead of Guns.* After all, Zablujena generacija has also frequently been using the metal sign – the extended index and little finger with the red star in the middle – in their visuals ever since they put it on the cover-page of their last album (2008).

Furthermore, the Yugoslav and Partisan content is added to the brico-lage of meanings and icons of contemporary popular culture. The latter comprises among other things the aesthetics of the Pink television channel, spaghetti westerns, various religious symbols, pop-celebrity glamour, the iconography of rebellion and, last but not least, new left-wing movements and ideas, from pop-leftism to anti-militarism and anti-Americanism. In the vocabulary of studies of post-modern art, it is a typical *pick'n'mix* or *mix'n'match* of socialist/Yugoslav/Partisan motifs and other historical content, aesthetic trends, political orientations and elements of contemporary popular culture. Hybridization proves that what is involved is not a simple reproduction of past cultural production and its ideological background, but a much more relaxed attitude towards both the past and the present. Since it is a deliberate, provocative play with what both sides see as the most sacred and incompatible themes, it may appear as sacrilege to both exclusivist camps, the Yugonostalgics and the pro-European Slovenian nationalists. It brings together what is apparently incompatible. Hybridization reflects the complexity of new transitional identities in which there is "a bit of both:" it says to domi-nant discourses that "we are both: the contemporary Slovenes and the former Yugoslavs, Europeans and the Balkan people, rock'n'rollers and Partisans."[11]

Another related question here is that of whether all this is about *conti-nuity, return, or new narrative constructions* of the images of *Yugoslavia, socialism, Tito and Partisanship.* As a matter of fact, all three are involved, but the manner of construction varies. Firstly, continuity is created through documentarism. Many songs and videos begin and end with original songs from the past (the Yugoslav anthem, "The Internationale," "Od Vardara pa do Triglava"), excerpts from speeches (mostly Tito's) or archival footage. The people and episodes that appear in them are real and historical personalities and episodes. For example, GUB begins their song Yugoslavia with the well-known footage of the statement by soldiers of the Yugoslav People Army at the beginning of the conflict in Slovenia in June 1991; Leni Kravac makes use of Tito's famous speech on the necessity of interconnection and cooperation for all Yugoslav nations; and Mirko from the one on the sanctity of brotherhood and unity. The documentary approach leaves an impression of authenticity and of continuity of the new production with the previous period. Old television footage, speeches, old song samplings and photographs are a kind of reality check – they say that *it was really like this*, and that new scenes are a continuation. That is to say, the old is upgraded with the new. The conjoining of two separate parts also manifests itself in technical details; the archival footage is black-and-white, while the contemporary one is in color; intermezzos in old songs are deliberately poor with a scratchy sound, while the new parts are technically flawless. Documentarism as an ideology of authentication therefore it further deepens present fiction while legitimizing it with through the past.

Secondly, the return to the past is achieved through imitation, repro, that is, faithful, mimetic reproduction of old music (e.g., in the repertoire of both choirs) or images (Rock Partyzani's performances and visuals). In this case, the strategy of authentication is remembrance which says, *this is the picture that is preserved in my memory*. Music is a non-material form of remembrance. Since in Slovenia the socialist and Yugoslav past does not have its material "places of remembrance" (as defined by Nora, 1996), these have been transported to the sphere of their non-material equivalents – the Internet, Yugonostalgic parties, the celebration of the former holidays and music – and legitimized through the aura of remembrance. To say it with the title of the radio show of several decades ago: *Still remember, comrades?*

Let me explain this in more detail. In other Yugoslavian successor states, there are many places of remembrance that have become sites of Yugonostalgic pilgrimages and historical tour destinations. By contrast, in Slovenia it is "soft memory" (personal memories, remembrances) that predominates over "hard memory" (monuments, buildings, symbolic places, etc.). The reason is that in Slovenia the most important sites of the Partisans' World War II struggles have recently been associated with the Slovenian rather than the all-Yugoslav anti-Fascist experience, while at the same time every association with the socialist revolution, which was an inseparable part of the liberation war, has been avoided. Put differently, there have been attempts to remove Slovenian Partisanship from its Yugoslav as well as its revolutionary framework.

Thirdly, the very fact that panegyrics to Yugoslavia appear in contemporary popular music is in a way paradoxical, defying the explanations that what is involved is simple inertia. Frozen images of *those times* are brought into the present time by the younger, post-Yugoslav generation, not by *old comrades*. In most cases these are completely new construc-tions of the Yugoslav past. In the new narrations, everything is possible, realities mix and anything goes – Partisans play electric guitars, young women in low-neck dresses sport the military look, the past is depicted as a time when everything was about dance, partying, love, victories and truancy, and we were all friends and had everything we needed. The performers are aware of and reconciled to their post-Yugoslav present day, but they have not forgotten their Yugoslav past.

The images of the past are therefore associated with those of post-Yugoslav and contemporary mass culture. In the song "Dežela" ("Country") of the above-mentioned rap trio, there is a line *I am a child of transition, embedded in new norms, but with my thoughts in Yuga*. Murat and Jose say that they *drink a toast with friends from all parts of the former Yuga*. Crucial elements here are humor, parody and semiotic play, not to mention irony, all of which are the basic characteristics of retro and postmodern culture in general. Scuffy Dogs "complain": *The state asked from me to throw into shit one year of my life, to do what they say, to be subor-dinate in a communist way. I want to serve in the Yugoslav People's Army!* Performers point out the now unimaginable but agreeable pathologies of socialism and everyday life (moonlighting at a work place, the protec-tive role of the state, the new speak of self-management socialism, etc.) whose public questioning in the past was ruled out.

Ambitions

The third group of questions is concerned with the *ambitions* behind this type of production, that is to say, the degree of political engage-ment. There are three kinds of engagement accompanied by matching narratives that derive from the Yugoslav socialist experience: nostalgic and neo-nostalgic[12] escapades ("the past was better"), the comparative-critical ("the present is worse than the past") and emancipatory engage-ments (*the struggle for old rights*, as an old song with the same name says).

One kind of engagement involves passive and unambitious contem-plation of the "lost paradise." GUB, for example, sings, *we didn't under-stand what was going on, only knew that other flags were fluttering around, adios Yugoslavia, adios socialism, brotherhood and unity, this will be capi-talism*. Rock Partyzani, in their remake of Springsteen's "Born in the USA" sing *Born in Yugoslavia, the country of happiness and love, you still live in our hearts, we'll never forget you*. Many reiterate the question and answer that has been asked many times since the disintegration of the common country: *and then I ask myself how we came to where we are now if all was good in Yugoslavia ... politics brought us here, seven nations that had been together now bleed,*[13] or ask the dead Marshall, who supposedly turns in his grave, *and now, comrade, tell me, we cannot go back, but where do we go, really? And where are we now? I don't expect you to tell me, but since everyone is silent, perhaps you know.*[14]

The second kind of engagement involves severe criticism of present social injustice, capitalism and the normalization of nationalism, while comparing the current situation with that of the past, which emerges as a better option. Paj says that *it's worse than in Yuga, we were alive then if nothing else, but now we are the living dead*; Zlatko says that *the country is in shit, all the time, they say it's because of Tito Broz, the train called recession has arrived.* Brendi *sometimes thinks to himself, while making salad, that all that is injustice, they took care of themselves but left little for us.* Zaklonišče prepeva are the most caustic critics: *new homeland protectors sweep our doorstep, we no longer like any of our former brothers, we now chase away these stinky bastards from our courtyards, enough of brotherhood and the former Yugoslavia*; the refrain of the song is *Ale, ale, ale ... Slovenia, Aufwiedersehen, Balkans.*

Finally, some performers' engagement consists in an appeal for change and revolution, with Rock Partyzani being the most adamant protesters. *Stand up, damned of the Earth, let us once more get together to liberate our homes!, from Siberia to the Balkans, from Germania to Greece, from the river Vardar to Mount Triglav, the voice of the revolution can be heard.* Blašković and Brecelj say that *land should be given to peasants, the factories should be given to workers, don't be numb, let's make a revolution, because a capitalist is a pig.* Leni Kravac thinks that *together we can do everything, let's gather our strengths and dreams.*

Various ambitions purported by these pro-Yugoslav musical pieces – contemplation, critique, a revolutionary spirit – clearly allude to the feeling of liminality in contemporary Slovenia, the feeling of living in an intermediate space between the known past and an unclear future; the feeling that "we are no more" and at the same time "we are not yet." They answer the old questions of how to proceed and where to go now. What should be done? The emergence and development of this music in Slovenia has therefore not been accidental, since, as Guffey has established, (2006, 166) retro is "a symptom, rather than an end; we are pulled to the past, because our visions of the future remain unformed."

The vertical approach: analysis of the ideological and political dimensions of this music

In previous paragraphs, I have categorized, briefly described and explained the cultural aspects of contemporary Slovenian "Yugophile" pop music, and I will now proceed with the analysis of its ideological messages and political reach. Since it explicitly or implicitly proceeds from the songs, visuals, statements and productions, in the ideal-type sense, the fundamental binary and antagonistic structure of Slovenian Yugoslavism that defines present day Slovenianness and former Yugoslavianness is as follows:

- Slovenia vs. Yugoslavia
- the present vs. the past
- Europe vs. the Balkans
- neo-liberal capitalism vs. self-management Socialism
- nationalism vs. multiculturality (*brotherhood and unity*)
- historical relativism vs. anti-Fascism
- ideology of individualism vs. socialist communitarianism and the welfare state
- hard work, workaholism vs. Socialist easy living
- new international organizations (EU, NATO, redefined UN membership) vs. old ones (the non-aligned countries, or the Yugoslav federation, for that matter)
- conformism vs. rebellion.

The Other created through this music is diametrically opposite to the Other in Slovenian dominant discourses: while in negative Yugoslavism Slovenia is the Self and Yugoslavia is the Other, in positive Yugoslavism of this musical production it is exactly the opposite – Yugoslavia (Socialism, Partisanship) is the Self, while Slovenia (capitalism, conformism) is the Other. The performers take sides with "Yugoslavia" and criticize "Slovenia" from that position: *it was better in the past.*

In new Slovenian Yugoslavism as a whole, identities are fundamentalized: on the one hand, we have negative Yugoslavism with hegemonic images of Slovenianness, or in other words, the condemnation of everything that smacks of *those times.* On the other hand, as an anti-thesis, the area of popular music presented here offers affirmative images of Yugoslavianness that are increasingly gaining ground. The "intellectual and spatial confinement" (Appadurai, 1988, 38) of Us and Them is being fixed: contemporary Slovenes are supposedly something quite different from the former Yugoslavs; we supposedly have nothing more in common with them and we are supposedly not similar at all.

In the case of contemporary Slovenia, it is precisely the "dangerous" temporal and spatial proximity to the socialist Yugoslavia and the Balkans that generates difference, since excessive similarity would be destructive for the new, dominant ideological self-image of Slovenia. It would annihilate the justification for *Slovenia's independence and secession from Yugoslavia*, and would completely destroy the self-legitimization of the transition ideology that is advocated by the "transition elites." Unpleasant questions would then ensue: if we are similar and if it was better before, why did we split at all? This is the source of obsessive insistence over the past 20 years on differences between and hierarchies among contemporary Slovenes and the former Yugoslavs. Put differently, any suspicion threatening the justification of dominant discourses must be eliminated.

The new Slovenian Yugoslavism creates and reproduces the impossible, split, dual attitude of the Slovenes towards Slovenia's socialist and Yugoslav past. It is not fixed or unequivocal in its content or purpose but rather contextual, adapted to various contemporary groups, circumstances and goals. Undoubtedly, Slovenian Yugoslavism says more about the Slovenes themselves, or rather, about their changing, not to say schizophrenic attitudes[15] towards their socialist and Yugoslav past, than about how socialism and Yugoslavia in Slovenia really were. The music presented here is then a kind of "magical window" into a past that had never been what it appears to be in its present simulations (to be read: reproductions or constructions).

Negative Yugoslavism in dominant discourses cannot be apprehended unless we also take into account its positive pole in marginal discourses that have been slowly turning into dominant ones. The exaggeration, on the one side, has a boomerang effect and leads to exaggerations on the other. Much as in Orientalism and Balkanism, this involves antagonistic ambivalences that counterbalance each other.[16] In Yugoslavism as a whole, meaning both its positive and negative forms, rejection goes hand in hand with fascination, demonization with delight, stigmatization with glorification, contempt with envy, attraction with fear (in the parlance of popular psychology, this would be called a love-hate relationship). It is a blend of the exotic and dangerous, wild and beautiful, tender and rough images of that enigmatic space and time called socialist Yugoslavia.

Since in this micro-analysis I concentrate on positive Yugoslavism within music, negative Yugoslavism is only briefly outlined, although it deserves a study in its own right. However, the two should definitely be studied together, and this particularly applies to ideological turns: when does a particular characteristic, period, value, personality or the like become positive, good or glorified, and when does it become negative, bad and condemned? Contemporary Slovenian Yugoslavism is not a homogeneous discourse that displays "cracks" at certain nerve points through which the positive images of Yugoslavia, socialism, Tito, Partisans and so on intrude randomly or sneak in. These are not haphazard incursions of external elements, or nostalgic escapades into a time and space that is today safely inaccessible. The duality of Slovenian Yugoslavism is constitutive. Positive Yugoslavism constantly compensates for the dark images of Yugoslavia put forward by negative Yugoslavism (as can be found in contemporary anti-Yugoslav Slovenianness).

Positive Yugoslavism – such as emerges from the "musical accompaniment" analyzed in this chapter – can be interpreted in more than one way. And yet, although I am aware of the many possible readings of this music, its heterogeneity, breadth and diversity of messages and layers of possible interpretations, I believe that it is nevertheless possible to identify two main trends within it. One is non-political positive Yugoslavism, a passive shift away from the controversial (Yugoslav) political history. The other is political Yugoslavism, conceptualized as a utopian alternative, as proof that a different political system was possible and that an alternative way always exists. As such, it has the potential to survive in the present "Slovenia-first" circumstances, and more importantly, it has the potential to initiate change.

The passivization strategy in positive Yugoslavism

In their attempt to depoliticize and dehistoricize Yugoslavia, socialism, Partisanship and the dominant images and slogans of that time, performers use several interconnected passivization strategies: reduction to entertainment, ranting over the present situation in the lumpen-proleteriat manner, simple nostalgic contemplation of a better past, aestheticization, ironic distance and finally, clear connections with neo-conservative ideologies. Let me explain this step by step.

The professed purpose of this specific popular music is *to party*. Socialist Yugoslavia looks like a time-oasis of entertainment which this music attempts to transport into the present time. For example, while Rock Partyzani indeed draw attention, in songs and in interviews, to social injustice, exploitation, the disfranchised masses, the rampant advance of turbocapitalism and historical revisionism, they are still simply a rock 'n' roll band appearing at the usual concert venues. In the words of their frontman, *we somehow coincided with this situation, they accepted us as theirs*. They point out that they *do not have political allegiances*, as is suggested by the inscription on their cover page, which reads: *An entertaining, not a political band*. Partisan songs are supposedly *not political songs ... but evergreens from a particular period of time, inspiring, songs that live in people's subconscious.*[17] Speaking about Pankrti's "Bandiera Rossa," Peter Lovšin says that *it is a good melody, it's a good piece. We like to sing it and that's all there is to it. It is what rock 'n' roll offers you.* A good song, that's what it is. Magnifico also asserts that he is *really not politically-minded.* Therefore, this is not the "Balkanization" of entertainment but its "Yugoslavization" (in the sense, "that was party time") and, on the other hand, the "Europeanization" and "sobering" of Slovenian contemporariness. The two are completely separate.

The second passivization strategy within the affirmative perspective on past times is *ranting over the present.* The condemnation of the current government and the entire social order, on the one hand, and the glorification of the past system in an apparently revolutionary spirit, on the other, obviously represent a profitable market niche. This is quite clear to Rock Partyzani. In the 1980s, their frontman was the leader of the band called Agropop, which had initially appeared to be a Slovenian counterpart of Bosnian *New Primitivism.* At the time of the radicalization of nationalist discourse in Slovenia during the late 1980s, they took on the role of alarm-bells and sang about the tragic fate of the Slovenian nation and the danger of its extinction; at that time, too, this discourse included self-victimization, self-pity and the necessity of resistance. The titles of Agropop's songs speak for themselves: "Slovenia," the "Most Beautiful Country," "Long Live Slovenian Women," "Whole Slovenia Dances," "Drinking in Slovenia," "Songs from Mount Triglav," "Slovenian Men for Slovenian Women," "Happy Slovenes," and "Slovenian Woman, You Will See." In 1993, they released a march about the Slovenian Army, entitled "Slovenia is With Us," including footage from the *war for independence.* The former Agropop frontman, now the Rock Partyzani frontman, is still convinced that Slovenes *always had to reassert their identity through their language, including in the former Yugoslavia.*[18]

Today the glorification of past times is much more popular and profitable than the glorification of Slovenia. Had it been something else, he would have been there to do the job, and he sincerely admits this: *I was thinking about T-shirts with the red star and Rock Partyzani text on the one side, and with the cross and inscription Polka Home Guards,*[19] *on the other. We would then turn the shirts around, depending on the situation.* Rock Partyzani's repertoire is indeed dominated by personal nostalgia (for youth, past loves, or the music of that time) and memories of everyday life, while purely political themes (social injustice, historical revisionism, etc.) are much less frequent, and even when addressed the diction is mainly that of the lumpenproleteriat and entertaining, along the lines of *bread and games* (*...yes, yes, give me a drink anyway*).

The above-mentioned song by Brendi invites similar conclusions. He remembers the times when *we ate and drank, and whoever worked was crazy, whoever didn't drink was not serious, and we were all stealing so much that we had itchy fingers.* The *criticism of the government* from the perspective of *an ordinary man* (and the footage of anti-government and student protests at the end of the past decade) can also be found in the song and video by 6Pack Čukur, "Good morning, Slovenia" (2011), in a series of Rock Partyzani's songs ("Workers boogie," "Cheated...") or in Lovšin's new album, *For a Change* (2012). All this points to intuitive ideological opportunism and an elaborate marketing strategy that counts on the vague but unmistakable sympathies for *those times* cherished by most Slovenes, and even more on their discontent with the present situation. Yet, all is forgotten the moment the concert is over, or some other musical genre becomes more profitable.

A similar pragmatic approach can be observed in Predin's songs. He has recently been adapting resistance songs and singing in Serbo-Croatian, but he also sings that *we live for Slovenia in good times and in bad, look, Europe, Slovenia goes on.*[20] And even the folk band Modrijani admit that Yugoslav music is good for a party (*We most enjoy it when we play yugo-rock, which someone might find offensive or get angry, because we first play, dressed in folk costumes, /Slovenian folk/ songs like You, My Rose, and In the Quiet Valley, and then we play /Yu-pop classic/Ružica /laughing/*).[21]

The third passivization strategy is *nostalgia*, which, says Reynolds, is (2011, xxiii), "after all, one of *the* great pop emotions." However, many musical groups emphasize that their music is not nostalgic. The Kombinat singers explicitly refuse such associations on their website: *we are not nostalgic, we sing with faith in values such as solidarity, faithfulness to the idea, gallantry and courage.*[22] A member of Dan D is also explicit: *We DID NOT color this video with nostalgia, at least not purposefully.* However, whether or not one likes it, every emotionally positive representation of the past is as a rule designated as nostalgia. The Carmina Slovenica conductor admits that a *certain nostalgia is always present with the music that we grew up with.*[23] How else could one understand lines such as *did we lack anything at that time?* or, *where are those golden times when we were happy?* or, *where our old love takes us, down there to the Vardar river, long live Yugoslavia.*

But again, nostalgia, too, is an excellent marketing niche; nostalgia sells everywhere in the contemporary Western world. Accordingly, Slovenian present-day marketing strategies also contain (un)intentional nostalgia, for example, the aesthetics characteristic of Yugoslavia, not to mention the "industrial heritage" and retro-chic in other areas of mass culture, arts, design, tourism and consumerism. Much as in other post-socialist societies, in Slovenia, too, retro-design leans on the three historical aesthetic genres unequivocally specific to Socialism: (Soviet) avant-garde, functionalism (especially in architecture) and Socialist realism.

Such an exploitation of yugonostalgia in contemporary music received severe criticism from the left: Damir Avdić demystifies the idealization of the ideology of brotherhood and unity that ended *in concentration camps and mass graves, with killing squads and mass slaughters*, through the telling verses, *nostalgic mother fucker! Fuck your Bijelo dugme, Fuck your Lepa Brena, Fuck your Džoni Štulić, Fuck your Paket aranžman, Fuck your communism and swastika, a-ha- a-ha Brotherhood and unity has ended! It's time to get to know each other the way we really are.*

Marketing motives are also responsible for the reduction of the political symbols and cultural production of the previous system to *mere aesthetics*. Much like commercialization, aestheticization too devours the original, revolutionary meaning of the images of those times. It disappears, becomes erased: what is left is a mere aesthetic form that "overcomes" the ideology of the past. Undoubtedly, such "aesthetic" erasure of former ideology is deeply ideological in itself in the sense of liberal/postmodern inclusivity, commodification and relativization, in which meta-narratives are reduced to their aesthetic shells, enabling endless play and pure enjoyment. The power structures – which should be afraid of otherness – are safe. Painless simulation is always more desirable than the original thing that carries political connotations; it is preferred by the audience, because the picture is more attractive and purged from unpleasant and controversial aspects, and by the groups in power, because the ideological turn transforms antagonistic images into a game, and the aesthetic preferences of the past become simply another style for the sake of style. Moreover, they earn money from such simulations, and can at the same time boast benevolence ("we allow different views" in a liberal spirit). Hegemonic victory is thus complete.

The next, fifth element of passivization is *ironic distance*, another constant trait of this production. Smith (1993, 79) shows that the "pleasures of retrospection are multiple, but among the more prominent of these are the sense of detachment and the luxury of indifference." The impression of distance enables relaxed joking with the Yugoslav past and the Socialist system, reducing it to an agreeable differentness rather than to a radical – and for dominant discourses dangerous – otherness. The alternative is turned into a joke. Irony thus becomes an end in itself, in the sense that "if we cannot accept or change the present, let us at least joke, and in the worst case provoke without causing pain." However, this same irony – which by definition "opens social convention to exploration and critique" (ibid., 86) – could also be the inception of social engagement, or at least of semiological diversion or semiological guerilla warfare.

The passive aspect of positive Yugoslavism also leaves the door wide open for the elements of neo-conservative ideologies, *nationalism and patriarchy*. Some performers emphasize only the Slovenian aspect of the story: they view the past and the social order of the time from the narrow, national perspective. Rock Partyzani – with the above-mentioned nationalist agenda – sings almost exclusively in Slovene, saying, for example, *at that time we danced all night, we sang Slovenian songs, we sang every night until dawn and Slovenia was for the party*, or they address exclusively the *Slovenian men and women*, or include lines from the Slovenian national song "Naprej zastava slave!" or call "*arise, Slovenian nation!*" Slovenia is mentioned in the titles of many of their songs and, after all, they *love it more than God*. This same song also mentions, indiscriminately, the name of the contemporary extreme nationalist organization Tukaj je Slovenija! (This is Slovenia!).[24]

The neo-conservative component of the visual repertoire accompanying this music also manifests itself in the images of sexualized, but passivized "Yugoslav women," which is fully consistent with the hierarchy in newly introduced post-Yugoslav partriarchy and neo-traditionalism. Two or more sexy young women dressed like Tito pioneers, or Partisan fighters, or female JNA soldiers, or female workers have a purely decorative function, appearing in the background, supporting the men in the front and never taking the initiative. Since the middle of the past decade, Slovenian turbofolk has standardized the inclusion of two exuberant blondes in low-neck dresses, and this practice was embraced by "pro-Yugoslav" pop and rock, which also makes use of blondes exclusively. Their image is similar to that of cheerleaders in American pop culture, with their uniforms and their young-girl look actually becoming the erotic symbol of adult women. These videos therefore reproduce rather than invert the patriarchal hierarchy of gender roles. On the other hand, the Carmina Slovenica and Kombinat female choirs clearly back up their songs with their looks. Carmina Slovenica singers perform the repertoire that relates to such topics dressed in nondescript uniforms that seem to be a combination of pioneer and Partisan uniforms, while Kombinat singers wear an "anarchic-syndicalist" black-and-red combination, with shirts featuring the name of the choir and the hammer and sickle; their posters also include images of active, independent women.

In conclusion, let me explain the passive and conservative aspects of this music. To a large extent, it depoliticizes, dehistoricizes, commodifies and through this neutralizes the original meaning of Yugoslav and Partisan themes, the rhetoric, images, symbols, and last but not least, the songs themselves. A resistance song thus becomes "only a song," a proletarian symbol "just another" symbol in an endless series of other contemporary symbols: the Partisan fighter uniform is a pure travesty ("a cloakroom community'" in Bauman's words (2000, 200)) and the pioneer cap and white shirt, an erotic outfit; the critique of the government is an entertaining charade; a revolutionary motif is reduced to an "aesthetic challenge"; radical political otherness becomes fun with the help of ironic distance and discrepancy; the everyday life of the SFRY is carnivalized and turned into a timeless masquerade or light comedy (albeit with a tragic ending, which is – *voilà* – a perfect point of departure for nostalgic escapades). A step-by-step explanation would be as follows: dehistoricization downgrades the Yugoslav and socialist past to *good old times*, de-contextualization turns them into isolated fragments, de-ideologization trivializes them into entertainment and easy life, while nationalism reduces them to the Slovenian-only experience.

Perhaps this is why this music practically never draws negative comments in public, or bans, or moral panic, or revolt. Everything is reduced to a party, toothless ranting, sentimental memories, "artistic pleasure" and reinforcement of current ideologies – a harmless venture, by all means. The repressive tolerance of contemporary societies ("everything is *in*") and pandemic commodification ("everything is on sale") have proved to be the best ways to suppress dissent and alternatives. The rebellious, pro-Yugoslav, proletarian music becomes just one among many styles, a weekend pastime; it is turned into a pop culture product just like any other.

The paradox of this music lies in the fact that the more it seems to be in favor of *those times, those people and that society*, the more it is dismissive of them all. The more it seems approving of Yugoslavia and socialism, the more it shifts away from them. Firstly, the revolutionary load is effectively numbed by insisting on party/nostalgia/lamenting/pure aesthetics/ironic distance/conventional views. Secondly, the continuity between *them/then* and *us/now* is erased through dichotomy – or moreover, it is antagonized. By confronting the two, a radical, antithetic and on top of that naturalized distinction is made between Slovenianness and Yugoslavianness, and between the contemporary Slovene and – allow me irony – *homo yugoslavicus*. Stanković has arrived at a similar conclusion with regard to the Balkan scene (2002, 235), saying that it reproduces "the set stereotypes about the region to the south of the Kolpa river, seen as the regions of 'non-European' irrationality, non-civilization and the like."

Positive Slovenian Yugoslavism creates dualities which separate the now from the past, and *us* from *them*. In this way, it indirectly justifies yugophobic dominant discourses and reinforces negative Yugoslavism. Such a dichotomy discreetly legitimizes the colonial approach to "solving" the otherness problem, which assumes a transition to dominant identity. *They* (the *Oriental people, the Balkan people, the Yugoslavs*) are supposed to become us (*the Westerners, Europeans, Slovenes*) through the evolutionary "civilizing" process, which, naturally, is never completed. Yugoslavia therefore appears as an enigmatic realm of agreeable adolescence, Arcadian remoteness, careless childhood and crazy youth, whose naïve joie de vivre we had, experienced, lived and finally left behind. And rightly so, since these are new times, new values, and a new order. At this point it seems appropriate to quote Duncan again (1993, 45), who says that "difference was increasingly converted into history and history explained in terms of evolution." The Yugoslav Other is an internal Other of the Slovenian Self, the Other from our past which we had to live behind in order to reach our Slovenian Self. Yugoslavism therefore inevitably implies a transition: it is a transitional ideology, not only an exclusivist one, given that it offers the option of change. It enables the Slovenes to legitimize their present, Slovenian position based on their discarding of the previous, Yugoslav position. Former pro-Yugoslavism and present anti-Yugoslavism both appear self-evident.

The emancipatory potential of positive Yugoslavism

I will now address another, different dimension of Yugo-retrospective music and positive Yugoslavism, one which rises above the passive and conservative stance. My point of departure is the understanding of the emancipatory potential and reach of everyday practices and mass culture as developed by Walter Benjamin, and the possibility of transcending the current state of affairs by way of cultural production, as put forward by another German Marxist, Ernst Bloch. Both saw in mass culture not only the prevalence of dominant ideology but also utopian motives, resistance strategies and concrete transformational activities. And although I abide by my critical attitude as described above, I am also aware of the subversive interpretations and the potential of this music to bring about change. This music refers to the actual state, its political system and the real historical experience, so its messages and content do not deal simply with imaginary, wishful utopias.

First, the very fact that this music *raises a delicate topic seen by many as taboo* (i.e., Slovenia's Yugoslav and Socialist past) is an unambiguous sign of its political connotations. Judging by the dominant contemporary interpretations, one would think that the history of Slovenia began in 1991. The use of retro is therefore not accidental, because it allows us "to come to terms with the modern past" (Guffey, 2006, 9). What the music analyzed here does is a kind of "musealization" of the Yugoslav and Socialist era, which does not have its permanent collection in any museum in Slovenia. Slovenian rock'n'retro is a virtual musical museum of the former common country. It therefore inspires one to think, it employs a relieving humor, and introduces into the public space speech about Yugoslavia that is undoubtedly as biased as that in negative dominant discourses. The authors and performers of this music are well aware of this arbitrariness, so their tone is mainly ironic – which, in turn, as I showed earlier in the text, soon takes us to passivization, unless there is a concrete political stance behind it. Everything depends on how humor is conceptualized: on whether it is an end in itself or invites deliberation and activity.

However, what is even more important is catharsis and the recovery of lost dignity, as pointed out on several occasions by the performers. The leader of Carmina Slovenica says that their rearrangements of Partisan songs have *the effect of catharsis and bring people together. ... The auditoriums were packed to capacity and the audience was extremely emotional. Not one concert went by without tears. The audience sang with us.*[25] The experience of the Kombinat singers is the same: *Very often a listener or a guest at a concert confides in us that he or she cried while listening to these songs. And it even happened that we all cried together, so moved were we ...* They are also convinced that they can *contribute, along with the recognitions they bring, to the creation of a more humane society.*[26]

Positive Yugoslavism in Slovenian music has the same ideological effects as what has come to be known as the Balkan scene. Pro-Yugoslav Slovenian music and the Balkan scene both say that part of contemporary Slovenianness is the former Yugoslavianness and contemporary Balkanness – and that the more we try to distance ourselves from them, the closer they are. This is what lies behind the insistence on the *we* rhetoric in this music: this *we* is the Yugoslav Self, which criticizes the present-day Slovenian Other from that position, or rather, criticizes all systemic injustice in contemporary Slovenian society.

Secondly, *the picture of socialist Yugoslavia is positive*. This music offsets the negative Yugoslavism that triumphs in dominant discourses – it forms a kind of "bad conscience" for contemporary Slovenes, pointing to what we have lost, what is no longer present, and saying that it was possible to live in a different way. It introduces into mainstream pop culture a kaleidoscope of what the latter sees as "unpleasant" images of the former dignified life, of the support that the former political system enjoyed, of everyday life pleasures, popular culture, but also a critique of what we have now. The things that were taken for granted in the past are now idealized, romanticized and nostalgicized. Undoubtedly, there are also other, more radical discourses and activist groups in Slovenia – and other musical productions – which much more directly criticize the current state of affairs and point to possible alternatives while taking other ideological points of departure rather than the Yugoslav past. Unfortunately, these penetrate dominant discourses only rarely, so their voice cannot be widely heard. On the other hand, the Yugoslav and Socialist alternative is well known to practically everyone.

An important emancipatory element is *resistance to historical revisionism* in contemporary Slovenia, which attempts to negate autochthonous anti-Fascism, criminalize the Partisan resistance and justify collaboration with the Fascists, while ignoring the social and economic gains of the socialist era (free schooling, social security and health care, quality of life, worker solidarity, etc.) and the pleasures of everyday life. The unspoken line that proceeds from the viewpoints and the atmosphere of these songs could be: *in good and in bad, it was our country.*

Fourthly, this kind of music – we could call it the soundtrack of positive Yugoslavism – never rises above its *utopian position*, although it destroys the self-complacent presentist image of *the best of all worlds* by presenting Yu-topian images of the former times.[27] These amusing simulations sketch the nonexistent, magical place and time, not telling anything about how it was then, but rather revealing how it never was. More importantly, these performances never cross the borders of the world of music – not one performer is a real, direct political activist (future-oriented or nostalgic, pro-Yugoslav). And yet, the very drawing of attention to injustice and the positive attitude towards something different, even if in the past, can have transformational potential, even if only utopian. The teaching is: "yes, a different, better world is possible, more humane values, lifestyles and goals do exist!"

The utopian image of Socialist Yugoslavia appears as an alternative that has already been implemented in practice (not so long ago), as something that really existed. In the words of the Kombinat singers: *There is a very simple reason behind our decision to start singing songs of resistance – in the present situation in which the reasoning that nothing can be done is gaining ground, we wanted to say, through the songs that are the carriers of values (solidarity, comradeship, courage, boldness, freedom and sympathy), that it is possible* [to do something]. *To say that the kind of society that has been forced on us is not the only possible option, and above all, that it is not just.*[28] The rapper Mirko joins in with, *what is important is to realize in practice what we carry inside, to stand up and say loudly what annoys us and what we want. Nobody will do it instead of us, neither the right nor the left wing in Parliament, we ourselves will win it, all of us together, and the true Fighters know this.*

In conclusion, let me say that the most powerful tool of this music is parody (and its techniques of comic inversion, carnivalism and exaggeration to the point of absurdity), which is today a frequently overlooked and despised form of political resistance. Humor has unfortunately and mostly been degraded to mere entertainment, and in the best case a solace for the weak, while its relieving potential and socio-critical achievements are forgotten. A very good example is Chaplin's burlesques that deliberately subvert social hierarchies.[29] The same can be said about the funny but positive images of Yugoslavia in this music: "the parody replicates some prior form and thereby makes that form an object of one's attention rather than a transparent vehicle for some other message" (Hariman, 2008, 253). With its witty exaggerations of the positive aspects of Yugoslavia, this music implicitly criticizes the seriousness of present-day anti-Yugoslav discourses and their stubborn exaggeration in the opposite direction.

Conclusions – sex and red stars and rock 'n' roll

Let me conclude this study by returning to the introductory question: does this pro-Yugoslav music pose a threat to present-day dominant discourses in Slovenia, or does it implicitly support them, regardless of how it appears at a glance? Put differently, what are the concrete political implications of these representations of the former state replete with audio and visual effects? To answer this question, I used a combination of the horizontal (the analysis of cultural breadth) and vertical approaches (the critique of ideology).

There is no simple answer to this question, among other things because it is "only" music. It can be a symptom of, or a litmus test for social developments and ambitions, but its political and cultural reach is limited: neither music nor humor can change/preserve the world on its own. To establish how serious the protagonists of this music are, we need only look at the venues where they appear and activities in which they engage. Just one example: Kombinat regularly appears not only at celebrations in commemoration *of those times*, but primarily at events that problematize present injustices and offer alternatives.

Similar observations can be made about other performers. But most of them "are not serious" and they do not stand behind their words/songs because there is no concrete political engagement behind these. The major part of this music adapts to the existing state of affairs and does not attack it seriously. While it indeed does not ignore it, it restricts itself to cursory condemnations, partying, nostalgia, pure aestheticization, irony and conservatism, all of which sell well. It offers escapism and compensation for the alienated and unjust present.[30] Viewed from this perspective, everything begins and ends with pure – and in some cases well marketed – provocation for the sake of provocation, nothing more. Therefore, a brief answer to the initial question is: yes, as regards the concrete political level, it rather supports than destroys the negative Yugoslavism of dominant discourses.

However, the main contribution of this music – regardless of whether or not the authors and performers are aware of it – lies elsewhere in my opinion. It contributes on the ideological level, by questioning and wittily counterbalancing current Yugophobic discourses, which have more or less convincingly dominated Slovenia ever since the late 1980s. Practically all leading political forces and institutions in Slovenia pursue the same basic ideology, nationalism and neoliberalism, with surprisingly few nuances. Part of it is negative Yugoslavism which is offset, among other things, by positive Yugoslavism in popular music and its parodic glorification of the socialist Yugoslavia. It opposes the centripetal force of contemporary Slovenian nationalism with the centrifugal force of images of life in SFRY. This has therefore re-entered public discourse in Slovenia as an already realized historical alternative in which the Slovenes actively participated.

As an internally contradictory ideology, Slovenian Yugoslavism binarizes the Slovenes' mixed attitude towards their own recent history. The complexity of this attitude exceeds the *pro and contra* antagonization symptomatic of societies in transition, which seek their new identity by revising previous ones. Such an attitude (un)intentionally obscures the multifold picture of the past on many levels, ranging from that of official, decreed historiography and anti-histories (i.e., alternative, self-critical, Howard Zinn-like historiography), to that of diverse collective and personal memories.

A mature attitude towards the past is one that rises above pure demonization or monumentalization. Slovenia should be able to adopt such an attitude, since the period of slightly more than two decades of independence makes its socialist past sufficiently distant and yet close enough. It could begin by discarding the binarisms that confine one to *pro* and *contra* reasoning; it should seek to uncover not only "the good and the bad" or "the good in the bad, or the bad in the good," but everything that makes up its past, in its full complexity, polyvalence and polyglossia. It should abandon ideological homogenization and repeatedly compare the past and the present, while exposing the heterogeneity of everything. It should devote special attention to the narrative of marginalized, ostracized and erased groups and episodes, past and present. It should consider that which was articulated and that which remained unarticulated, memories and amnesias, the words and the silence, and compare the discontinuities, turns and contingences, past and present. In so doing, it should embrace self-reflection and self-criticism. In this concrete example, this requires both negative and active remembering, as defined by Kuljić (2012, 242, 214). The former proceeds from the fact that "remembering can be humanist and democratic only when it also includes the history of injustices and crimes for which we share responsibility, or in which we participated," while active remembering "is preserved by way of constant remembering of the shadows of the past, primarily those hanging over one's own nation."

The Pro-Yugoslav music analyzed in this chapter is therefore not an answer to the ideological binarisms of Slovenia's transition, but it does help challenge these. By taking an uncritically positive view of Yugoslavia, it counterbalances and calls into question the uncritical, negative views poured over it from dominant platforms. Through the parodic simulation and emphatic reproduction of the ideological elements and images that were dominant in the past, it undermines the self-sufficiency, bias, pathos and endless repetition of the present ones. Although politically harmless and devoid of political activism, it unintentionally, and frequently humorously, reveals Slovenia's recent history, indicating ways to think about the future and prepare ourselves to cope with it. It raises the question of resistance in a world of pandemic conformism and opportunism. It points to the real, although miserably failed alternative, so that we can become aware of those alternatives that are available today.[31]

Notes

1. In this text, the slogans and lyrics, the billboard texts, the statements taken from interviews or daily newspapers and ideological syntagmas are rendered in *italics*.
2. According to (neo)colonial ideology, one of the essential characteristics of the *aboriginals* is that they are locked in their space, time and lifestyle, meaning that they practically do not change.

3. Put differently, "the discourse of mimicry is constructed around *an ambivalence*; in order to be effective, mimicry must continually produce its slippage, its excess, its difference" (Bhabha, 1994, 122).
4. Interview Za Domovino s Partyzani!, Stop, Lj., 16.1.2008, 21, 22 and the cover page.
5. *Na juriš* is a warrior's exclamation, meaning *Charge!*
6. A contemporary slang that combines Slovenian and Serbo-Croatian vocabulary, syntagmas and pronunciation style. For self-ironization of the čefur-subculture in Slovenia, see for example Magnifico's video Kdo je čefur? (Who is a čefur?).
7. A journalist for national television described the popularity of this music at the Rock Otočec Festival 2012 using a telling title: A Paradise is a paradise only if accompanied with good, old (yugo)rock (http://www.rtvslo.si/zabava/ glasba/foto-raj-je-raj-sele-ob-dobrem-starem-jugo-rocku/286452, accessed July 4, 2012).
8. Rock Partyzani are distinguished for this kind of stage travesty in their performances or photos, in the style of the Village People of the 1970s.
9. Certain opinions are more premeditated. The Roy de Roy singer, Nikolaj Grilc, commented on the inclusion of these topics in their music as follows: *since the addressing of the topic of Yugoslavia is sooner or later a polarized issue, it should be understood as follows: Yugoslavia stretches not only from Mt Triglav to the Vardar river, but also from Goli otok to Bleiburg. Nostalgia is a choosy fox with selective memory.* Interview, 3.8.2012. Mirko, who *remembers Tito's heroic acts and mistakes*, in addition to criticizing the present exploitation, also raps a critique of Tito: *differences have been too large since the system collapsed, workers in the mud, capitalism on the advance, I don't have illusions when I write to you that you were the biggest capitalist in the socialist era.*
10. Irony is, according to Smith (1993, 86), "a representational discrepancy, a symbol out of place."
11. Even yugophobes and balkanophiles at the same time, according to a cynical verse in the song Country by the above-mentioned rapper trio, *I am fucking sick of those patriots who spit on Yuga, but all raise their hands when they hear the trumpet.*
12. For more on neonostalgia, i.e., "new nostalgia" see Velikonja (2008, 29, 30).
13. Klemen Klemen, Slovenija.
14. Mirko, Druže stari.
15. This is clear from Rock Partyzani's Slovenija 'ma jajca (Slovenia Has Guts): *little bit to the right, little bit to the left, a bit in Europe, a bit in the Balkans.*
16. The Balkan binarism, the symptomatic *and* that stands between the two extremes, the beautiful and the ugly, the good and the bad, is a bestseller within global popular culture as well. Let me mention just Bregović's "Weddings and Funerals Orchestra" and Jolie's movie *The Land of Blood and Honey.*
17. Interview Za domovino s Partyzani!, Stop, Lj., 16.1.2008, 21, 22
18. In the interview Lepa pesem za slabe čase (A Nice Song in Bad Times), Dnevnik, Pilot, Ljubljana, 26.11.2011, 8, 9.
19. Domobranci, The Home Guard, were a Slovenian Quisling formation in the World War II.
20. In the football fans' anthem for the Football Championship 2000, "Slovenia Goes On," with Kreslin and Lovšin. The turn appears even more radical in

the light of his very courageous and sharp criticism of the Slovenian skiing euphoria while he was the frontman of Lačni Franz, when he sang, *we are not afraid if skiers are with us* (White Symphony, 1983).
21. http://www.rtvslo.si/zabava/druzabna-kronika/modrijani-letos-bi-razproda-li-stozice-v-treh-dneh-brez-reklame/293689 (accessed January 22, 2013).
22. Interview, 28.3.2012.
23. Šilec, ibid.
24. See http://www.tu-je.si/, accessed April 17, 2012.
25. Šilec, ibid.
26. Interview, 28.3.2012.
27. In the words of experts in retro-marketing: "Perhaps most important, the retro brand must be capable of mobilizing a Utopian vision, of engendering a longing for an idealized past or community. In this respect, the brand must inspire a solidarity and sense of belonging to a community" (Brown, Kozinets, Sherry, 2003, 30).
28. Interview, 28.3.2012.
29. These could be understood in a non-political manner (as a pure sitcom), but also as subtle social criticism. The protagonists of his stories are the lower classes of the then Western society – vagabonds, homeless people, immigrants, orphans and paupers – who resist their miserable position and the authorities (often symbolized by a tall, fat policeman), and overcome it.
30. This is excellently encapsulated in a slogan that was part of the invitation to the *Grand Yu Spectacle* by Rock Partyzani on November 29 (2012), the Day of the Republic in Yugoslavia; *Better one Yuga day than this dismay.*
31. This is a short version of the text that was first published in Serbian in a book co-authored by V. Perica and M. Velikonja entitled Nebeska Jugoslavija: Interakcija političkih mitologija i pop-kulture (Biblioteka XX vek; Beograd, 2012).

References

Althusser, L. (1980). "Ideologija in ideološki aparati države", in Z. Skušek-Močnik (ed.), *Ideologija in estetski učinek*, Ljubljana: Cank.založba, 35–99.
Appadurai, A. (1988). "Putting Hierarchy in Its Place", *Cultural Anthropology*, 3, 36–49.
Barthes, R. (2003). *Učna ura*, Ljubljana: Apokalipsa.
Bennett, A. (2003). *Cultures of Popular Music*, Maidenhead, Philadelphia: Open University Press.
Bhabha, H. (1994) *The Location of Culture*, Abingdon, New York: Routledge.
Brown, S. (1999). "Retro-marketing: Yesterday's Tomorrows, Today!" *Marketing Intelligence & Planning*, XVII (7), 363–376.
Brown, S., R. V. Kozinets, and J. F. Sherry Jr. (2003). "Teaching Old Brands New Tricks: Retro Branding and the Revival of Brand Meaning", *Journal of Marketing*, LXVII, 19–33.
Bauman, Z. (2000). *Liquid Modernity*, Cambridge, Oxford, Malden: Polity.
Duncan, J. (1993). "Sites of Representation: Place, Time and the Discourse of the Other", in J. Duncan and D. Ley (eds), *Place/Culture/Representation*, London, New York: Routledge, 39–56.

Guffey, E. (2006). *Retro – The Culture of Revival*, London: Reaktion Books.

Hariman, R. (2008). "Political Parody and Public Culture", *Quarterly Journal of Speech*, XCIV (3), 247–272.

Kuljić, T. (2012). *Kultura spominjanja – Teoretske razlage uporabe preteklosti*, Ljubljana:Znanstvena knjižnica FF.

Mandić, I. (1976). *Mitologije svakidašnjeg života*, Rijeka: O. Keršovani.

Nora, P. (1996). "Between Memory and History", in P. Nora (ed.), *Realms of Memory: Conflicts and Divisions*, Columbia University Press, 1–20.

Reynolds, S. (2011). *Retromania – Pop Culture's Addiction to Its Own Past*, London: Faber and Faber.

Smith, J. (1993). "The Lie That Blinds – Destabilizing the Text of Landscape", in J. Duncan and D. Ley (eds), *Place/Culture/Representation*, London, New York: Routledge, 78–92.

Stanković, P. (2002). "Uporabe 'Balkana': Rock in nacionalizem v Sloveniji v devetdesetih letih", *Teorija in praksa*, XXXIX (2), 220–238.

Velikonja , M. (2007). *Evroza – Kritika novog evrocentrizma*, Belgrade: XX vek.

Velikonja, M. (2008). *Titostalgija – A Study of Nostalgia for Josip Broz*, Ljubljana: MediaWatch.

Velikonja , M. (2009). "Povratak otpisanih – Emancipatorski potencijali jugonostalgije", in I. Čolović (ed.), *Zid je mrtav, živeli zidovi!*, Belgrade: XX vek, 366–396.

4

Heroes of a New Kind: Commemorations and Appropriations of Yugoslavia's Sporting and Pop-Cultural Heritage

Vjekoslav Perica

> Out of about a hundred people who led us to democracy, some 50 of them ended up at the Hague tribunal's most wanted lists; 30 others have been tried by national criminal courts; about a dozen or less seem to be honest people, and for the rest, sufficient evidence for criminal prosecution has hitherto not been found.
>
> Boris Rašeta, Writer,
> Croatian weekly *Novosti*, 710, July 26, 2013, 31

> The naming of a street in our city after the popular rock performer Milan Mladenović, is an honor and recognition of a remarkable generation that began thriving in the last decade of socialism in Yugoslavia. But the memory of this epoch and this generation has been brutally suppressed during the 1990s.
>
> Statement for the media by the Chairman of
> the Municipal Committee for naming of streets and
> public places in Zagreb, Croatia, 2012

> The common Yugoslav cultural space does not need to be restored because it never ceased to function although the post-Yugoslav regimes have made every effort aimed at destroying it.
>
> Marko Brecelj, Slovenian rock musician and
> conceptual artist, in an interview, 2012

Heroes wanted: post-Yugoslav nations' struggle for a symbolic nationhood

Post-Yugoslav nations under construction struggle with one another over many things, collective identities included. They are also pained with surviving symbolic legacies and cultures of memory of the Socialist Federated Republic of Yugoslavia after whose destruction they were created through wars. More than 20 years after the end of the Socialist Federated Republic of Yugoslavia (SFRY), the post-Yugoslav states continue to deal with selection, appropriation and re-distribution of the common state's cultural property, myths, symbols, heroes, memorials and historical legacies that resist revisionism. Most of these cultural clashes take place in domains of popular culture including sport, pop and rock music and film in which the socialist-era nation was prolific and internationally recognized. Since heroic cults from pre-modern ethnic history do not suffice for the construction of new nationhood, post-Yugoslav nations need national icons from the most controversial historical periods such as World War II, the socialist era, and the wars and transition of the 1990s. Popular culture and sport are both part of an attractive and usable past. Late Yugoslav-era popular culture and sport, especially from the 1970s to the 1980s are a treasury of the usable past.

Nationalisms of the Yugoslav socialist-era as well as post-Yugoslav ethnic nationalisms differ in the crucial multiethnic integration of all-Yugoslav ideology versus monolithic ethno-confessionalism but are similar in their emphasis on hero worship and mythmaking. In modern nationalist narratives heroic myths and cults are indispensable (Mosse, 1991; Smith, 2003; Hosking and Schöpflin, 1997; Kolstø, 2005). In the history of the Yugoslav peoples most common are the following archetypes of heroism: the warrior-hero, the bandit or guerilla-hero, the strongman leader-hero and the martyr-hero (Bracewell, 2003, 22–36; Perica and Velikonja, 2012, 15–54). Yet, modernity introduced new heroic types such as scientists, sport stars, writers, rock and films stars and so on. In the last decade of the SFRY heroes of pop-culture, particularly rock 'n' roll, film, professional sport, satirical journalism, television series and so on emerging "from below" were markers of the great change (Perković, 2011; Perica and Velikonja, 2012, 67–253). As ethnic nationalism came to the fore, particularly during the wars of the 1990s, new ethno-national hero cults were manufactured and the old Titoist-era heroes were demonized and removed from public discourse (Čolović, 1994; Žanić, 1998). The new regimes imposed new heroic cults such as ethnic paramilitary leaders, adventurers, common criminals and con men released from foreign prisons to become political leaders or patriotic fighters in the Balkan wars, political demagogues and mavericks, gangsters turned-war criminals – all portrayed by the regime-controlled media as great patriots (Čolović, 2011, 34–61; Kuljiš, 2006). There was also a noticeable revival of the pre-modern bandit-type of heroism (Čolović, 1994; Žanić, 1998; Bracewell, 2003, 22–36). The new heroic cults celebrated even gangsters and former ordinary criminals turned into war criminals but promoted by state propaganda as heroes of what was portrayed as liberation wars (Čolović, 2011, 34–61; Kuljiš, 2011).

In the sphere of popular culture during the 1990s, tensions rose between the nostalgic fans of the socialist-era rock music versus ethnonationalist folk music (e.g., the Serbian "turbofolk" sound or the Croat "Thompson" ethno-rock). This clash was observed by a reporter for the *Christian Science Monitor* while visiting Belgrade in 2008. He wrote as follows:

> Modern politics here has always had a soundtrack. There was the '80s rock embraced by a generation shrugging off the shackles of communism. The turbo-folk of Serbian aggression in the 1990s gave way to more alternative pop fare – hip hop, electronica, indie rock – tied to the revolt against Milosevic, who was toppled by street protests in 2000. But turbo-folk's popularity never completely waned, even during the years when Milosevic was on trial for crimes against humanity. The genre's younger generation of fans, who can sing along with the turbo-folk anthems of the 1990s, say the music has shed its nationalistic undertones and now worships only commercial success. (*The Christian Science Monitor,* 2008)

Post-Yugoslav states have been designed as ethnically homogenous societies with a majority religion in a symbiosis with the ruling ethnic regime, that is as the antithesis for what socialist Yugoslavia used to be but also in mutual competition over common history and kin cultures. However, continuous pressure from leading western democracies in cooperation with domestic human rights advocates on the post-Yugoslav regimes made ethnic nationalistic mythmaking ineffective. The wars of the 1990s have been simultaneously exposed to the world as massive criminal enterprises in the shadow of which rose "mafia capitalism" instead of heroic liberation wars as ethnic nationalistic propaganda tried to portray them. The Serb nationalist leader and prime mover of the wars of the 1990s, Slobodan Milošević was ousted from power in 2000. Prosecuted before the International War Crimes Tribunal (ICTY) in The Hague, he died in prison in 2006. Two other ethnic nationalist top leaders, the Croat Franjo Tudjman and the Bosnian-Muslim Alija Izetbegovic, also died before formal indictments were made public. These leaders and their parties were further discredited by evidence about the criminal privatization and corruption. In 2012 a Croatian court passed a ten years prison sentence against the former Croatia's Prime Minister Ivo Sanader for corruption and war profiteering. Meanwhile in Serbia, the state managed to detect and prosecute the guilty for the 2003 assassination of the pro-western liberal Prime Minister Zoran Ðinđić.

The dark side of the wars of the 1990s was unveiled through the execution of international justice. From 1996 to 2012, the ICTY prosecuted 161 cases out of which 146 were found guilty and sentenced for war crimes and crimes against humanity receiving between 7 and 46 years of imprisonment and 1 life sentence for genocide (UN/ICTY webpage, 2012). Life sentence verdicts are also expected for the two major genocide suspects, the Bosnian Serb top leaders Radovan Karadžić and Ratko Mladić. Moreover, two political leaders of the ethnic parties after having been sentenced committed suicide: the Bosnian-Serb leader Nikola Koljević and wartime president of the Croatian-Serb enclave Milan Babić. The trials unveiled an extremely brutal and criminal character of these wars in which primary targets and most victims were civilians. Such wars could not be utilized by the post-Yugoslav ethnic regimes as nation-founding wars of liberation. Likewise, the ethnic regimes found it difficult to maintain patriotic heroic cults made out of ethnic armies and militias' commanders military leaders if many of them were sentenced for war crimes and some also for unlawful privatization and corruption. Croatian philosopher Srećko Horvat wrote that there is the obvious elites' desire to impose the perception of the 1991–1995 war as a pure, just liberation struggle through which came the birth of the nation, or, as he put it "Croatia's Immaculate Conception" (Horvat, 2012). Likewise, Serbia, as the prime mover of the crisis that escalated into the wars of the 1990s, despite all its political and church leaders' denial of such a role, insists on the spur-of-the-moment civil war thesis or blames equally the movements led by Milošević and Tudjman and Bosnian-Muslim and Kosovo Albanian nationalists.

All things considered, the post-Yugoslav nations faced the following contradiction: as the world and objective insiders view it, these nations have been conceived in shame during a country's collapse followed by brutal civil war and genocide; yet, they cannot imagine post-war successful national development without strong sentiments of collective pride. Contrary to the western European nation-building pattern, in this case from the southeastern periphery of Europe, patriotic symbols, myths and heroes are apparently more important to these peoples than regaining what they have lost in socialism, making economies strong, building states based on rule of law and strengthening a middle class instead of now dominating small political and clerical elites with a few tycoons. Yet, both these elites and the frustrated masses need mechanisms to make them proud at least symbolically. Hence they now search for both war heroes without criminal backgrounds and all kinds of heroic figures and myths that could boost pride and confidence in these small nations. For example, the 2012 state-sponsored celebration honoring the two Croat generals released by the Hague tribunal due to lack of evidence for a genocide conspiracy, the regime presented as the world's recognition of the 1991–1995 war in Croatia as just and honorable. After the release of these two generals a pompous parade in the capital was staged. Effigies of the freed generals appeared in a church's Nativity scene during the 2012 Christmas holidays. General Ante Gotovina (blamed in Serbia as the perpetrator of the 1995 expulsion of some 200,000 Serbs from Croatia) is the most popular and his public appearances trigger euphoria orchestrated by rightist parties. A similar hero-manufacturing attempt was staged in 2009 by the government of Serbia – in this case with ambition for designing a nation of martyrs and heroes (Historical Museum of Serbia, 2009). Interestingly, when the Hague tribunal in 2013 acquitted two close Milošević aides also due to lack of evidence for Belgrade's regime assistance to the Serb militias during the 1991–1995 war, the Belgrade government did not stage a celebration but quietly transferred the two to Serbia. However, the evidence about massive war crimes including attempts of genocide is still so plentiful that it is difficult to maintain cults of heroes constructed out of patriotic leaders and military commanders from the wars of the 1990s. In addition, heroes of one ethnic community are usually considered villains by the others so that official state-sponsored commemorations of such controversial figures run risk of a perpetual enmity and instability and also thwart the postwar rapprochement called for by the international community and dictated by economic recovery plans. Consequently, in contrast both to the official heroes of former Yugoslavia who all come out of World War II as military and political leaders, and also the most recent ethnic nationalist hero construction unsuccessfully seeking flawless military and political leaders from the war of the 1990s – in post-Yugoslav states many popular heroes emerged spontaneously "from below" and were neither politicians nor military leaders. Many of them were icons of pop music, film, sport and popular culture in general which is a novelty in the history of hero-worship in the Balkans. Moreover, many of them also belong to a common cultural heritage and collective memory of generations across ethnic divisions. Seeking a proper way for dealing with these hero cults emerging from below or inherited from the socialist era, the new ethnic nations' official patriotic ideologies ignored or even tried to defame selected hero figures while appropriating suitable others.

Reasons for the small south Slavic nations' difficulties with manufacturing ethnic hero-cults are many. For example, an intertwined akin population, similar languages, two common Yugoslav states and earlier common imperial settings, millions of persons with multiple identities, widespread interethnic marriages, and so on. Consequently, many prominent historic figures in this part of the world have such backgrounds and achievements (in common Yugoslav states and worldwide) that they cannot be exclusively appropriated by any post-Yugoslav ethnicity. They need to be shared by the local groups and world's cultural heritage alike. For example, the American scientist Nikola Tesla and the Yugoslav Nobel prize winner for literature Ivo Andrić, are impossible cases for "ethnicization." Tesla's birthplace is an Austrian province which is today Croatia and his father was a Serb-Orthodox priest. In the interwar period, Tesla was a patriotic Yugoslav-American. He was educated in Western Europe and spent most of his life in the United States as an American citizen speaking English and writing his scholarship in English or in German. Today both Croatia and Serbia claim Tesla as a great man of their histories and national cultures. However, Serbian nationalism has recently moved toward exclusive appropriation of Tesla's memory. To this end, the Serbian Orthodox Church is preparing for his canonization and his relics has been recently transferred from a museum to the national cathedral St. Sava's Temple in Belgrade. This is the established clerical method for managing historical controversies and various political, moral or cultural disputes.. of appropriation and exclusion of contestants. Likewise, Serbian nationalism appropriates the Bosnian-born Catholic writer Ivo Andrić, the only Yugoslav Nobel Prize winner for literature under the pretext that he lived and wrote most important works in Belgrade in the linguistic idiom spoken there. Yet, Andrić wrote mostly about his native Bosnia-Herzegovina in the language called Serbo-Croatian considered then and even now by some linguists as one single language (Kordić, 2010). He declared himself a Yugoslav by nationality, was in the interwar Yugoslav Foreign Service and during the socialist era even a Communist party member and cultural policies co-creator. He repeated many times that he had contributed to the Yugoslav peoples' common culture. Similarly, most of the icons of pop-culture and sport mentioned in this chapter belong to the common cultural heritage of the federated multiethnic socialist Yugoslavia and cannot be "ethnicized" regardless of their family background or birth-place or even their temporary political activity. In addition, as in the cases of Tesla and Andrić, many of them have also been internationally recognized, lived for many years and succeeded abroad thus also belong to the world's cultural heritage.

Consequently, post-Yugoslav national heroic pantheons still wait to be staffed particularly by appropriate cults from the most controversial recent history. Idolized figures from the Yugonostalgia subculture and particularly the icons of pop culture from the socialist-era revival of the 1980s have been all the time a plausible alternative to the ethnic nationalist contested cults that perpetuate conflict. Icons of rock music, film and sport – even though few of them can be exclusively ethnicized – have unifying and reconciling potential. They are an easier material for induction to the vacant national pantheons than contested cults or historical figures that unambiguously rehabilitate Yugoslavia, notably the Tito cult (Velikonja, 2010). In sum, the new nations' extremists have failed to construct new symbolic forms of nationhood against both the common state and their neighbors as the negative others. The redeeming potential of the icons of popular culture from the socialist era remains to be exploited.

The greatest generation: an outline for an alternative heroic pantheon from the socialist era

The icons and cults from the Yugoslav-era popular culture and sports to be presented in this section are a sketchy representative sample out of a more detailed and lengthier version presented in other studies (Perica and Velikonja, 2012). They are alternative heroes – the commu-nist mythology preferred warriors and martyrs of the antifascist libera-tion war. As mentioned in the opening paragraph, the criteria for the selection starts from the premise about the symbolic representation of nationhood through hero-worship. The selected heroic types are also alternatives to the traditional hero-types. Furthermore, although pop-cultural production is much broader (and after all, it would be useful to expand the analysis to culture in general, i.e., beyond pop-culture), I narrowed my analysis' focus to sport, rock music and film, mostly produced during the great urban pop-cultural revival of the 1980s (Petrović, 2012). Speaking of sport, it is the least represented topic in scholarly literature on the Yugoslav case (Perica, 2001). This is odd because in Yugoslavia and post-Yugoslavia sport has been one of the most important social institutions (the so-called "most important secondary issue in the world"). By contrast, there are numerous, useful books written about Yugoslav cinema and rock music (Goulding, 2002; Levi, 2007; Pavičić, 2011; Crnković, 2012; Luković, 1989; Popović, 1990; Perković, 2011; Janjatović, 2007). I have earlier written about the "school" of Yugoslav sporting development and the sports style out of which some of the icons described below emerged (Perica, 2001). This school, style or system was organized in the SFRY in the early 1960s and produced top word-class results through the 1970s and 1980s. Some western countries successfully copied this system and others recruited most talented post-Yugoslav young athletes or imported high quality final products, i.e. internationally recognized athletes and coaches. The term "system" is not an exaggeration although many find it difficult to use for it may refer to the entire socialist system under communist rule. Nevertheless, it was a well designed and efficient system of sporting development operated under the socialist socio-economic system in the multiethnic united federal Yugoslavia relying on its diverse and rich resources. Elaborating on this system and using the term "ystem" and "organization",, Žan Tabak, the head basketball coach of the *Caja laboral* from Sevilla, Spain, and former professional basketball player in Europe and the NBA, explained the success of basketball in socialist Yugoslavia at a conference (which I also attended) in Sevilla, Spain in 2011. He emphasized the functioning of a "system," school or style of national sporting development which borrowed the best from both US and Soviet models and added some Yugoslav innovations. Spain, for example, borrowed ideas from the Yugoslav school of basketball and recruited many outstanding players and coaches from the unfortunate country after its collapse and during the wars of the 1990s. As a result, Spain, which played mediocre basketball until the 1980s, dominated the world in the game outside the United States by the early 2000s. Likewise, since the late 1980s thousands of athletes from the Yugoslav space have played professionally in Western Europe and the United States.

The same school influenced post-Yugoslav world-class athletes born in the region since the late 1980s. For example, Novak Đoković, currently the world's number one tennis champion publicly emphasizes his post-Yugoslav patriotic Orthodox Serb image although his precursors are socialist-era Yugoslav tennis players of ethnically diverse origins (e.g., Nikola Pilić, Bora Jovanović, Željko Franulović, Boba Živojinović, Monika Seleš and Goran Ivanišević) some of whom discovered, inspired and even coached him. Likewise, the 2012 Croatian Olympic gold medal-winning water polo team was built on the capital of six Olympic medals won by the SFRY national team in the 1970s and 1980s. At any rate, even in cases where the Yugoslav state ethnicizes and appropriates international sport trophies, their athletes and coaches won far more international trophies with the Yugoslav national team from the 1960 to 1980s. These trophies cannot be balkanized or ethnicized – definitely not in team sport games but individual sports are also the product of teamwork and in SFRY it was always multiethnic. SFRY sport trophies of the socialist era can be properly preserved only in a single sport museum preferably located in Sarajevo as the only Yugoslav city that hosted the Olympic Games (Perica and Velikonja, 2012, 193).

The particular personalities selected below, symbolically represent Yugoslav popular culture, socialist modernization and multiethnic federalism but above all, the changes of the 1990s and their impact on the postwar memory and identity across the post-Yugoslav space. Their tragic fates also mirror the country's fate. They come from one of neglected products of socialist modernization and Yugoslav multiethnic federalism namely, a talented generation coming of age in a modernized, relatively stable and democratized society from the 1960s to the 1980s. The role of this generation encourages further research beyond the standard scholarship on national, ethnic and religious groups – arguable on generations have been relevant social and historical factors (Kuljić, 2009). In other words, the story of this generations is no less historically relevant and worth of conceptualizing and placing in primary focus of analysis than histories of nations, ethnic or religious groups otherwise extensively exploited by scholars. Members of this generation were born roughly during two decades, the 1950s and 1960s, to have come of age during the late 1970s and the antebellum 1980s. They belong to the younger of the two most influential generations that made history from World War II through the socialist era. I call these generations under consideration here the Partisan generation (that successfully fought in World War II and later against Stalinism) and the "Post-partisan genera-tion" (Perica and Velikonja, 2012, 244–247). I argue that these two gener-ations' achievements belong to an indivisible common cultural property of the Yugoslav revolution and socialist-era Yugoslavia. Finally, I selected personalities that have been honored not only by subculture currents and alternative means of communication (e.g., internet networks) but also by various public memorials, official tributes and established forms of remembrance. This is possible because many of them are no longer alive so that they have been posthumously recognized through memorials, monuments, statues, street-naming, biographies, documen-tary films, specially dedicated songs, books, awards, and so on. What I found most impressive are internet comments from teenagers testi-fying about an inter-generational transfer of culture and values. It is also obvious that many of these comments come from post-Yugoslav diasporas which is another phenomenon suppressed from public knowledge by the post-Yugoslav regimes. These regimes celebrate as national myths glorifying stories about ethnic diasporas allegedly persecuted under communism – without mentioning terrorist groups among these ethnic diasporic communities – and after the fall of Yugoslavia happily returned to their countries of origin in order to fight liberation wars and invest in economic recovery which never came (Perica, 2011, 113–132). As a matter of fact, many more people were forcibly exiled or voluntary left post-Yugoslav space during the 1990s including a sizeable intellectual-academic diaspora (while exodus of young people continues) than those who returned from exile. These migrations have already drawn a considerable scholarly interest and are yet to be further examined (Jović, 2003; Brunnbauer, 2009; Valenta and Ramet, 2011).

In the process of selection for the provisional pantheon sketched below, besides standard resources such as books, newspapers and journals from the period of the creativity examined, I relied particularly on Internet resources (mostly YouTube) taking into account the number of video clips uploaded and the number of views. I found especially instructive content analysis of the viewers' comments that affirm the exceptional lasting cult status, glorification, attributing prophetic, messianic and martyred characteristics and using these cults as proof for the existence of a better past and as fuel for protesting against the "Dark Nineties," the sad present and absence of hope or vision for a better future. These comments came from people of diverse national origins including members of the formerly warring ethnic groups but while exchanging insults and outbursts of chauvinism elsewhere on the Internet; here they are unanimous in openly paying respect to these icons and heroes of pop-culture regardless of their ethnic origin.

The following are the icons of the socialist era that belong to the Yugoslav and post-Yugoslav legacies that can possibly be reconciled thus contributing to a new synthesis in the balkanized cultural sphere.

Mate Parlov, boxer (1948–2008)

There is no way I could be a nationalist. Nations are only particles of the whole world. And, for God's sake, I've been champion of the world!
Boxer Mate Parlov, in a 1990 interview,
remembering his 1976 World's boxing championship title
and commenting on the crisis in the country.

Mate Parlov was the all-time best Yugoslav boxing champion and one of the best European boxers in the worldwide competition among amateurs and professionals alike. Born in the Croatian town of Imotski, in northern Dalmatia, Parlov spent most of his life in Istria's town of Pula and died of cancer in Zagreb. Among many prestigious trophies, he won the Olympic gold medal for the SFRY in 1972; the amateur World Championship Tournament in 1974; and twice was the continental champion of Europe. As a pro, Parlov won the European championship title in 1976. The crown of his career came in 1978 when he became World Champion in the light heavyweight category. Parlov fought 29 pro matches and won 24 – 12 by knockouts. He lost 3 fights with 2 draws..After retiring as a boxer, Parlov became a boxing coach. As the SFRY national team's boxing head coach, Parlov won the gold medal at the 1984 Olympic Games. Until his death Parlov was one of the coaches in the region's most prestigious boxing school in the Croatian town of Pula. The Croat Parlov was more popular in Serbia, Bosnia and Kosovo than in his native Croatia. The Tudjman regime did not consider him a "proper" Croat according to the new ethnic nationalist standards. To them he was too cosmopolitan and too Yugoslav. However, memorable clips from his matches, glorifying messages and in memoriam tributes to Parlov on the Internet come from all around the world and are signed by members of all ethnicities in the region and numerous foreigners describing him as a boxing legend, a man of extraordinary honesty and integrity, a lover of art, particularly poetry, and a reserved, quiet person. The city sport center in Pula is named after him. It is obvious that he merits a more appropriate memorial in his native Croatia. It seems that the problem is with his image as a warrior-hero type which he as a personality never was. In the post-Yugoslav setting he was expected from the new ethnic nationalistic patriotism in his new country to enter the ring of interethnic relations knocking down members of the hated group. He would probably have a monument in the Zagreb downtown had he fought for the ethnic nationalist cause. Thus, the greatest Yugoslav boxing champion Mate Parlov left a void in the post-Yugoslav sport and pop-cultural imagery because the pubic needed memorials to warriors and fighters such as boxers. This void has been filled in rather bizarre ways: in the Herzegovinian city of Mostar a local group of activists had a statue built representing the kung-fu celebrity Bruce Lee. Similarly, in Serbia, a monument was built honoring the worldwide popular film character "Rocky," a fictional professional world boxing champion.

Belatedly, an intriguing but noteworthy public recognition for Mate Parlov in his native Croatia surprisingly came from the Catholic Church.

On the occasion of the fifth anniversary of Parlov's death, on July 27, 2013, the Archdiocesan Seminary in Parlov's native city of Split, held church services and public commemoration for the sporting legend. Similar ceremonies were held in the nearby north Dalmatian city of Imotski from where the Parlov family moved down to the Dalmatian coast after World War II. The seminary's rector Rev. Prof. Dr. Mladen Parlov, the deceased champion's cousin, officiated at the services and spoke to the media which publicized this event. He recalled how popular Mate Parlov was among the local children of the Imotski region and how excited he was after the handshake with the champion when the great Mate visited his parents' native village that celebrated Parlov's most recent victory by the traditional north-Dalmatian roasted ox feast. The Reverend Parlov also mentioned the champion's famous public statement about incompatibility between nationalist ideology and his world championship titles and added that some right-wing clerical circles never forgave him this (*Slobodna Dalmacija*, 2013, 6).

Krešimir Ćosić, basketball player and coach (1948–1995)

He was 25 years ahead in terms of quality, coordination and height. Another example of the fantastic players of the former Yugoslavia. I must sicsay he was the evidence that the most important thing in basketball are the fundamentals, cause he mastered all of them. Excellent player, and even excellent coach. He died too early, too young.

Krešimir Ćosić was my idol, like basketball player. I was born in Belgrade, former Yugoslavia. I remember Kreso when he was in Belgrade, and visiting basketball court well known, in New Belgrade as a ranch. It was in year sometime 1970. With, Moka Slavnic, Jelovac, some other guys from former best team ever.sic Great memory. Kreso was one of the first, if not the first who went to USA, became great name there also. He was such a great man, and top basketball player of all times!

Comments on the internet

Krešimir Ćosić could be called a Tesla of basketball. This 6'11" center dominated international basketball in the 1970s; he was even drafted as one of the earliest non-Americans in US professional leagues, and was probably the first in the history of the game who attempted to reinvent the role of the "big man." As a player and later successful coach, he argued that even the tallest players in the game of basketball should not be confined to the "down low" position under the rim waiting for passes by the little, quick, technically superior (and supposedly smarter) guys. He envisioned that with advancements in the game many players of his own or greater size would someday be able to play the same way as the players of smaller size; through proper selection and training they would acquire all the athletic, long-distance shooting and ball handling technique requirements. As an active player in the 1970s he even tried to apply this vision in the game and to promote the new role of the "big man." Yet, he was so ahead of his time that both players on court and spectators seemed confused. Legend has it that one of his teammates of the Cougars stole the ball from him when Ćosić was trying to dribble down the court in order to pass the ball to another teammate running the fast break.

Krešimir Ćosić knew that his dream came true when the 6'9" tall point guard Earvin "Magic" Johnson dominated professional basketball in the 1980s to become one of the all-time best in the game. Unfortunately, Ćosić did not live long enough to see the 7'0" versatile forward and long-distance shooter Dirk Nowitzki elected the most valuable professional player in the world in 2010 or two years later to see the 6'8" guard LeBron James dominate the elite NBA pro league and as of this writing James is still the best among the best. However, Ćosić was one of the teachers, coaches and co-creators of the all-time best tall guard/forward in the Yugoslav school of basketball, Toni Kukoč (6'11") who excelled in Europe in the 1980s and played an important role in US professional basketball in the 1990s. When the 19-year-old Kukoč began leading his teams as a playmaker point guard, nobody believed that a 6 feet and 11 inches tall athlete could play in this position but Kukoč was doing it better than the typical small point guard. Soon the game would change so that most players except for a minority of extremely tall or short ones would become athletically and technically capable to play any position on the court. The 2008 US-made documentary film "An Off-Court Story: The Life of Kresimir Cosic," directed by Lindsey Jurdana, recognizes Krešimir Ćosić as a basketball visionary who was the first to attempt to introduce these changes into the game.

Ćosić was born in Zagreb, Croatia, but spent most of his life in the basketball center of Zadar on the Dalmatian coast from where his family originated. To the 1968 Olympic silver medal with the Yugoslav national team, he subsequently added 15 additional prestigious international trophies in the 1970s and also successfully coached several clubs and the Yugoslav national team in the 1980s. Ćosić was one of the greatest in European basketball and also recognized as world-class in the game. He was also among the earliest pioneers of European stars who ventured to America, the game's native land. From 1970 to 1973 he excelled on the court playing for the Cougars of the Brigham Young University in Provo, Utah. He was offered professional contracts twice, first by the Portland Trailblazers and then by the famous Los Angeles Lakers. He declined, returned to Europe, played and coached there. The reason was his conversion to the Church of Jesus Christ of Latter-day Saints. His missionary and spiritual work was as important to him as his sporting career. He founded the first Mormon communities in Eastern Europe and had the Book of Mormon translated into Croatian. When war broke out in Croatia in 1991, the president Tudjman appointed Cosic to a senior position at the Croatian Embassy in Washington D.C. in order to seek the support of the United States for the cause of Croatian independence. In this capacity he passed away in 1995 while being treated for cancer at Johns Hopkins hospital in Baltimore. The Tudjman regime exploited his May 1995 funeral in Zagreb for propaganda as they had done two years earlier when the basketball superstar Dražen Petrović died. Many international sporting dignitaries and famous players were in attendance including Ćosić's former teammates from Serbia. Long speeches by the Tudjman regime's officials glorified Ćosić's trophies he had won "for Croatia" and "the Croatian people" although his 16 most prestigious trophies all had been won for the Socialist Federated Republic of Yugoslavia. Yet, on this occasion (as it is still the practice in Croatia today), the word Yugoslavia was not mentioned. Given the fact that Ćosić died as a Croatian diplomat during the war he was declared a national hero and great patriot, which he certainly was although he was never affiliated with any political party or ideology. A basketball arena and two city plazas were named after him with a bronze statue built in front of the arena in Zadar. In 2007, he was inducted into the Basketball Hall of Fame in Springfield, Massachusetts. He is still admired and commemorated in all post-Yugoslav states and also in the countries where he played and coached (e.g., Italy) but especially in the United States. His alma mater, the Brigham Young University and the Mormon Church celebrated his jersey retirement with a spectacular sporting event in Provo in 2006 and since have occasionally commemorated this man as some kind of a Mormon saint using his fame and international popularity for promoting the faith. For example, the BYU-produced documentary "An Off-Court Story, The Life of Kresimir Cosic," which is available on YouTube, and some other propaganda films and writings about Ćosić produced in post-Yugoslav Croatia, allege that Ćosić was persecuted by the Yugoslav communist regime for his religious beliefs. This is untrue and makes no sense. Mormonism, as a non-traditional imported religion as opposed to the major traditional Yugoslav religions

(Serb Orthodoxy, Croat Catholicism and Bosnian Islam), was not associated with any ethnic nationalism and therefore the regime did not perceive such a minority religion as a security threat. Not to mention that in the liberal phase of Titoism the government that enjoyed a considerable international reputation as a country-leader of the Nonaligned movement, would not make such a blunder as to mistreat its international star athlete for such trivial reasons as personal religious beliefs.

Mirza Delibašić, basketball player (1954–2002)

Mirza Delibašić was one of all-time best players from the world-class Yugoslav school of basketball. Born to a Bosnian-Muslim family in the eastern Bosnian city of Tuzla, he spent most of his life in Sarajevo. With the Yugoslav national team he won eight major European and world championships including an Olympic gold and World Championship gold plus two European championships. In 1979 he – already one of the best European point guard playmakers, led the club *Bosna Sarajevo* to the first championship title in the European professional league. Subsequently as a pro he excelled with the Real Madrid. During the war in Bosnia-Herzegovina (1992–1995), Mirza took up the position of the head coach of the Bosnian national basketball team. Except for occasional trips to international games, Mirza otherwise remained in Sarajevo during the entire siege and destruction of the city by the Bosnian-Serb army. While the city was under heavy shelling, Bosnian radio boosted the defenders' morale by broadcasting Mirza's phone talk with the vice president of the Real Madrid in which he explained why he was staying in besieigned Sarajevo to support its defenders and therefore declining the offer for political asylum and coaching job in Spain.

Mirza died from complications after a stroke at the age of 47 and was buried at the Sarajevo cemetery next to his best friend, the legendary Sarajevan rock musician Davorin Popović. In the Sarajevo city center, there is a park "Mirza & Davor" with a children's playground and statues of the two good souls of Sarajevo, Delibašić and Popović. In 2000, Mirza was voted "athlete of the century" in Bosnia-Herzegovina and the Bosnia-Herzegovina's national basketball cup tournament has been recently named after him. Despite Bosnia's effort in Mirza's hero-cult construction – and he truly is a hero of the new Bosnia perhaps in the first place a hero of Sarajevo as it was before the war – he also remains a socialist-era Yugoslavian and international sport hero. Like most urban Bosnians he cannot be exclusively ethnicized based on his familial background which is Bosnian Muslim mixed with the others further Mirza was married to a Serb woman. Mirza himself never declared his identity in exclusive ethnic or religious terms. Furthermore, all the most prestigious trophies he won for the SFRY plus several international successes with Real Madrid. He is particularly admired and remembered in Spain but also in other European countries as evident from Internet comments in various languages. Recently in an interview, Sergey Biriukov, once prominent basketball player for the Soviet Union, revealed that Soviet players, due to a bitter rivalry, did not like the Yugoslavs except for the good man Mirza. Yet, in his case, as in the previous case of Parlov and most of the cases to follow in this section, Mirza's multiple heroism is not mutually exclusive but compatible with the other identities including ethnicities and particularly important belonging to urban communities. Hence Mirza and his achievements belong to the common indivisible property of the SFRY, of international sports and of Sarajevo and Bosnia which tried to defend its multiethnic character and values of interethnic harmony against ethnic nationalism. However, Mirza Delibašić is a symbol of Sarajevo (and Bosnia) as it used to be. The war changed demographics, forced people into sectarian enclaves and destroyed Bosnian society's multicultural fabric. The one-time fascinatingly diverse Sarajevo is now nearly homogenous ethnically and religiously although minarets are still there intertwined with church towers. Delibašić's former teammate on the Yugoslav national team and in Real Madrid, the Hall of Famer Dražen Dalipagić, a native of western Herzegovina who has lived since the 1970s in Belgrade, Serbia, when asked in a 2012 interview if he still sometimes visits Sarajevo, replied: "Unfortunately I don't... because I don't have any close friends left there; once I had Mirza – the most wonderful person who ever lived in this world, but he is gone forever..." (*Dnevni Avaz*, 2012).

Dražen Petrović, basketball player (1964–1993)

Since his tragic death in a car accident at the age of 29 while at the height of his career, it has been debated whether Dražen Petrović is the very best player of all times who came out of the prestigious, socialist-era Yugoslav school of basketball. At any rate, he was for sure a global, European, American, Yugoslav and Croatian basketball superstar. While it is debatable if he is the all-time best Yugoslav basketball player, he is definitely on of the greatest and probably internationally best recognized. Petrović became some kind of a sporting and in some cases national and global cult. He is a hero-athlete with probably more memorials in his native country and worldwide than any other athlete in the rich history of Yugoslav and post-Yugoslav sports. These memorials include, among other honors, three statues, two plazas, one school and two sport centers named after him in his native Croatia; another statue at the Olympic Museum in Lausanne, Switzerland; a memorial in Germany on the site of his death; enshrinement to the Basketball Hall of Fame in Springfield, Massachusetts; a best-player trophy at the most prestigious international junior players' tournament; a folk song from his native Dalmatia composed and dedicated to him; and a documentary film about him produced by the leading world's sport TV channel ESPN. Not to mention numerous Internet clips with glorifying comments in many languages and from various corners of the world including the usual accord in such matters and outburst of fraternal sentiments among the people from post-Yugoslav lands who in other websites exchange hateful messages, insults and conflicting interpretations of history.

Dražen Petrović was born in Croatia's coastal city of Šibenik. He declared himself a Croatian but his father, as a local police chief with a last name very common in Serbia and older brother Aleksandar (another name more frequent among the Orthodox than Catholics), have been appropriated in Serbia as Serbs. In Serbia they now consider Dražen a half-Serb although the likely culprit for this misunderstanding (because Petrović's family probably is not ethnically mixed) is Croatian nationalistic propaganda according to which all police and military leaders in pre-war Croatia were ethnic Serbs. At any rate, Petrović's achievements are global and international exceeding all ethnic and national boundaries. The statistics speak, however, that he won several dozen of the most prestigious sport trophies from the SFRY and only one Olympic medal for the independent Croatia. He is therefore in the first place a socialist-era Yugoslav athlete, captain of the most successful basketball generation playing under the flag with the red star and in the second place he is an international and global superstar of professional sport who excelled in world-famous clubs such as Real Madrid and the New Jersey Nets. During the war in Croatia, the Tudjman regime exploited Petrović's outspoken patriotic support for his country's independence and also his death that was commemorated as a national tragedy. This makes Petrović a much-needed hero for the new Croatia but it is clear that he cannot be ethnicized or appropriated exclusively by a single country. As a matter of fact, he, as a basketball star above all, received the greatest basketball honors in the country where the game was invented, where the most competitive game is played and where he achieved the best games of his career, that is, in the United States. His significance for American sport history is noticeable insofar as he led the first large group of foreign players, which in the early 1990s were recruited to compete in the earlier homogenous American National Basketball Association (NBA) as the most competitive professional basketball league in the world. Thus he symbolizes the transformation of what is now a large and highly profitable global corporation in which players from more than 60 countries have performed. Yet his career is also suitable to the US national mythology because this East European immigrant (although then a best-paid athlete outside the United States) initially struggled and did not even get enough playing time to prove himself; yet, he chose the American way by keeping the hope and he persevered, worked even harder and finally excelled in his two last seasons as one of the best in the league. Both causes of importance coupled with benevolent intentions to contribute to post-war reconciliation in post-Yugoslav states inspired the 2010 ESPN-NBA produced documentary film *Once Brothers*. The film became influential in the United States after its prime time TV premiere in 2010. Thus Petrović representing foreign athletes received public recognition. The film is about Petrović but the narrator and main actor playing himself is the Serb professional basketball star Vlade Divac (currently chairman of Serbia's Olympic Committee). The story is based on the mythical archetype about civil wars that separate best friends but they eventually reconcile (e.g., mythology of the American Civil War). The film ends with a symbolic reconciliation performed by Divac who visits Croatia's capital Zagreb and prays at his teammate's grave. Divac also accurately tells the story about a great generation of Yugoslav athletes and the beginnings of the early East European professionals in American basketball. Yet he marred the largely successful project by instilling in the movie the Serb nationalistic perspective on the causes of the 1991–1995 war blaming Slovenia and Croatia's secession from Yugoslavia as the war's principal cause. Nonetheless, the Petrović hero-cult was perceived in the United States as an effective reconciling mechanism plus a heroic story of growth of a worldwide popularity of basketball and the transformation of the NBA league into a global corporation. The NBA commissioner David Stern spoke of Petrović as not just a member of the Basketball Hall of Fame but as a trailblazer of this new era in the game's history (*NBA Encyclopedia Playoff Edition*, 2011). The Petrović cult also helped the development of the post-Yugoslav re-integration process through the international professional league ABA. Since 2001 it has involved teams from the entire post-Yugoslav space and even a wider area of Europe and the Middle East.

Milan Mladenović (1958–1994) and Margita "Magi" Stefanović, rock musicians (1959–2002)

Mladenović and Stefanović in rock music, like Dražen Petrović in sport, have become the main lasting symbols of the Yugoslav school of rock due to their premature tragic deaths followed by cult construction along the matrix of glory plus martyrdom such as in the cases of Jimmy Hendrix, Janis Joplin, Jim Morrison, Kurt Cobain, and so on. Milan Mladenović, lead singer-songwriter and guitarist, and Margita "Magi" Stefanović, on the keyboard, were key figures of the Belgrade-based new wave or post-punk rock band Ekaterina Velika (a.k.a. EKV). Mladenović was born in Zagreb, Croatia, but spent most of his life in Belgrade, Serbia. Stefanović, in addition to playing the keyboard, piano and backup vocals, also did most of the musical design for the band. A versatile artist, Margita graduated from the University of Belgrade's Musical Academy and School of Architecture. The band's most creative years are from the mid-1980s to the early 1990s. Confronted with the threat of war in 1991, the EKV band frequently performed at peace rallies and wrote songs calling for peace and condemning violence. Unfortunately, drug abuse marred these gifted artists' careers. All EKV band members, including Mladenović and Stefanović, struggled with drug addiction. In 1994, Mladenović was diagnosed with pancreatic cancer and after a short struggle with the illness he passed away. "Magi" Stefanović continued musical and other artistic work (writing, painting, filmmaking, etc.) during the 1990s but could not cure her drug addiction. Losing eventually all her family possessions to drugs and unsuccessful attempts to continue creative work, she spent the last months of her life in a homeless shelter in a Belgrade suburb where she died in 2002.

Social recognition for both artists came belatedly but the cult has been growing constantly over the last decade. The Internet, of course, was the major cult-constructing tool and unifier of all rock fans (and their children) from various parts of socialist-era Yugoslavia and the post-Yugoslav diaspora. The city of Belgrade honored Mladenović by "Milan Mladenović Plaza" in the city center near a once popular concert hall. In November 2012, city authorities in his native Zagreb named a street after him thus giving an impulse for improvement of Serbo-Croatian relations. In a similar vein, Croat folk singers from Dalmatia released EKV's signature hit "The Land" ("Zemlja," originally written by Stefanović) in 2009 in the local dialect of the mid-Dalmatia (YouTube: "Zemlja – Klapa Iskon vs EKV"). Mladenović's first biography was published in 1999 (Žikić, 1999). Meanwhile YouTube saw a flood of video clips with Magi, Mladen and EKV's concert performances, interviews, funeral scenes, and so on. These video clips are accompanied with glorifying comments from an ethnically diverse audience from all post-Yugoslav lands domestically and abroad and as usual they are all in accord about the great generation and the remarkable era of the last socialist decade – except for sporadic exchanges of hateful barrages with lovers of the local country music (turbofolk). There are also two biographical books in several editions about Margita Stefanović (Ilić, 2008; Nikolić, 2012) and an important reprint special journal issue "Rock legends of the 1980s" (Popović, 1990) featuring an interview with Margita Stefanović. In this interview she states that she had written the rock anthem "Zemlja" ("The Land") in 1987 aware of the growing ethnic tensions. Therefore she used the term "land" as an object of love and belonging: "this is the land for us, this is the land for all our children ...." She explained that she intended to overcome the politicized exclusivist ethnic labels for the notion of a country namely the Croat *domovina* and the Serb *otadžbina* (EKV Ljubav blogspot, 2012).

These books, interviews and memories – regardless of polemics about authenticity of the sources and some contested facts – are, like, for example, post-Yugoslav Serbian cinema (Crnković, 2012), resourceful tools for understanding these chaotic historical changes. These biographies or more precisely hagiographies (books about lives of the saints) – like all the heroic cults described here – portray a dramatic degeneration of the one-time prosperous and dynamic society with a rich human capital groomed under socialism to take over the country's leadership when the "old guard" of communist revolutionaries is gone. In particular these two tragic rock biographies portray Serbia's society during the "Dark 1990s" when this country was under international sanctions, and their governments, staffed by cynical ex-communist converts to ethnic nationalism including the war criminals ran the country in cooperation with the Balkan mafia. They jointly fueled and funded the wars in order to make profits on them and they also allowed the expansion of drug trafficking, human trafficking, political corruption, criminal post-socialist privatization and other forms of social pathology. That was the time when the spread of drug trafficking destroyed many young lives and affected many families particularly in urban centers that used to be hubs of the 1980s cultural revival. The other post-Yugoslav states were not familiar with this situation in Serbia – for most of them Serbia was perceived primarily as the primary source of evil that is, the fountainhead of the movements and policies that dragged all into war. This is correct, but the Serb people also suffered, particularly the common people and everyone without ties to the new elites, power holders and the mafia. In other words, through the tragedies of the two young people preserved as a cult in the domain of rock 'n' roll urban subculture it is possible to learn that "the Dark Ages of the 1990s" in post-Yugoslavia were not so much darker outside Serbia than within although it is true that prior to the NATO intervention of 1999 Serbia did not see bombshells falling on its cities. When TV Slovenia showed a documentary film about the lives of Margita Stefanović, Milan Mladenović and their rock band in 2012, the charismatic Slovene singer-songwriter Zoran Predin wrote and released a moving tune dedicated to Magi and her "angel's touch" he saw in one of his dreams about the better past (YouTube: "Zoran Predin Kosa boja srebra (Margita)"; E-novine, 2012).

Branimir "Johnny" Štulić, rock musician (1953–)

The Macedonia-born Štulić (of Croatian family background) spent his most creative years in Croatia's capital Zagreb but never declared any ethnic affiliation. Since the late 1980s he has lived in The Netherlands. After war broke out he left and virtually never set foot on his native country's soil. He is today much more than one of the leading rock stars of the post- punk/new wave rock currents of the late 1970s and 1980s. This withdrawn and ascetic man is considered a guru, poet-philosopher who, after producing a massive rock 'n' roll opus, he also published multivolume translations of classical Greek thinkers and is working on new publications. His lyrics, aphorisms, metaphors and prophecies are part of the intellectual discourse in post-Yugoslav states. He is quoted not merely by rock fans, journalists and Yugonostalgiacs. This college dropout is also quoted by many leading intellectuals, such as a president of a Croatian university in a polemic with the incumbent Education Secretary over reforms in higher education (*Slobodna Dalmacija*, 2012). He is some sort of a cult figure prominent in cyberspace with thousands of video clips appended by his admirers. Their comments exaggerate to the point of calling the Azra a religion and Johnny a prophet. Johnny composed hundreds of songs, including the song "Balkan" ("The Balkans," 1979), which is one of the anthems of the age of the ex-YU school of rock music. Last but no less important, Johnny is viewed by his fans as some sort of a Messiah. He has been for more than 20 years in a self-imposed exile. His fans call upon him to return, put on a series of concerts in every corner of the region, unify millions of people, preach and set into motion some kind of a cultural revolution symbolically uniting the country as imagined by its urban population coming of age in the 1980s. A 2010 internet comment in the Macedonian language passes to the world the following message: "If this man [Štulić] returns and puts on a concert, I think that the whole of Yugoslavia would get together in one place: Serbs, Bosnians, Croats, Macedonians, Slovenes..., Nikola, Skopje, Macedonia" (YouTube, 2010, "Azra Balkan").

"Johnny, please come back!" and "Johnny, come back, we're alone and darkness is all around here" are slogans that can be found among graffiti on the walls in almost every major city across what used to be the SFRY (Perica and Velikonja, 2012, 214–219). While songs by Štulić and his band *Azra* released from 1978 to 1991 remain rock classics frequently heard in the media, and have been resold time and again and transferred to younger generations, Štulić has remained committed to non-appearance in concert, yet he has recently undertaken something new. People familiar with his knack for seeing reality more clearly than ordinary people while also demonstrating clairvoyance, considered his recent moves symbolic anticipation of a renaissance of the culture, values and the spirit of the great generation from the SFRY of the 1980s. Many would like to see this as another chance to continue some kind of a "cultural revolution" halted by the ascent of ethnic nationalists, their wars and the Dark Ages of the 1990s. For two years now Štulić has been posting on YouTube hundreds of his recognizable rock-fashion rearranged evergreens and pop-rock classics from the socialist era and folk songs in all languages and traditions of the Yugoslav peoples. Štulić is also commemorated in several documentary films, books, clubs and cafes named after him and his band *Azra*. His family background is Croatian but he declared himself a "Balkanian." He was one of the first among several prominent figures of Yugoslav pop culture who in his songs idealized the Gypsies (later to be copied, notably by Goran Bregović and Emir Kusturica). Born in Macedonia's capital of Skopje, after SFRY's end, he, according to tabloids, applied for a Macedonian passport yet for unknown reasons his request was declined. When Serbia, followed a couple of years later by Croatia, offered him their passports and citizenships, it was he to decline. Allegedly he has no Dutch passport and is in fact an *apatride* (a stateless person) confined to his small town near Utrecht. He remains an icon of the integrated ex-YU school of rock and belongs to the continuous Yugoslav cultural space. His brand of rock and his philosophy have also influenced the post-Yugoslav rock, pop, rap and hip-hop. His cult and his opus are part of the common heritage of the SFRY and the synthesis that is developing transcending the dark and struggling post-YU decades and inspiring positive perspectives of the future.

The curious cases of Đorđe Balašević and Emir Kusturica

The two pop cultural icons of the socialist ear both belong to the "greatest generation" born from the 1950s to the 1960s and both created cultural production of a lasting value. Regarding their attitude toward the socialist period and changes of the 1990s, the two are also controversial figures each in his own right. Đorđe Balašević (Novi Sad, Serbia, 1953–) who in his youth wrote odes to the Tito cult, become a disillusioned Yugonostalgiac, critical of Titoism as an unmasked dictatorship and even more critical of post-Titoist ethnic nationalism. Although he had to suffer a dose of ridicule and parody for his songs about Tito some of them have artistic value and became generational anthems, Balašević remained massively popular, loved and respected in the entire Yugoslav space. Subsequently, with the post-Yugoslav revival of the Tito cult (Velikonja, 2010) his Titoist anthems were exploited by this nostalgic current although he would only sporadically referred to Tito with sardonic jokes. Unfortunately, those songs (especially the 1978 "You can count on us" or "Računajte na nas") have not been to this day placed in a proper socio-historical context. As a matter of fact, Balašević's apparently supportive message to the Titoist elite could be also interpreted as a continuation of the "clash of generations" from the turbulent 1968 when the children of the revolution urged the old guard to democratize faster and with greater confidence transfer power to the young.

Emir Kusturica (Sarajevo, Bosnia-Herzegovina, 1954–), represents the few pop cultural figures who began with a critique of Titoism but have gone into extremes of ethnic nationalism. In the 1990s Kusturica – born to an all-Muslim Bosnian family although his father, ironically, bore the name of one of principal villains from Serb ethnic mythology – passionately converted to extremist Serb ethnic nationalism. He spoke out justifying Serb nationalists' war crimes in World War II and the wars of the 1990s. Explaining the Yugoslav tragedy, he blamed all non-Serbs particularly the Croats, Slovenes, Bosniaks, Albanians and of course, Tito and the communists for allegedly plotting against the Serb people by inventing the policy of brotherhood and unity in the federal Yugoslavia. He sparked outrage and massive disappointment although people never devalued his memorable movies of the 1980s keeping them as part of the culture and identity they wanted to preserve. This is evident from the Internet comments: while everyone loves Balašević and all his songs including the Titoist anthems; only Serb nationalists glorify Kusturica and all others insult him as a person but still praise his best movies made in the 1980s.

The Novi Sad, Serbia-born singer-songwriter, poet, political satirist and antiwar activist Đorđe Balašević (1953–) was one of the most prolific pop-rock musicians in socialist and post-socialist Yugoslav lands. From the late 1970s continuously to this day he has performed across the entire Yugoslav space before crowded concert halls. Even during the Serbo-Croat war in Croatia, for example, thousands of Croats travelled to this Serb's concerts in neighboring Slovenia and emotionally welcomed his post-war concerts in Croatia – a documentary film recorded his 2001 return (YouTube: *Balaševic – Na stanici u Puli*). Balašević openly regretted his youthful ballads glorifying the Tito cult, later he criticized the dictator and other flaws of socialism by writing songs critical of Tito and satirizing the failures of socialism. Yet, concurrently Balašević vehemently opposed war, targeted ethnic nationalists as principally responsible for the Yugoslav tragedy and never said anything offensive about the other groups. Therefore he has remained loved and respected by all which is evident in the continuing popularity of his music, massive attendance at his concerts across the entire region, several documentary films produced and books written about him including his own contribution in writing poetry and documentary filmmaking.

The Sarajevo-born filmmaker Emir Kusturica (1954–) is the single best internationally known Yugoslav and post-Yugoslav film director who received more prestigious international awards than anyone else in the profession from this part of Europe. Unfortunately he was unable to preserve dignity like Balašević in handling the traumas of the 1990s that for sure was hard for both as for many others. Kusturica's behavior is difficult to understand although whatever he does he still remains one of the greatest filmmakers of the Yugoslav school. Yet, he never stopped public political provocations advocating extremist Serbian nationalism. He did not want to see the aggression and genocide behind the Serb militia's bombardment of his native Sarajevo and ethnic cleansing targeting Muslims and Catholics. Kusturica left his native city, and after a short stint in exile, moved to Serbia when the regimes of Milošević and Koštunica funded his projects. The government even awarded him an "ethno-village" for organizing international film festivals and doing propaganda for the Serb nationalist cause. In addition to frequently causing public scandals by his extremist nationalistic statements and biased pro-Serb interpretations of controversies from Yugoslav's recent and World War II history, Kusturica eventually shocked the troubled region by converting to the Serbian Orthodox Church, abandoning his Muslim name and rejecting his familial Bosnian-Muslim tradition. He took the Christian name Nemanja (after the medieval Serb ethnic dynasty). He justified this move by genealogy arguing that his thorough research revealed that his ancestors were Orthodox Christians before converting to Islam. The Serbian Orthodox Church and also conservative circles in Russia with whom Kusturica came into contact did not wait long before organizing spectacular tributes to Kusturica awarding him various medals and honors for promoting their causes and celebrating their culture. Yet, this "born again" experience had a negative impact on Kusturica's development as an artist. Starting with the 1995 Golden Palm-winning film "Underground", he often displays his political partisanships and nationalist views in his production, not to mention his provocative and sometimes chauvinistic public statements. The Slovene philosopher Slavoj Žižek wrote an essay deconstructing *Underground* in which he compared

Kusturica to the principal war crimes and genocide suspect Radovan Karadžić (a psychiatrist and aspiring poet from Sarajevo). The product is a grotesque "poetry of ethnic cleansing" generating a film as a mix of its authors' personal psychological frustrations with uncritical espousal of the ethnic nationalistic stereotypes and propaganda which all combined to play into the hands of the then-dominant Western perspectives such as *balkanism* and *orientalism* (Žižek, 1997, 61–68).

Kusturica and Balašević's fates are exemplary cases in the context of our broader theme. They highlight various dimensions of the Yugoslav tragedy and diverse responses to the trauma while also sustaining the continuity argument. Both artists were the outgrowth of the swan song of the SFRY pop cultural scene in the 1980s which left the legacies and values that outlived the end of the multiethnic state and influenced the new constructions of nationhood. However, Balašević emerged as a survivor of the hard times of the 1990s. After two decades he has emerged as a driving force of the slow but visible reintegration of the war-torn space. He has been invited to and warmly welcomed in all parts of what used to the SFRY, holding concerts, encouraging and unifying people. By contrast, Kusturica, has since the 1990s never made a film comparable in quality with his best works of the 1980s particularly with films he made in cooperation with the renowned Sarajevan author Abdulah Sidran. Confined to his "ethno-village" in Serbia awarded to him by the discredited Serbian regimes and supposed to host international film festivals, Kusturica lives in frustration. He is not welcome in his native city of Sarajevo or anywhere in the region outside Serbia. Even in Serbia's largest cities he is hated by liberal and leftist intellectual circles with which he exchanges insults and lawsuits. Nevertheless, his entire opus including prestigious awards belongs to the common heritage of the SFRY and its greatest generation of children of socialism. Not even Kusturica's conversion to the Serbian Orthodox Church can change this.

Conclusion

Subversive legacies, selective appropriations and the restructuring of nationhood

> Heroes! We need no bombs and guns; Just pure heart and have no fear!
>
> Croatian Hip-hop band TBF, *Heroyix*, 2004

> There is no escape from Yugoslavia.
>
> Birgithe Kosović, Danish author in an interview, 2011

The issue of continuity and change is one of historians' constant preoccupations. In the light of this theme, the Yugoslav case is particularly instructive. The continuity via cultures of memory and symbolic commemorations of the Socialist Federated Republic of Yugoslavia (SFRY) as it existed in the 1970s and particularly in the 1980s in the post-Yugoslav ethnic states that attempted to construct themselves against the SFRY, will be was in the focus of this essay. Arguably, the SFRY after the completion of the disintegration process from 1990–1992, has continued life through various remarkable cultures of memory, symbolic commemorations and survival of the common cultural heritage that in many respects remains indivisible according to ethnic nationalistic criteria. Although the post-Yugoslav nations made a great deal of effort to construct new national identities against the SFRY manufacturing new and different (counter)myths, symbols and heroes, most of the old proto-national material, to borrow Hobsbawm's term, that is, pre-modern ethnohistories and myths that the ethnic regimes revived, proved inadequate and could not serve the management of the most controversial past. Some of the Yugoslav heritage had to be exploited although selectively. Besides, it proved more durable and appealing than the new regimes expected. The SFRY was developing integration through various mechanisms and there was also a longer experience of interethnic integration not only in the two common states but also in many multiethnic communities with longer traditions of cultural pluralism than those fostered by the state. For the post-Yugoslav ethnic regimes, it might have been even more difficult to find enough ethnically pure great historical figures and national heroes than to create ethnically homogenous territories in the wars of the 1990s. Various types of heroic icons representing the diverse multiethnic Yugoslavia are not easily reduced to ethnic symbols via exclusion and based on each person's family origin, religious tradition or birthplace. Many of them are products of the Yugoslav interethnic and inter-confessional synthesis through longer periods of time. In our case-study, during mature socialism through the country's last two decades, modernization and urbanization provided additional impulses to identity mutations in favor of interethnic integration and multicultural sentiments. The icons of popular culture and sports of the two decades are only hypothetically usable for the post-Yugoslav nation building but in reality they proved difficult for "ethnicization." This is not a new phenomenon. For example, the Nobel Prize winning author Ivo Andrić belongs to older generations but he also represents this indivisible all-Yugoslav cultural heritage. According to the author and literary critic Ivan Lovrenović, speaking on the occasion of the 150th anniversary of

Andrić's birth, Andrić as a person was politically a Yugoslav; his literature is in the first place part of history and culture of his native Bosnia although the other Serbo-Croatian speaking peoples can also share Andrić; finally, in Lovrenović's words, his opus is "the most brilliant expression of inter-culturalism in South Slavic literature" (*Jutarnji list online*, 2012). A similar example is found in the earlier mentioned scientific inventor Nikola Tesla. The same, *mutatis mutandis*, applies to the urban youth pop-culture of the SFRY. Both Andrić and Tesla, and the above-named icons of the socialist-era rock and pop music, film and sport exemplify the all-Yugoslav synthesis and internationally competitive achievements as one of its products.

A number of pop cultural icons and sporting champions have been recognized, celebrated and appropriated by the post-Yugoslav regimes. To be sure, some of these icons were "too Yugoslav" and could not serve present-day political purposes and ideologies. Hence they have been ignored and left for commemoration by the Yugo-nostalgia subculture. It celebrated and commemorated everyone and everything that was prominent in everyday life and popular culture in the socialist era – even anti-heroes and ironical interpretations of the system (Adrić et al., 2004). Yet, Yugonostalgia also remembers selected figures and their legacies within different contexts of socialist federalism invariably as a proof that the common multinational framework (including socialism, too). It is represented as a "superior culture" and sophisticated urban culture as opposed to the post-Yugoslav "rural primitivism" that shaped the new ideologies and is expressed in pop-cultural phenomena such as racism and violence in football arenas and music such as "turbofolk" and "Thompson." In a longer historical perspective, these heroes of a new kind can serve as evidence of the Socialist Federated Republic of Yugoslavia's relatively successful modernization compared to both its precedents and post-Yugoslav states. Country to what used to be one of poorest and most backward places in Europe and then devastated in World War II, over the ensuing four decades it achieved unprecedented levels of modernization, probably never to get surpassed. Icons of sport, rock music, film and other forms of popular culture and urban life from the last two decades of socialism symbolize this modern society that facilitated their accomplishments. Despite some symbolic similarities, their hero-types differ from the traditional great, strong man-hero, warrior-hero or the martyr-hero which dominated both ethnic nationalist and communist mythologies. These urban icons were making history not by wearing military uniforms or ethnic attire and using sabers and guns but by wearing athletic shoes and using electric guitars in an advanced stage of socialism when their native multiethnic country seemed happily united, modernized and more open and westernized than any other East European society. They left to posterity the subversive "happy together" message which naturally the post-Yugoslav ethnocentric regimes despise and fear. Not to mention that the level of modernization reached in the SFRY in the 1970s and 1980s is for the post-Yugoslav semi-colonial states a long shot which they probably will never accomplish despite Europeanization or perhaps because of it.

Representing a radical Yugo-nostalgic view considering post-Yugoslav regimes as a cultural degeneration against which the "superior and sophisticated" socialist-era urban culture is still holding out, the rock-icon of the 1980s, Marko Brecelj, after glorifying popular culture and an overall level of freedom and sovereignty in the SFRY compared to what came afterward, concluded in a 2112 interview: "the common Yugoslav cultural space does not need to be restored because it never ceased to function although the post-Yugoslav regimes have done every effort aimed at destroying it..." (*E-novine,* 2012). Progressive factions in the post-Yugoslav elites occasionally try to cash in on Yugonsotalgia in order to present its liberal image. For example, the 2012 naming of a street in the Croatian capital Zagreb after the rock icon Milan Mladenović. He was a Zagreb native of Serb descent but spent his artistically most productive years in Serbia in the 1980s. This move was initiated as a civic and conciliatory policy by the Croatian Social Democrats (SDP) upon their coming to power in 2012; it is also celebrated by the Yugonostalgia subculture and also by liberal and leftist circles in Croatia and Serbia but opposed by the nationalist Croatian HDZ party. Or, in the case of the tragically deceased international basketball star Dražen Petrović, present-day Croatia celebrates him as a Croatian national icon and great patriot while Yugonostalgia subculture appropriates him for the nostalgic memory of the lost multiethnic homeland. Yet, Petrović as an athlete was so successful internationally that he is also celebrated in the United States as a pioneer of the globalization of basketball which is significant for the game's history and is basically incompatible with the idea of ethnic nationalism that emphasizes boundaries and fears globalization. Finally, Petrović has also been appropriated by the Serbian ideology that denies Serbia's principal responsibility for the Yugoslav wars of the 1990s as in the case of the basketball star-turned politician Vlade Divac and the US-made documentary film "Once Brothers" (2010), which Divac used to express his views. Another similar type of controversy was hotly debated in Croatian media early in 2013 when local authorities refused to approve naming of a newly built sport center after the worldly recognized swimming marathon champion Veljko Rogošić on the pretext that he conspicuously wore and used to say he was proud of a wrist watch awarded to him by the Yugoslav leader Josip Broz Tito in honor of Rogošić's sport successes. These local authorities in Rogošić's native small town of Kaštela in Dalmatia near Split, are dominated by hard line Croatian nationalists. They would rather delete the memory of the most world-famous citizen in the history of their small town than honor what they see as a "collaborator" with the communist dictator they hate. Yet they by no means represent a liberal or democratic political viewpoint that hates dictatorships. They hate Tito primarily as a creator and symbol of a multiethnic country rather than as a dictator per se because they otherwise commemorate and consider as national heroes some notorious right-wing dictators and authoritarian leaders of the ethnically homogenous Croatian movements involved in massive war crimes and crimes of genocide. One prominent Croatian who publicly responded to this controversy was the basketball legend Željko Jerkov, former mayor of Split, Croatia, in a 2013 interview. He, as a successful businessman, wanted to remain ideologically neutral as he used to be as a successful athlete when he was in his prime. He did not speak for the Yugonostalgia movement when he criticized those who refused to honor this meritorious athlete but wanted to assert the integrity and autonomy of internationally successful athletes and by extension by all individuals who thanks to their extraordinary talent and achievements rise above communities of their ethnic and national origin. In that interview Jerkov said as follows:

> Great athletes who won most prestigious international trophies are in the first place great athletes regardless of whatever country one comes from. I belong to the generation of Yugoslav athletes that won a number of Olympic medals and other international trophies, awards and titles in the 1970s and 1980s and I am proud of it. The single greatest athlete of this generation was in my opinion the boxing champion Mate Parlov. Of course, there are many others almost as great as he was because the Yugoslav sporting school was internationally competitive and its top class recognized worldwide. I want to say the following on behalf of some of us internationally awarded athletes that are now Croatian citizens: we could not have won these titles and trophies for an independent Croatia because at the time it did not exist as such. It existed only as a part of Yugoslavia and therefore we won those international trophies under the Yugoslav flag. And I want politicians to understand it and stop revising history,

dividing us, appropriating us as individuals and appropriating our medals and trophies according to present-day ethnic or national criteria. After all, each and every great internationally recognized athlete surpasses whatever national, ethnic or similar boundaries... (*Slobodna Dalmacija*, 2013).

Nevertheless, similar cultural clashes and disputes continue and some of them are rather bizarre. Thus in 2013, Croatia celebrated administrative and legal proceedings that eventually recognized the classic socialist-era film *Battle at the Neretva* (1969), as cultural property of Croatia. Even Croatian right-wing parties welcomed what they saw as an all-Croat and all-time great national victory (primarily against Serbia) because the film is about a World War II battle in which the communist-led Partisans, including many Croatians, decisively defeated the Serb nationalist Chetnik forces. So, although the film glorifies the communist idol Tito and his Partisan resistance fighters and promotes values of multiethnic brotherhood it serves contemporary purposes even for ethnic national-ists when it is adjusted to current political needs and changed circum-stances. The film director is Veljko Bulajić, an ethnic Montenegrin who lived and worked mostly in Croatia and the film cast is all-Yugoslav multiethnic. Bulajić came under attack from Bosnia and Herzegovina which claimed the film as commemorating a historical event that took place on Bosnian soil and therefore should belong to Bosnian cultural heritage. At any rate, according to the current constellation of the forces of post-Yugoslav nationalisms, whatever can help the cause of demon-strating any form of positive image, advantage or superiority of one feuding group against another is politically usable and welcome.

All things considered, the resilience and modernizing evidence of the common multinational interethnic pop-cultural heritage of the SFRY is a variable that analysts of transitional Eastern Europe need to take into account. In addition, these cultures of memory, at least symbolically, prolong the long process of Yugoslav disintegration. Yugoslavia appar-ently is no longer a nightmare (or "the communist inferno" as Franjo Tudjman used to call it) that must be forgotten. From its heritage remain things to be remembered. For some, the SFRY is perceived as a lost para-dise, while the "lost generation" from which this pantheon was selected and the urban pop-cultural revival of the 1980s were seen as great prom-ises and the swan song of a talented and resourceful country that had a bright future but was subsequently destroyed by ethnic nationalists and communists turned-nationalists. For others, it is "the communist inferno" (e.g., for the Catholic Church in Croatia or right-wing ethnic parties throughout the region). And for the pragmatic neoliberal elites it is something to be downplayed but exploited as usable material for whitewashing the new ethnic nationhood and legitimizing the neoliberals as tolerant and progressive. It is only in Croatia, for its right-wing politics and the Church, that Yugoslavia remains a "forbidden word" as it has been since 1990, which the author Dubravka Ugrešić pointed out in an interview (Kovačević, 2007). Yet, in Slovenia, Bosnia-Herzegovina, Macedonia and Serbia, the word Yugoslavia is normally in use and often with nostalgia and positive connotations. The remembrance of Yugoslavia is a rather complex sociological phenomenon (Kuljić, 2006; Velikonja, 2010; Perica and Velikonja, 2012). There is evident influence of ex-Yugoslav film (Crnković, 2012;), sport (Perica and Velikonja, 2012), and pop-culture of the 1980s on the post-Yugoslav hip-hop, rap and rock music (Perica and Velikonja, 2012) or simply the lasting and vital impact expressed in many forms of Yugoslav heritage, culture and legacies (Petrović, 2012). Many leading post-Yugoslav athletes (notably the global tennis superstar Novak Djoković) speak affirmatively and with gratitude about the socialist-era Yugoslav school of sport. Some of the leading post-Yugoslav rap and hip-hop artists such as TBF, Edo Maajka and Dubioza Kolektiv are vehemently anti-nationalist, delegitimizing the post-socialist "mafia-regimes," often also playing the socialist-era nostalgia card and making references to the pop-rock production of the 1980s. Another recent and quite intriguing contribution came from the hip-hop artist "Priki" (Haris Rahmanović). His 2012 video titled "Yustalgija" (or "I wanna everything's okay with all of us") with nearly 100,000 YouTube views so far including mostly Yugonostalgic comments glorifying especially the pop-culture and lifestyle of the 1980s, features a counterfactual history. It's a happy imaginary world in a post-1989 restructured Yugoslav democratic federation that never experienced the wars and horrors of the 1990s (it was not forgotten but never happened) but instead evolved into a prosperous proud European country preserving nonaligned foreign policy by staying outside the EU or any other great power influence while domestically celebrating the interethnic unity as the key value. In an interview, the young artist "Priki" explains: "My song and video are not about any particular politics – I did not feel the SFRY as my parents did but I can feel the good spirit of the 1980s, the love, the culture, and all the geniuses of the sport and the music of that remarkable period ... " (YouTube, "Priki Yustalgija").

A recent research project published in Germany that involved a sample of 2,000 young people born between 1971–1991 in the countries of the Western Balkans, shows that even the young post-Yugoslav generation invokes the SFRY as an alternative to what has existed since the early 1990s. According to this poll, more than a half of those polled say that the SFRY should have been preserved as a system which would have secured a better life to its citizens ("Istraživanje," 2012). Furthermore, SFRY values have also been revived by a number of people's refusal to declare the official ethnic labels. Again, rock icons have been prominent rebels. In a recent interview, the Slovene Marko Brecelj – one of the icons of the ex-YU rock scene of the 1980s, declared himself a Gypsy (Marko Brecelj, *E-novine*, 2012). It is a reminder of the rock star Štulić's once having referred to his nationality as a "Balkanian." In the most recent census in Serbia, thousands of people write under the ethnicity/nationality categories labels such as Indians-Native Americans, Martians, Jedis, Extraterrestrials or Teletubbies. Likewise, according to the 2011 census in Croatia, the number of people who chose regional/provincial identities over the majority ethnicity has tripled in comparison to the last census (*Index.hr online*, 2012). This coincides with a revival of local dialects especially prominent in contemporary hip-hop and rap music across the entire post-Yugoslav space. The same census in Croatia unveiled a significant increase in the number of citizens who declared themselves atheists and non-religious, which is a likely a response to Croatia's national Catholicism's alliance with the largely discredited ethnonationalistic regime of the 1990s.

All things considered, the phenomenon of SFRY's symbolic continuity through pop-culture and the new-types of heroism is a unique experience that has much more to teach than the standard East European post-communist nostalgia theme (Todorova and Gille, 2010). Likewise, continuing manifestations of the Tito cult (Velikonja, 2010) represent only one among many forms of post-Yugoslav dealings with the past. Tito symbolizes an ideology which is no longer as influential as it used to be. In addition, Tito belongs to the Partisan generation that paved the way for the revolution in the sphere of culture accomplished by the post-Partisan generation. Yet, this generation needs finally to get out of the old guard's shadow. A number of post-Yugoslav Titoist biographies and documentary films produced in the West overrate the "Balkan strongman who kept Yugoslavia together" while obscuring and underrating the greatest Yugoslav generation and its contribution to the country's cohesion and legitimacy. This is partly due to superficial analyses of the Yugoslav case; partly because of the colonial and post-colonial perspectives that are still vital in the West; and also partly due to the ideological bias that does not allow recognition of any progressive achievements of socialist revolutions even in the case of a relatively

West-friendly Titoism. However, Tito was by no means the only cohesive force of Yugoslavia. Actually, in the eyes of many members of the post-Partisan generation that commemorates the SFRY and identifies with it via the remarkable pop-cultural revival of the 1980s – Tito is perceived as an avatar of Sacha Baron Cohen's caricature from his 2012 film *The Dictator*. After all, the 2004 *Lexicon of YU Mythology* has indicated that the changing meanings of Yugoslavia and the new type of belonging to it as outlined in the 1980s are complex and dynamic cultural phenomena in which the Tito cult and the Partisan mythology had already been demystified, caricatured and overcome although antifascism and interethnic solidarity survived as values (Adrić, Arsenijević and Matić, 2004, 306–308).

Thus, the (post)Yugoslav pop culture and its derivates, legacies and continuities (including its influence on new forms of expression in the genre in post-Yugoslav states), help to construct a hardly imaginable and surprisingly durable community of memories and values while also building a bridge among the three generations that I labeled the Partisan, the post-Partisan and the post-Yugoslav generations. Thus Yugoslavia lives though film, in sports, rock, pop and most recently hip-hop and rap music (Perica and Velikonja, 2012, 55–253). The living hero-worship of a new type as exemplified here, showcases only a part of the pop-cultural production of the SFRY; also indicate a possibility for rehabilitation of the SFRY as a nation. In other words, the living SFRY cult is something more than a set of symbols, myths, memories, films and nostalgic tunes. It does not mean rehabilitation of the Titoist system. After all, during the socialist period, Yugoslav pop-culture came from below, not from above. It was never under the regime's control but enjoyed considerable autonomy. Pop culture was some kind of a tolerated opposition except in some cases such as notably international sport and partisan-theme films. Besides, the grand revival in the sphere of urban pop-culture in the 1980s fully expressed itself after Tito's death and among other things also entailed anticommunism and an impulse for democratic reforms but turned against the ethnic nationalists as soon as these came to power. The generation which carried out this revival was a reminder of the young rebellious generation of 1968 that challenged the old guard unwilling to more radically democratize society including through a transfer of power to the younger cadres. Of course, the methods differed: as opposed to the radicals of 1968 which still pursued revolutionary politics, the younger alternative expressed itself through pop-culture shining bright from the late 1970s to the early 1990s. The revival represented here by the sample of pop-cultural icons is also an imagined, improved version of the SFRY. This one, among many perceptions of Yugoslavia, was, according to the words of the historian Latinka Perović – one of the young liberal party leaders purged by Tito in the 1970s – Yugoslavia as "a missed historic opportunity" (*Novi plamen*, 2011). The greatest generation – at least its urban youth bound by belonging to the pop-cultural movement described here – dreamed about the possibility of an improved, democratic and further modernized Yugoslavia capable of preserving both land and pride. This presupposed preservation of values and legacies included antifascism, anti-Stalinism, interethnic solidarity and nonaligned foreign policy. Ethnic and clerical nationalists did not like the urban youth pop culture of the 1980s except perhaps sports but with modified functions and without the all-Yugoslav national team in international competition that showed the strength in interethnic cooperation. Some of the icons of pop culture, sport and the cultural revival of the last country's decade, especially those with tragic personal fates, remarkably represent this missed historic opportunity.

References

Books

Adrić, I., V. Arsenijević and Đ. Matić (eds) (2004). *Leksikon YU mitologije*, Belgrade: Rende; Zagreb: Postscriptum.

Bracewell, W. (2003). "'The Proud Name of Hajduks': Bandits as Ambiguous Heroes in Balkan Politics and Culture", in Norman M. Naimark and Holly Case (ed.), *Yugoslavia and Its Historians: Understanding the Balkan Wars of the 1990s*, Stanford, Calif.: Stanford University Press.

Brunnbauer, U. (ed.) (2009). *Transnational Societies, Transterritorial Politics: Migrations in the (Post) Yugoslav Region, 19th–21st Century*, Munchen: Oldebourg Verlag.

Čolović, I. (1994). *Bordel ratnika : folklor, politika i rat*, Belgrade: I. Čolović; I. Mesnere; Slovograf).

Čolović, I. (2011). *Za njima smo išli pevajući: Junaci devedesetih*, Zagreb: Pelago.

Crnković, G. P. (2012). *Post-Yugoslav Literature and Film: Fires, Foundations, Flourishes*, London: Continuum International Publishing Group.

Goulding, D. J. (2002). *Liberated Cinema: The Yugoslav Experience, 1945–2001*, 2nd edn, Bloomington: Indiana University Press.

Greenfeld, L. (1992). *Nationalism: Five Roads to Modernity*, Cambridge, Mass.: Harvard University Press.

Horvat, S. (2012). "Budućnost je mrtva, ali imamo Mastercard", *Zarez*, no. 346. Zagreb

Hosking, G. and G. Schöpflin (eds) (1997). *Myths and Nationhood*, New York: Routledge.

Ilić, A. (2008). *Vrati unatrag: razgovori sa Margitom Stefanović o EKV*, 2nd edn, Belgrade: Dragon Music Production.

Janjatović, P. (2007). *Ex YU rock enciklopedija: 1960–2006*, Belgrade: Čigoja štampa.

Jović, D. (ed.) (2003). "Postjugoslavenska akademska dijaspora", in the *Reč*, special issue: "Nova Generacija: Postjugoslavenska akademska dijaspora", June, no. 70/16, Belgrade. 42–57.

Kolstø, P. (ed.) (2005) *Myths and Boundaries in Southeastern Europe*, London: C. Hurst & Co.

Kordić, S. (2010). *Jezik i nacionalizam*, Zagreb: Durieux.

Kovačević, N. (2007). "Yugoslavia, an 'Almost Forbidden Word' cultural policy in times of nationalism – interview with Dubravka Ugrešić", *Women & Performance: A Journal of Feminist Theory*, 17 (3), 23–39.

Kuljić, T. (2006). *Kultura sećanja : teorijska objašnjenja upotrebe prošlosti*, Belgrade: Čigoja štampa.

Kuljić,T. (2009). *Sociologija generacije*, Belgrade: Čigoja štampa.

Kuljiš, Denis (2006). *Majmuni, gangsteri, heroji, geniji, lupeži & papci: 52 lika u povijesnom spektaklu*. Zagreb: Metro.

Levi, P. (2007). *Disintegration in Frames: Aesthetics and Ideology in the Yugoslav and post-Yugoslav Cinema*. Stanford, Calif.: Stanford University Press.

Luković, P. (1989). *Bolja prošlost: prizori iz muzičkog života Jugoslavije: 1940–1989*, Volume 1, Estrada, Belgrade: Mladost.

Mosse, G. L. (1991). *The Nationalization of the Masses: Political Symbolism and Mass Movements in Germany from the Napoleonic Wars through the Third Reich*, Ithaca: Cornell University Press.

Nikolić, L. (2012). *Osećanja. O. Sećanja*, 2nd edn, Belgrade: Čekić.

Pavičić, J. (2011). *Postjugoslavenski film: stil i ideologija*, Zagreb: Hrvatski filmski savez.

Perica, V. (2001). "United They Stood, Divided They Fell: Nationalism and the Yugoslav School of Basketball, 1968 – 2000", *Nationalities Papers*, 29 (2).

Perica, V. (2011). "Mit o dijaspori u konstrukciji novog hrvatstva i srpstva", *Politička misao*, 48 (4), 13–132.

Perica, V. and M. Velikonja (2012). *Nebeska Jugoslavija. Interakcije političkih mitologija i pop-culture*, Belgrade: Biblioteka xx vek.

Perković, A. (2011). *Sedma republika – pop kultura u jugoslavenskom raspadu*, Zagreb: Novi liber.

Petrović, T. (2012). YUROPA: *Jugoslovensko nasleđe i politike budućnosti u postju-goslovenskim društvima*, Beograd: Fabrika knjiga.

Popović, P. (ed.) (1990). Journal *Ćao*, special issue: Rock legends of the 1980s, Belgrade: March–April, 7–23.

Smith, A. D. (2003). *Chosen Peoples: Sacred Sources of National Identity*, Oxford; New York: Oxford University Press.

Todorova, M. and Z. Gille (eds) (2010). *Post-communist Nostalgia*, New York: Berghahn Books.

Valenta, M. and S.P. Ramet (eds) (2011). *The Bosnian Diaspora: Integration in Transnational Communities*, London: Ashgate.

Velikonja, M. (2010). *Titostalgja – studija nostalgije za Josipom Brozom*, Belgrade: Biblioteka xx vek.

Žanić, I. (1998). *Prevarena povijest: guslarska estrada, kult hajduka i rat u Hrvatskoj i Bosni i Hercegovini, 1990– 1995*, Zagreb: Durieux.

Žikić, A. (1999). *Mesto u mećavi : priča o Milanu Mladenoviću* [fotografije Goranka Matić … i dr.], Novi Sad: Matica srpska.

Žižek, S. (1997). "The poetry of ethnic cleansing", in Žižek, S. *The Plague of Fantasies*, London, New York: Verso.

Internet resources

"Marko Brecelj: Yugoslavia was replaced by slavery", *E-novine*. Accessed on November 25, 2012 at http://www.e-novine.com/intervju/intervju-drustvo/75254-Jugoslaviju-smjenilo-ropstvo.html?print

The Christian Science Monitor, May 5, 2008, "Turbo-folk music is the sound of Serbia feeling sorry for itself". Accessed July 4, 2010 at http://www.csmonitor.com/World/Europe/2008/0505/p20s01-woeu.html

UN/ICTY "Judgment list". Accessed on December 4, 2012 at http://www.icty.org/sid/10095

Exhibit "On heroes, winners, losers and victims"– *O herojima i pobednicima, žrtvama i gubitnicima* – at the Historical Museum of Serbia, 2009.

"Krešo Ćosić mix", You Tube. Accessed on November 29, 2012 at http://www.youtube.com/watch?v=f2k40KmUYE0

An Off-Court Story, the Life of Kresimir Cosic (Original), YouTube. Accessed on November 29, 2012 at http://youtu.be/aAR3-H-EjXA

"Dalipagić: U Sarajevo ne svraćam otkad nema Kindžeta", *Dnevni Avaz*, May 5, 2012. Accessed on November 2, 2012 at http://www.dnevniavaz.ba/sport/kosarka/93771-drazen-praja-dalipagic-za-sport-u-sarajevo-ne-svracam-otkad-nema-kindzeta.html

NBA Encyclopedia Playoff Edition. Accessed on May 17, 2011 at http://www.nba.com/history/players/Petrović_bio.html

YouTube: "Zemlja – Klapa Iskon vs EKV". Accessed on November 2, 2011 at http://www.youtube.com/watch?v=sgSX9glsdMM; live version at "Klapa Iskon – Zemlja za nas" (live) http://www.youtube.com/watch?v=rd0dhQz0Vxk.

EKV Ljubav blogspot. Petar Popović, "Margita Stefanović interview". Accessed on October 2, 2012 at http://ekvljubav.blogspot.com/2011/05/margita-stefanovic-interview.html

YouTube "Zoran Predin – Kosa boje srebra (Margita)", http://www.youtube.com/watch?v=4g0T-tgfbdg&feature=player_embedded# Accessed on November 25, 2012. See also E-novine, September 6, 2012, "Pesma o Margiti Stefanović: Kosa boje srebra", http://www.e-novine.com/kultura/kultura-tema/70980-Kosa-bo-je-srebra.html

"Nadahnuto pismo Jovanoviću", *Slobodna Dalmacija*, December 3, 2012. Accessed on December 5, 2012 at http://www.slobodnadalmacija.hr/Hrvatska/tabid/66/articleType/ArticleView/articleId/195613/Default.aspx

"Tribute to the champion: Archdiocesan seminary marks anniversary of the famous boxer's death: Mate Parlov could not be a nationalist because he was a poet", *Slobodna Dalmacija*, July 28, 2013, 6.

YouTube video "Azra–Balkan". Comment in translation from the Macedonian. Accessed on October 3, 2012 at http://www.youtube.com/watch?v=vVOUrPyNfh8

Balašević – Na stanici u Puli (2001). Accessed on July 4, 2012 at http://youtu.be/ A2SE8eB5BlE

Jutarnji list online. Interview with Ivan Lovrenović. Accessed on December 21, 2012 at http://www.jutarnji.hr/ivan-lovrenovic – gospodo-iz-vile-arko – ne-ra-zumijete – andricu-bosna-nije-zemlja-mrznje – istina – niste-prvi – to-je-mislio-i-radovan-karadzic/1073949/ "Dvorana nije dobila ime po maratoncu: Zbog Titova sata na ruci, Rogošić ostao bez počasti u Kaštelima". *Slobodna Dalmacija*, online edition, April 6, 2013 at http://www.slobodnadalmacija.hr/Hrvatska/tabid/66/articleType/ArticleView/ articleId/206856/Default.aspx

YouTube Priki – Yustalgija (official video). Accessed December 23, 2012 at http:// www.index.hr/black/clanak/yustalgija-podigla-prasinu-srbe-razljutilo-fiktivno-odvajanje-vojvodine/654080.aspx; http://youtu.be/V_G5rnIlyhM

"Istraživanje predstavljeno u Berlinu: Mladi na Zapadnom Balkanu: Bilo bi bolje da je SFRJ opstala". Accessed on March 8, 2012 at http://www.sara-jevo-x.com/vijesti/bih/mladi-na-zapadnom-balkanu-bilo-bi-bolje-da-je-sfrj-opstala/120308048

24 sata online. Accessed on December 2, 2012 at http://www.24sata.hr/cudne-vijesti/jeste-li-znali-u-srbiji-zivi-185-vanzemaljaca-ali-i-640-jedija-291837

Index.hr online. Accessed on December 17, 2012 at http://www.index.hr/vijesti/ clanak/rezultati-popisa-stanovnistva-i-dalje-nepotpuni-hrvati-sve-starija-naci-ja-pada-broj-katolika-raste-broj-ateista/652676.aspx

Latinka Perović: "Jugoslavija je bila historijska šansa koja je samo delimično iskorišćena, pa onda ispuštena". Novi plamen, no. 16, 2011, str. 101–104, http://www.noviplamen.org/#

5
Diasporas and Contextualized Transnationalism
Maria Koinova

Introduction

How does the political context of a host-land influence the transnational mobilization of conflict-generated diasporas?[1] This question is highly relevant in a globalized world where migrants are the economic, social and political link between different countries. But the question is still poorly understood by relevant streams of thought, such as transnational migration, conflict studies and foreign policy analysis. Migration studies traditionally focus on how migrants integrate into their respective societies, and more recently started to pay attention to their day-to-day activities across borders. Conflict and post-conflict studies have started to factor in the impact of diasporas on conflict and post-conflict processes, but have not yet understood how the context of receiving countries impacts on their transnational practices. Foreign policy studies have focused on how ethnic lobbies influence the foreign policy of a country, but remain embedded in a statist paradigm, avoiding a discussion on diaspora transnationalism. This chapter aims to integrate insights from these streams of thought.

I develop ideas about how processes in world politics become contextualized in domestic affairs, and how these contextualized factors in turn influence the transnational activities of diasporas. I pay special attention to foreign policy issues and the presence of the International Criminal Tribunal on Yugoslavia (ICTY) in the Netherlands. I argue that despite being viewed by the Dutch majority in monolithic terms as the "post-Yugoslav population," those individuals who identify as Bosnian Muslims (Bosniaks), Croats, Serbs, and Yugoslavs engage in different transnational mobilization patterns. In a previous piece I identified that a focal point for mobilization of Bosniaks has been the failure of

Dutch peace-keeping forces to protect the Srebrenica enclave in 1995. Here I further develop the argumentation and presentation of evidence to demonstrate that this theme dominates interactions between the Bosniak community and the Dutch state, the strong "transnationalism from below" linking the Bosniak community with Bosnia-Herzegovina, and the emerging "transnationalism from above" where Bosniak social entrepreneurs sporadically engage the EU level. Such a core theme does not exist for the mobilization of Croats and Serbs. For them remembering and forgetting the wars of Yugoslavia's disintegration takes place when triggered by sporadic events related to ICTY proceedings or during communal events organized by the respective Catholic and Orthodox churches. For them "transnationalism from below," or the linkages between people across borders, rather than high politics is dominant. Finally, there are individuals who identify as "Yugoslavs," a multicultural category which existed in socialist Yugoslavia but does not exist today. They create transnational networks with other "Yugoslavs" and cosmopolitans and pursue "transnationalism from above." For them the ICTY proceedings are important as a means of transitional justice. Yet they voice their messages in atomized ways, mostly through academia and international organizations.

The rest of the chapter continues by clarifying definitions of "diaspora" and different types of transnationalism. It further engages a theoretical literature on migration and transnationalism, conflict and post-conflict processes, and foreign policy analysis. The chapter's core is dedicated to comparative exploration on how the different communities filter the political context of the Netherlands into their transnational mobilization. I conclude by demonstrating the theoretical gains of this discussion to the understanding of how diasporas' embeddedness in a specific political context influences their transnationalism.

Definitions: diasporas, transnationalism

The term "diaspora" differs from the more widely used term "migrants" by emphasizing the *transnational connectivity* of migrants with their countries of origin rather than their migrant status in a foreign country. I adopt a definition of Adamson and Demetriou:

> A diaspora can be identified as a social collectivity that exists across state borders and that has succeeded over time to: 1) sustain a collective national, cultural or religious identity through a sense of internal cohesion and sustained ties with a real or imagined homeland and

2) display an ability to address the collective interests of members of the social collectivity through a developed internal organizational framework and transnational links. (2007, 497)

While diasporas can live in areas adjacent to the original homeland, of interest here are those who reside in liberal countries in distant locations, which Anderson called "long-distance nationalists" (1998). Diasporas are not monolithic entities, and are often constituted of competing groups. I use the term "diaspora" to refer to the social collectivities, and the term "diaspora entrepreneur" to designate individual and institutional social entrepreneurs who declare to represent these collectivities and make political claims on behalf of their original homelands.

Although in this chapter I talk about Bosniaks, Croats, Serbs, and Yugoslavs, I do not consider their "ethnic labels" in essentialist terms (Wimmer, 2011). There has been an enormous diversity among people of mixed marriages, places of origin or migration and identities. Hence, this chapter designates as diasporas only those individuals who make political claims about Bosnia-Herzegovina, Croatia, Serbia or the former Yugoslavia. They can be of different generations, institutions, networks, interrelated families, home towns and political orientations.

Political claims are voiced in the transnational space through different modes of engagement. Without making references to political claim-making, but speaking generally about migrant transnational practices, Luis Guarnizo and Michael Smith (1998) distinguish between "transnationalism from above," or the processes of globalization represented by multi-national governmental and non-governmental organizations, and "transnationalism from below" focusing on the day to day realities of migrants (quoted in Steigenga, 2006). When engaging with "transnationalism from above" migrants make political claims to circumvent the states in which they live by forging direct links with international organizations such as the UN and the European Union, and by lobbying them to exert pressure on their host-states or original home-states. Influential international relations works of Keck and Sikkink (1998) and Risse et al. (1999) explained how through "boomerang" and "spiral effects" human rights activists engage international organizations to pressure their home-states to adopt human rights reforms (Keck and Sikkink, 1998; Risse et al., 1999). This pattern can be observed by diaspora entrepreneurs as well, but with two caveats: one is that migrants are identity-based actors for whom human rights are often interpreted in ethnic terms, and second is that they can pressure home-states, as well as host-states. Less often do diaspora entrepreneurs resort to using global market forces or international corporations to pursue their political claims. Nevertheless, such have been observed in a UK-based campaign to boycott Israeli goods derived from the West Bank, joined by members of the Palestinian diaspora (Koinova, 2009), and challenges to the policies of the international corporation "Arcelor Mittal," considered problematic by a Bosniak diaspora seeking transitional justice at the site of a former concentration camp in Bosnia-Herzegovina (Koinova, 2013). "Transnationalism from above" requires from migrants a high degree of institutional organization, within specific states and within multi-sited "transnational social fields" which, as Levitt and Glick-Schiller observed, "encompass those who move and those who stay behind" (2004, 2).

In contrast, "transnationalism from below" is more common. This form of transnationalism bypasses the state through person-to-person interactions taking place usually in a transnational social field where political organization is not always necessary. Individuals can send remittances to their families in the original homelands and thus to support their livelihood, but can also support political or social organizations with whose causes they sympathize. As Levitt argued, migrants can send "social remittances" exposing families and friends in the original homeland to democratic and economic practices learned in their new locations (Levitt, 2001). These practices can also induce conflict and post-conflict processes, the latter being of more interest to this chapter. Political claim-making in this form of transnationalism may be less organized, and more difficult to capture, but is still powerful in presenting political alternatives to state policies and exerting influences across borders.

Theories and their links to diaspora transnationalism

A cluster of theories addresses to what degree diaspora transnationalism is rooted in specific contexts. Early sociological scholarship asserted that the emergence of new transnational spaces uproots diasporas from both host-land and homeland contexts (Glick-Schiller et al., 1992; Basch et al., 1994). More recently it has been claimed that transnational diaspora politics can be de-territorialized in some aspects but anchored in others. This distinction is especially relevant to conflict-generated diasporas, which can be mobilized in transnational processes but advance specific goals tied to a homeland territory (Lyons, 2006). Diaspora activists may use global norms to frame specific issues (Ostergaard-Nielsen, 2003; Kozlowski, 2005), but act as "rooted cosmopolitans" in specific social contexts (Tarrow, 2005). Moreover, activists may form a global political movement around shared goals but act in a local "division of labor" that gives comparative advantage to segments in a specific territory (Lyons and Mandaville, 2010).

Two other streams of thought can offer further insights. The retraction of multiculturalism in Western societies after the terrorist attacks of 9/11 has been already documented (Hoffman et al., 2007; Vertovec and Wessendorf, 2010). The retraction of multiculturalism can create resentment among different populations and make them more prone to pursue transnational activities. The theory of segmental assimilation has opened the "ethnic label" box, and claimed that different segments of a migrant ethnic group can make different choices on how to assimilate into their new society. They can seek upward mobility through assimilating into a mainstream majority, undergo downward mobility by assimilating into other minority strata, or become "selectively acculturated" (Portes and Zhou, 1993). Both theoretical streams relate primarily to the legal and socio-economic aspects of migrant integration, but do not factor in how they influence the political claim-making of migrants during their transnational practices. Morawska's theory comes the closest by arguing that transnational engagement is more likely to occur in the private sphere if migrants had followed an "ethnic" and "mainstream downward" paths to assimilation, and more public and multi-sphere if they followed a "mainstream upward" path to assimilation (2004, 1396). However, this work does not concern political processes.

There is a recent burgeoning literature seeking to analyze how diasporas relate to conflict and post-conflict processes. The central question is whether diasporas are agents of conflict or peace. The findings have been primarily based on identifying practices and are far from conclusive. A stream of early scholarship found that diasporas can sustain conflicts with their financial contributions to rebel factions, drafting soldiers from diaspora ranks, demonstrating in favor of radical causes, or lobbying for them (Collier and Hoeffler, 2000; Shain, 2002; Adamson, 2005; Koinova, 2011). They can also import conflicts in their host-lands, as in the case of the Turkish-Kurdish conflict (Baser, 2012). Others found that diasporas can act as moderate factors and peace-makers (Bercovitch, 2007; Smith and Stares, 2007). Since this study aims to understand how the diasporas of the former Yugoslavia, and particularly those linked to Bosnia-Herzegovina, Croatia and Serbia, act more recently, it is important to focus on their practices from the point of view of a "snap-shot" analysis in the post-conflict reconstruction period.

I argued elsewhere that scholarship has identified a number of such practices (Koinova, 2010). Diasporas can reframe traumatic identities of conflict parties in the homeland, and contribute to reform as did the

Ethiopian diaspora in the United States vis-a-vis the Ethiopian-Eritrean conflict (Lyons, 2006). According to Bercovitch, diaspora members can be agents of healing of psychological traumas, as did some in the aftermath of the conflict in Sierra Leone. Diaspora entrepreneurs can also participate in problem-solving workshops, as did Jews and Palestinians prior to and in the aftermath of the 1993 Oslo process. They can aspire to strengthen civil society by transmitting norms, values and institutions characteristic for a democratic polity (Bercovitch 2007). They can engage in the formation of new constitutions, as did the Kurdish diaspora for the provision of Kurdish autonomy in the future Iraqi state (Natali, 2007). They can provide monitoring of external elections, and participate in referendums, as did the Kurds and the Macedonians on different occasions. They can also provide much needed political leadership for new governments as in the cases of post-conflict Armenia and Nagorno-Karabakh, Kosovo and Iraq. Women, although sidelined by male domination during the development of peace initiatives, can also contribute to peace-building, mostly through grass-roots organizations (Al-Ali, 2007).

Diasporas are major agents of development during post-conflict reconstruction. Beyond remittances which are crucial, their human capital is immense (Brinkerhoff, 2008). Diasporas participate in "informal economic systems" driven by the "moral economy of the diaspora," and are motivated by obligations to help family and friends (Radke, 2005, 12–14, quoted in Turner 2008). They can send humanitarian aid, medicines, clothes and food and contribute through investments and philanthropy (Škrbić, 2007, 233; Bamyeh, 2007, 101 quoted in Turner 2008). They can also contribute to the post-conflict economy with their recurrent returns and tourism, and their knowledge transfer facilitated through short-term programs of international organizations, such as the United Nations and the International Organization on Migration. Although burgeoning, this scholarship is still focused on identifying diaspora practices in specific cases. Comparative exploration is rare, as is research focusing on how these practices are linked to contextual factors in the country of settlement. Understanding how the foreign policy of a host-land is associated with transnational diaspora mobilization practices is only emerging (Koinova, 2009, 2011; Baser, 2012).

Traditionally, foreign policy analysis has theorized about ethnic lobbying, primarily in the United States. According to Haney and Vanderbush (1999) successful lobbying is likely if diasporas promote policies that the government already favors (there is "strategic alignment" of goals) or are able to find points of "permeability of and access to the government" (1999, 345). Rubenzer used crisp-set qualitative comparative analysis to isolate characteristics conducive to a relative success in ethnic lobbying from scholarship suggesting different explanations for different cases. He identified two criteria related to diaspora attributes – organizational strength and high levels of political activity on US foreign policy issues – which are necessary conditions for successful diaspora influence (Rubenzer, 2008, 172, 179–180).

This scholarship is statist and does not capture transnational mobilization processes. In a recent article using a comparative analysis of the mobilization of Albanians in the US and the UK for Kosovo independence I demonstrated that the dynamics in the original homeland drive the overall trend towards radicalism or moderation of diaspora mobilization in a host-land: high levels of violence are associated with radicalism, and low levels with moderation. Nevertheless, *how* diaspora mobilization takes place is a result of the conjuncture of the level of violence with two other variables: diaspora linkages to a strategic center in the homeland, and accessibility of a strategic center to influence host-state support for the sovereignty goal (Koinova, 2012a).

This chapter aims to take scholarship further. Instead of simply thinking about "strategic convergence" and "divergence" of foreign policies and diaspora's goals, I aim to look at how specific contextualized aspects of the foreign policy influence the types of transnational mobilization, and whether transnationalism is pursued from "above," through the nation-state channels or from "below." I do not make causal claims, but discuss associations between state policies and diaspora behavior as identified through interviews with more than 40 respondents. I conducted this research between December 2011 and June 2012 in the Netherlands and solicited information through a questionnaire including a combination of structured and open questions, which took close to one hour to complete. I interviewed formal and informal leaders, the latter being public intellectuals, owners of cafes and bars or ethnic shops, among others. I developed the concept of "informal diaspora leadership" previously (Koinova, 2013). Several of my interviewees expressed satisfaction that this research was conducted by a person who is neither of former Yugoslav origin nor Dutch, and can potentially bring a neutral presentation of current processes and their analysis.

The theoretical space explored in this chapter can be visualized as follows (Figure 5.1).

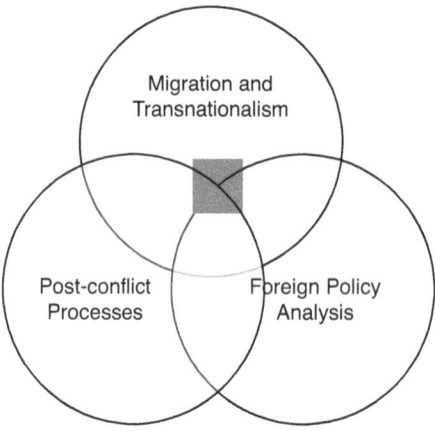

Figure 5.1   Theoretical Space

Diasporas of former Yugoslavia in the Dutch political context

Migration from the former Yugoslavia in Western Europe took place in three major waves. The first was driven after World War II by the need of booming Western economies to hire excess labor, matched by the development of policies to export labor from the cash-strapped Socialist Federated Republic of Yugoslavia (SFRY). These policies were rather open compared to the restrictions on travel and foreign residence which other communist states imposed on their citizens. Especially after the mid-1960s, guest workers with Yugoslav citizenship were hired massively in Western Europe, while others found their way to the US, Australia and Canada. In 1981 more than 875,000 Yugoslavs were working abroad, primarily in West Germany and Austria. The Netherlands hired Yugoslav guest workers as well, and organized them in "Yugoslav clubs," where all nationalities socialized with each other. A major hub for guest workers was Rotterdam, a city heavily bombed during World War II and in need of complete rebuilding. Amsterdam and other major cities also attracted guest workers.

The second wave was related to the wars of disintegration of the Socialist Federated Republic of Yugoslavia. In the late 1980s and early 1990s when ethnic polarization was on the rise, men of military age escaped drafts into the Yugoslav military by joining families or friends of already existing guest workers in Western Europe, mostly as tourists, and then claiming refugee status. Speaking of the Bosnian diaspora specifically, Valenta and Ramet (2011) mention that a major wave of migrants followed on two occasions: when the war broke out in 1992 and after the 1995 massacre of 8,000 men and boys in the Srebrenica enclave. The war triggered the most significant migration wave among Serbs, Croats and other nationalities. Initially the migrants received temporary protection status in Western countries. It was changed to a permanent one in many, except for Germany. The authors consider migrants who went to Germany "the most unfortunate" ones, because of the rapid expatriation procedures which followed the war's end, and then triggered a second wave of migration of Bosnian refugees to third countries (2012, 9). The third wave followed the end of the war, and took place mostly through family unification and other individual migration patterns, given that migration restrictions became more stringent and a reverse trend was already on the rise: Western countries sought to encourage return migration.

The Dutch migration context has been rather open. During the early 1990s when the major migration took place, the Netherlands granted refugee status to forced migrants shortly upon their arrival. As Al-Ali et al. mention, the state granted the refugees clear opportunities to acquire residency and citizenship in five years (2001, 582). This allowed for quick integration, at least when official documentation was at stake. Many individuals interviewed in this study univocally expressed their gratefulness to the Netherlands and their satisfaction that they had found asylum in this country. Yet migration policies and societal attitudes have been changing. In recent years, the hurdle to citizenship acquisition became higher with the introduction of language exams and sophisticated citizenship tests. Also, a creeping challenge to multiculturalism took place in the public domain. In the early 2000s the Liberal Party called for the return of all Bosnians to Bosnia-Herzegovina, claiming that their country is safe, and triggering massive press coverage, as well as feelings of betrayal among the migrants (Al-Ali et al., 2001, 588). When asked about how the attitudes of the majority have changed towards them during the past ten years, respondents of this study, regardless of their ethnic origin, overwhelmingly claimed that they were earlier viewed as guest workers or refugees who are entitled to stay. Currently they are often asked whether they intend to return back to their original homelands.

The rise of the right-wing politician Geert Wilders in the late 2000s and his Party for Freedom's (VVD) political support in 2010–2012 for the coalition of the minority cabinet of Prime Minister Mark Rutte (People's Party for Freedom and Democracy, VVD) and Deputy Prime Minister

Maxime Verhagen (Christian Democratic Appeal, CDA) added insult to injury.[2] Although Bosniaks who are of Muslim origin feel the most insecure given Wilders' anti-Muslim and anti-immigrant statements, interviewees of all ethnic backgrounds – but primarily from the first generation – identified a dangerous discursive pattern independently of each other. They claimed that Wilders' hate speech reminds them of the hate speech of emerging nationalist leaders during the late 1980s and early 1990s in socialist Yugoslavia. At the time when they used hate speech to galvanize citizens for their nationalisms, many individuals did not believe that hate speech could be as dangerous as to become instrumental to the outbreak of a war. Several interviewees claimed that most of the citizenry of socialist Yugoslavia did not take hate speech seriously, as does the Dutch majority at present, but hate speech can be highly detrimental to a society. Some Bosniak interviewees went as far as making discursive linkages between Wilders and war criminal Radovan Karadzic (Koinova, 2013).

In this context, an interviewee of Serbian origin questioned the human capacity to learn from mistakes. He told a story about a friend from Lebanon who was visiting him in Belgrade in the late 1980s, and who mentioned that the hate speech of Yugoslav politicians reminded him of the situation in Lebanon preceding the onset of the civil war (1975–1990). At that time my interviewee also did not take his friend's words seriously, because he believed that people who had lived for four decades alongside Yugoslavia's slogan of "Brotherhood and Unity" would not resort to war. The interviewee argued that currently he warns his Dutch friends about the same, but his words fall on deaf ears (Respondent 2, 2012).

These discursive linkages are indicative of the impact of current political events on the traumatic identities of refugees, which we need to understand in more depth. Scholarship on conflicts and post-conflict reconstruction mentions that traumatic identities maintain conflicts over time. Such identities become embedded in diaspora institutions, and maintain feelings of victimhood and "myths of return" preventing migrants from fully integrating into their new societies (Faist, 2000; Shain, 2002; Lyons, 2006). However, scholarship is not clear on when such identities are sustained, when they dissolve, and how they affect diaspora transnationalism.

The politically relevant environment (PRE)

I develop the concept of the *Politically Relevant Environment (PRE)* inspired by ideas of Maoz (1996) about the Politically Relevant International

Environment (PRIE) and bring to transnational diaspora politics. For Maoz the PRIE denotes "the set of political units (state and non-state units), whose structure, behavior and policies have a direct impact on the focal state's political and strategic calculus" (38). In my account, certain global, regional or local factors become contextualized and structure the behavior of diasporas' political and strategic calculations vis-à-vis their original homeland. These may be actor-based or structural conditions stemming from the host-state and the homeland environments, international system or the transnational field in which diasporas operate across borders. I focus on conditions politically relevant to the host-land environment. With regard to the host-state such factors can be contextualized through the territorialization of global issues and processes and can also be derived from domestic politics while having wider transnational repercussions.

This chapter is particularly interested in understanding the relationship between diaspora transnationalism and two contextualized political aspects which go beyond the domestic politics of the Netherlands: the proceedings of the ICTY and Dutch foreign policy towards the successor states of the Socialist Federated Republic of Yugoslavia. One can argue that ICTY is an international organization and concerns the Netherlands as much as other countries. My approach points to how global processes can become embedded in specific countries as they *become contextualized.* The importance of the ICTY could be on the radar screen of policy-makers of all countries that are signatories to the ICTY, but it assumes special importance in the Netherlands where it is territorialized by being given special attention with intense media coverage and engagement in the public sphere. Also, the somewhat existent self-perception among Dutch that The Hague is the "legal capital of the world" [3] also contributes to this successful contextualization.

It is beyond the scope of this chapter to follow in detail all the ICTY proceedings and fluctuations of Dutch foreign policy towards the successor states of the former Yugoslavia and how they affect diaspora transnationalism. While opening avenues for further research, this chapter wants to understand *how diaspora entrepreneurs perceive these factors* and how they act upon them in the transnational space. Thinking about perceptions is important because individuals can be removed from understanding the intricacies of foreign policies, and may or may not update their daily knowledge of foreign policy developments. But they can *develop stable perceptions about these foreign policies* upon which they can base their behaviors. The following section will identify specific perceptions and transnational activities among formal and informal leaders interviewed in this study.

Transnational activism within the Bosnian diaspora

This chapter argued earlier that the ethnic label will be used primarily as a designation for activism for specific original homelands, rather than to essentialize identities. Hence, all statistical numbers mentioned in this and subsequent sections need to be taken with caution, since they do not designate all who organize and make political claims. They are necessary to understand the migration landscape from which activism eventually follows. According to Valenta and Ramet whose study on the Bosnian diaspora is the most comprehensive so far, Bosnians in the Netherlands are around 24,700 (2012, 5). The official statistics do not distinguish between refugees by ethnic origin but data exist on their birthplaces. The largest refugee numbers originate from Sarajevo (2,753), Zenica (1,919), Prijedor (1,117), Tuzla (1,055), Banja Luka (704), Mostar (512) and Srebrenica (497) (Mulalić et al., 2008, 37). In the Netherlands the Bosnian refugees were dispersed throughout different cities in order to prevent spatial segregation, but were assisted through various welfare agencies (Koprivova, 2011, 6). Despite antagonisms of older guest-worker generations to absorb the newcomers, especially among the Croats and the Serbs who had more guest workers, the Catholic and Orthodox Churches of the respective communities became a meeting ground for these groups in the Netherlands. The most active claim-making with regard to Bosnia-Herzegovina has been made by the Bosniaks (Bosnian Muslims). Hence this chapter continues to further concentrate on their transnationalism.

The global distribution of Bosnian emigration

Valenta and Ramet stress that Bosnian authorities consider this overview inaccurate due to problems with the comparability of numbers, but it is the best to be offered at this stage (Valenta and Ramet, 2011, 6). These numbers also do not capture how many of these refugees were Bosniak (Bosnian Muslim), Bosnian Serb, or Bosnian Croat or had mixed, Yugoslav, or translocal identities.

As discussed previously elsewhere, Bosniaks in the Netherlands are very well organized.[4] The BiH Platform is the umbrella organization of 30 smaller organizations located in Utrecht, The Hague, Delft, Amsterdam, Rotterdam, Gouda and smaller cities. The BiH Platform acts as the official representation of the community primarily on non-religious matters, and has a sub-section for the second generation called "Mladi BiH." Bosniaks are also very well organized through their own Islamic-cultural Association,

Recipient country	Number of migrants from Bosnia-Herzegovina
Australia	50,000
Austria	132,300
Belgium	8,000
Croatia	60,000
Canada	60,000
Denmark	21,000
France	5,000
Great Britain	10,000
Germany	157,200
Italy	40,000
Luxembourg	6,000
Netherlands	24,700
Norway	15,500
Slovenia	100,000
Serbia (and Montenegro)	137,000
Sweden	75,000
Switzerland	50,600
USA	390,000
Other 28 countries	14,300
Total	**1,356,600**

Source: Valenta and Ramet (2011, 5).

which since 1995 incorporates ten organizations in Amsterdam, Rotterdam, Arnhem, Utrecht, Eindhoven, Enshede, Den Bosch, Nijmegen, Roermond and Veenendaal.

Three-pronged transnationalism: "from above," through the nation state and "from below"

Transnationalism within the Bosnian diaspora takes place through multiple channels. The failure of Dutch peace-keeping forces to protect the Srebrenica enclave in 1995, when more than 8,000 Bosnian Muslim men were killed by paramilitary units of Republic Srpska, is the core issue for activism.[5] It shapes the diaspora's relationship with the Netherlands, and its two modes of transnationalism: from below (linking people directly with Bosnia-Herzegovina) and more recently from above (linking diaspora institutions to the EU level). It is important to understand the process of contextualization of this factor into the Dutch political environment. In 1995 the failure of the Dutch peace-keeping unit (Dutchbat) was a failure of a UN peace-keeping mission. Yet the issue created a trauma within Dutch society for which Srebrenica became a symbol for loss of power and humiliation (Žarkov 2002; Rijsdijk, 2012). Towards the late 1990s, dwelling on this failure became embedded in procedures of local institutions and the public sphere. In 2002 the Netherlands Institute on War Documentation (NIOD) produced an investigative report about the role of Dutchbat, and media and academics continued with further investigations. The television series "The Enclave" was featured in 2002, and became highly rated (more on this in the chapter by Dubravka Žarkov).

The failure at Srebrenica also became embedded in Dutch foreign policy and particularly in its development cooperation program and the work of NGOs which receive 20 percent of the bilateral Overall Development Assistance funds (OECD, 2011). Development cooperation is one of the most important pillars of Dutch foreign policy. The Netherlands is among the five biggest donors of international aid to Bosnia-Herzegovina after the United States, Austria, Sweden and Spain. Its funding budget is almost the same as that of Turkey (EU Framework Contract Commission 2009, 16). In 2003 the budget was EUR 17.2 million. Dutch development cooperation funds are spent especially in the field of governance, human rights, peace-building, refugee return and Srebrenica-related aid. Also Dutch NGOs such as the Inter-church Peace Council Netherlands (IKV), Press Now and the Netherlands-Srebrenica working group have been very active on the ground (ibid., 74). The sectoral focus including aid for specific Srebrenica-related issues is clear when compared to a different focus towards Macedonia, a country in the Western Balkans on which the Netherlands also spends a considerable amount of foreign aid. In Macedonia the focus is on education, rural development and the implementation of the peace-building Ohrid Framework Agreement.

The Srebrenica issue shapes the political relationship between Bosniak diaspora entrepreneurs and the Dutch state. The annual commemoration of the Srebrenica events on July 11 is the biggest event that gathers no less than 1,000–1,500 Bosniaks in the Netherlands, their Dutch friends and sympathizers in front of the Parliament in The Hague. The BiH Platform and other organizations are the major organizers of this event. Diaspora entrepreneurs in the Netherlands clearly frame the Srebrenica massacre as "genocide," compare it to the Armenian "genocide" and seek acknowledgement on these terms. Their claims have been grounded in an ICTY judgment in the case of Radislav Krstić who was convicted of committing genocide (ICTY, August 2001). Hence, some of the rulings of the ICTY also became central to the diaspora activism within the Netherlands and beyond it.

The Netherlands have aspired to compensate for the Srebrenica massacre with foreign aid, but not with an apology towards survivors and their families. This attitude has fueled long-term activism targeting the state. Most notable is the activism of Hasan Nuhanović, a former UN interpreter stationed with the Dutch peace-keepers in Srebrenica, whose entire family was murdered, and who for the past 16 years has "waged a lonely campaign," as Dobbs put it, to "force the Dutch state to accept at least some responsibility for the deaths of his family members" (Dobbs, 2011). He filed a court case in the Netherlands against the Dutch government in 1995 which he holds responsible for handing over his family members to the paramilitaries of Ratko Mladić, currently on trial at the ICTY. In a precedent-making decision, in July 2011 the court ruled in Nuhanović's favor. This individual victory can further open opportunities for other genocide survivors to inaugurate court cases.

The "transnational from below" among Bosniaks is still highly driven by the need to cope with the traumatic events of the war, with the failure at Srebrenica taking an important stage, but also ICTY rulings and other occasions to commemorate traumatic events. The July 11 commemoration of the genocide at Srebrenica is becoming an all-Bosniak event to be attended whether in the Netherlands or in Bosnia-Herzegovina during the summer holidays (Respondent 3, 2012). This commemoration is a communal expectation and individual obligation of diaspora members and the second generation is not exempted from it. The rulings of the ICTY are usually rarely subject to media activism but more embedded in private conversations that flow in discussions with family members across borders, and when diaspora members go on return visits to Bosnia. The predominant attitude among diaspora members includes satisfaction with the capture of war criminals, but dissatisfaction with the media that war criminals are given so much space to voice their opinions, and with the authorities that they give them so many comforts – such as TV and different kinds of care – which a regular person in Bosnia often cannot afford. The Srebrenica issue also attracts other trauma-related diaspora activism. There is a group "Guardians of Omarska" organized by the concentration camp survivor Satko Mujagić, which seeks a change of policies of the transnational corporation "Arcelor Steel." The corporation bought the mines on the site of the former concentration camp "Omarska" in Prijedor in Republica Srpska, and initially promised to build a memorial, but has retracted from this promise and has prohibited access to the site on a regular basis. Seeking restoration of transitional justice and public apology, diaspora members invest energy and finances in organizing for the recognition of these trauma-related events. Some individuals have gathered information about the lives of concentration camp inmates or have been in the process of doing so. Yet, financial drives take place also for less politically charged phenomena, but still related to the war. Various networks, including Islamic ones, often organize drives to support sick people, individuals with dire needs and orphans in need of special care and education.

"Transnational from above" builds on the strong organization of the Bosniak diaspora within the Netherlands, but is still emerging and is related to lobbying the EU. Lobbying is framed both in terms of the power of the EU to exercise political leverage for European integration, as well as with regard to its symbolic power. In this endeavor a viable relationship has been essential between the BiH Platform and its youth organization Mladi BiH with the European Parliament (EP) representative Emine Bozkurt, a second-generation Dutch politician of Turkish origin and representative of the Dutch Labor Party, part of the Social Democrats in the European Socialists. Bozkurt has worked on social and women's rights since 2004, and has also been involved with European enlargement since 2009.

In her capacity as spokesperson on Bosnia-Herzegovina for the Social Democrats she pioneered together with Mladi BiH and the BiH Platform the first conference of the European diaspora in the European parliament in September 2010 (CNAB, 08/03/2010). According to Bozkurt, this conference gathered in Brussels more than 300 Bosnians from the Netherlands, Germany, France and Sweden and other countries to discuss how diaspora members, and especially the young generation, could contribute to the future enlargement of the country. The willingness of diaspora members to contribute to Bosnia-Herzegovina was a major discussion point, as was their feeling of often being excluded from the political and social processes taking place within Bosnia-Herzegovina. Bozkurt attributes the development of the Ministry of Human Rights within Bosnia-Herzegovina as a result of this conference. Another issue on which she has been active is a double nationality law envisaged for 2013 which could potentially exclude Bosnians from the diaspora from Bosnian citizenship and voting rights. Bozkurt considers her discussions with top policy-makers in Bosnia-Herzegovina as important so that a further development of this law does not take place (Telephone Interview, 06/27/2012).

Bozkurt has been supportive of Bosniaks' claims of genocide. During two events in which I did participant observation in 2012 – the 20th Year anniversary of independence of Bosnia-Herzegovina in March 2012, and the commemoration of the Omarska concentration camp in May

2012 – Bozkurt was supportive of statements that the voices of genocide survivors need to be heard on the EU level. In a more recent debate in the EP she also stated that Bosnia-Herzegovina needs to deliver quick and well considered reforms on many policy areas, including finding a durable solution for the refugees. She also emphasized that it is the "obstruction of justice, denial of [the] history of genocide, that is the bringing the country backward not forward" (EP Debate, 03/14/2012).

Transnational activism among the Croatian diaspora

Comprehensive information about Croatian migration to the Netherlands has been offered so far by a 2011 opening lecture of Ivan Kantoci during a symposium "50 years Croats in the Netherlands." In his account, Croats were already present in the mines of Limburg since 1920, while the majority of the 1,184 people counted in 1929 who arrived from Royal Yugoslavia were Slovenians, Croats, and the least were Serbs (2011, 1). One needs to be circumspect about the ethnic label used by Kantoci, not least because nationalist consciousness specific for the 1990s did not exist at the time. In Kantoci's account, before World War II Limburg was the center of gravity for Croats, while The Hague and Nijmegen experienced sporadic settlements. After World War II further migration took place towards Limburg mines and ship-building businesses in other cities. The most massive migration took place in the early 1970s when more than 25,000 working permits were issued for Yugoslav "guest workers." The Croats among the Yugoslavs came from industrial and harbor cities. This migration wave, which also included a following family unification, settled in Rotterdam, Amsterdam, Utrecht and The Hague. These cities retain the highest Croatian population at present (2011, 2).

Kantoci's account is indicative of trends during the 1990s in the Netherlands which other scholarship on the Croatian diaspora has already engaged regarding other political contexts (Hockenos, 2003; Ragazzi, 2009). With the 1992 outbreak of the war rapid dissimilation started taking place among the Yugoslav population. Although no reliable statistical data exist, an Alders and Nicolas 2002 study argued for the existence of 4,700 Croats in 1992 and 7,300 in 2002 and a Mulalić, Harmsen and Oudhof (2007) study found 9,800 Croats in 2004, not including Croat refugees from Bosnia-Herzegovina (quoted in Kantoci, 2011, 3). The latter number remains unclear, since refugees were statistically considered as coming from Bosnia-Herzegovina.

Towards the end of the 1980s Croats in the Netherlands started dissociating themselves from the "Yugoslav clubs," where – as Kantoci argues – Croats were present, but Serbs held the leadership roles. The mushrooming of new organizations started in 1991. During the war of Yugoslavia's disintegration and its aftermath 25 Croatian organizations emerged. In 2003 there were cultural and sports clubs, clubs for friends of Croatia, organizations offering supplementary education to children, a Croatian radio station in Rotterdam, humanitarian and women's organizations. Most notable, however, was the emergence of numerous branches of the nationalist Croatian Democratic Union (HDZ) of Franjo Tudjman with offices in Rotterdam, Amsterdam, and Enkhuizen responsible for North Holland. Branches of the Croatian Social Liberal Party and of the Croatian Christian Democratic Union emerged as well (Kantoci, 2011, 6–9). As Ragazzi and Balalovska point out, by considering the Croatian diaspora as part of the polity if it had citizenship of the socialist Republic of Croatia or were of Croatian ethnic origin, but disregarding residence, Croatia adopted a post-territorial citizenship regime (2011, 7). This pro-active attitude towards the diaspora also facilitated the development of official ties between parties in Croatia and the diaspora.

With the end of the war in 1995 many organizations ceased to exist, including branches of Croatian political parties and the Croatian radio in Rotterdam. In 2011 only 14 of them remained active. At present the power to organize the diaspora has shifted towards the Catholic Church, the main of which is in Rotterdam, and cultural organizations. The influence of political parties, most notably the HDZ, has certainly toned down compared to the previous period.

Throughout the 2000s Dutch foreign policy was adamant that Croatia deliver top Croatian generals indicted for war crimes to the ICTY. Hence, Dutch foreign policy was focused on an issue with which many Croats in the diaspora openly or tacitly disagreed. Yet, sustained mobilization to change the foreign policy of the Netherlands did not take place. There was an ad hoc diaspora mobilization on the premises of the ICTY when Croatian general Ante Gotovina was delivered to the tribunal in 2005 after 4 years of hiding. As one of my interviewees recalls, there was a large demonstration of Croats, but people from the Croatian diaspora in the Netherlands did not lead the effort. There was reportedly a mobilization effort exerted from Croatia proper and from other organizations of Croats in Europe, most notably from Germany (Respondent 4, 2011).

Several reasons could possibly explain the lack of sustained mobilization on the state level or with regard to the ICTY. Unlike in the Bosniaks' case, the Dutch political institutions were not implicated in a national trauma able to fuel further mobilization. Moreover, although the ICTY became the site of protest, diaspora members generally respected its choices even if they did not agree with them. It certainly helped that many Croats in the diaspora have been well integrated into Dutch society. Despite voicing that they remained and were reminded that they are foreigners, Croatian interviewees actively sought integration. They experienced rather positive majority attitudes, especially if compared to the majority attitudes towards other post-Yugoslav groups or migrants from the Middle East. A respondent even claimed that Croatian diaspora members exerted pressure on him to quickly integrate in order to avoid creating negative externalities for others (Respondent 5, 2012). Another interviewee argued that had it not been for the ICTY, Croats would have integrated into Dutch society even faster (Respondent 6, 2011). A third diaspora entrepreneur mentioned that the tight links between Dutch foreign policy and requirements to deliver indicted individuals to the ICTY created unintended consequences. Instead of being seriously investigated for their war-time crimes in Croatia, indicted individuals developed a new clout in Croatian politics: they once again "offered themselves" for their nation, this time for the sake of EU integration (Respondent 5, 2012). This pattern became even more visible in November 2012, when Gotovina was acquitted and was accepted in Croatia as a hero, while the acquittal was condemned in Serbia and became highly questioned in various international circles. A similar pattern spread regarding all successor states of the former Yugoslavia, and did not contribute to the delivery of transitional justice in these post-conflict societies (Subotić, 2009). Finally, while some diaspora individuals became active in the cultural sphere to bring more attention about Croatia in European institutions and networks, sustained diaspora "transnationalism from above" to pursue Croatia's EU integration did not take place. A respondent claimed that some lobbying activities involved the Christian Democrats and the Green Left, but they were also sporadic (Respondent 7, 2012). In 2010 Dutch foreign policy dropped its long-standing veto on the opening of EU accession talks with Croatia (Vogel, 2010). Sustained diaspora lobbying became more or less obsolete.

In recent years "transnationalism from below" has been the dominant mode of engagement across borders. Person-to-person interactions have been taking place through telephone, Skype, and the social media. Rulings of the ICTY were rarely discussed on the telephone unless an indicted individual was captured or a specific ruling concluded. Most of the conversations flowing across borders focus on issues of unemployment, the corruption of Croatian politicians, and the involvement of the Catholic Church in domestic politics, including with the diaspora. War-time events are not discussed at length, but conversations occur occasionally in long-distance communication, and more profoundly during return visits usually taking place 1–3 times a year. My interviewees confirmed a general trend among Croats abroad, discussed also in Valenta and Ramet's (2011) book with regard to other European cases, that Croats buy second homes in Croatia, especially alongside the Adriatic coast. As in the Bosnian case, an outspoken frustration exists among diaspora Croats that it takes the ICTY too long to convict war criminals. But in contrast to the Bosnian case, there is often a voiced disapproval that war criminals were not tried in Croatia. One interviewee even argued that the prosecutor, not the judge has the major say, and that he has the power to influence European states whether Croatia would become part of the EU or not (Respondent 8, 2012). Alongside other interviewees this respondent openly disapproved of the blurring between international law and politics, and considered the linkage between Croatia's EU integration and the ICTY "a mistake."

Transnational activism among the Serbian diaspora

Patterns of Serbian migration during the guest-worker generation have been similar to those of other peoples from the former Yugoslavia. In the early 1990s there were a considerable number of men from Serbia who evaded drafts from the Yugoslav army, and sought asylum in the Netherlands. Although most of my interviewees argued that the Serbian diaspora is not well organized compared to other groups from the Balkans, ethno-national dissociation from the previous Yugoslav clubs took place among those who considered themselves Serbs during the 1990s, and separate clubs were established. Currently, there is an umbrella organization, Serbian Information Network, two Serbian schools – "Vuk Karadžić" in Rotterdam, and "Stefan Nemanja" in Utrecht – and a number of clubs in Utrecht, Katwijk, Vlissingen, Hengelo and others. The Serbian Orthodox Church in Zandaam is considered a major hub for communal activities, with the church in Rotterdam playing a secondary role. There are other smaller churches in Utrecht, Nijmegen, Ede, and Emmer-Compascuum (Srbi u Holandji, 2012).

The Dutch foreign policy has been aligned with other NATO countries viewing Milošević in Serbia as part of the solution to the wars in the former Yugoslavia until the mid-1990s, and then as part of the problem, culminating in the Dutch support for NATO's military intervention in Kosovo in 1999. At the time of the intervention, numerous Serbian organizations in the Netherlands organized protests against it. In the present narratives of numerous interviewees, NATO's 1999 military intervention in Kosovo remains a serious traumatic event, discussed and commemorated on Facebook and other websites. As a respondent put it: "Dutch won't be happy to cede parts of Amsterdam to Morocco," alluding to a strong concentration of Moroccans in parts of the Dutch capital, and making linkages to the situation between Serbia and Kosovo where Albanians are concentrated and in the majority.

Yet most problematic in all interviewees' narratives remains the perceived criminalization of the Serbs in collective terms in the Dutch public discourse, capitalizing on events related to individual Serbian mafia bosses – such as Sreten Jocić aka "Joca Amsterdam" – who operated out of the Netherlands for several years. It is not the focus of this chapter to unravel underworld activities and whether they relate to diaspora politics. Yet it is still worth mentioning that several interviewees claimed that they did not want to engage in organized activities in the diaspora, because of penetrations of influences from the homeland that they did not want to be associated with.

One cannot ascribe criminal activities to specific ethnic groups. As a respondent argued: "People from the underworld are not driven by ethnic affiliations and often cooperate with each other" (Respondent 9, 2012). This person echoed an argument of Peter Andreas (2008) and others, who have claimed that various individuals in the Balkan underworld have actually cooperated during the wars in former Yugoslavia. Also one respondent of Croatian origin argued that the Dutch have given Croats the label of criminality (Respondent 7, 2012), but more Serbs voiced such a concern from the interviewed in this study. The latter claimed that they have been ascribed the image of criminals together with the image of the "villain" in the Balkan wars. As the respondent put it: "I very much sympathize with the Germans and how they have been perceived after the Second World War. As a Serb one has to carry the cross of all the atrocities other people have committed" (Respondent 9, 2012).

The perceived stigma magnified the mistrust towards diaspora political participation, characteristic for many people from former communist countries, and inhibited the Serbian migrants to organize politically in a systematic way. Hence, many of the existing organizations have been driven by cultural concerns. This does not mean that political activities were missing. Migrants with Serbian consciousness were generally dissatisfied that Milošević and other indicted persons were tried in The Hague, and not in local courts. Their attitudes did not diverge much from the attitudes of the population in Serbia. The extradition of Milošević to the ICTY triggered demonstrations in 2001 in The Hague (Respondent 10, 2011). When Radovan Karadzic was captured in 2008, there was some resistance about his delivery to the ICTY at a mass rally in Belgrade (Traynor, 2008), but – as some respondents claimed – the diaspora was not very active. The ongoing trial of Voijislav Šešelj is followed in the diaspora, but discussions remain confined to close circles and do not translate into sustained activism.

"Transnationalism from below" has been the dominant mode of connectivity between diaspora members and their original homeland. Many discussions on sensitive issues are rarely voiced on the phone. Migrants have been weary of wire-tapping during the Milošević rule, and maintain this habit until the present. Such issues are discussed in private during return visits, primarily during the summer months. For those who organize through the Orthodox Church, the latter becomes a major venue for charity activities, and commemoration of events. The strongest connections between Serbia and the diaspora are maintained through the Orthodox Church, and less so through official embassy channels. There is a general sentiment among Serbian migrants that Serbia is interested in them only when it comes to sending remittances. Hence, many maintain personalized attitudes towards their families and circles of friends in the original homeland, and avoid organizing for Serbia.

This minimal political activism translates into minimal political engagement with regard to EU enlargement issues. An interviewer claimed, Dutch foreign policy has not been neutral and has been blocking Serbia's entry into the EU. This "is not based on animosity for Serbia," which has been democratizing after the 2000 downfall of Milošević, but is somewhat driven by the trauma which "the Dutch have with regard to Srebrenica" (Respondent 9, 2012). It is worth noting that my respondents did not attribute Serbia's actual performance on coop-eration with the ICTY as a reason behind Dutch foreign policy. They generally considered the ICTY an international court highly intertwined with great power politics.

While political activism has been emanating minimally from the Serbian diaspora in the Netherlands, there are more recent attempts from Serbia to organize the diaspora in the Benelux (Belgium, Netherlands, Luxembourg) to which some diaspora institutions have responded. The Netherlands-based Serbian Information Network hosts several links to organizations active on these issues, most notably the site milosevic. eu. It is in Serbian only and is organized by a young diaspora activist, Ana Milošević Tassone, elected as a Benelux Serbian diaspora delegate for the Serbian parliament. The site features Serbia's 2011 draft law on the diaspora, information about activities of Serbian politicians in European institutions, photos from a meeting of the Serbian diaspora in the European Parliament, current initiatives such as a summer camp for diaspora Serbs to visit Serbia, and a student contest about the importance of Kosovo and Metohija as the "heart of Serbia" (milosevic.eu 2012).

Transnational activism among "Yugoslavs"

The group of diaspora individuals who identify themselves as "Yugoslavs" is the most diverse and fluctuating. Compared to the transnationalism of earlier discussed diasporas, that of "Yugoslavs" is driven by values more open to "human rights for all" (and not only for a specific ethno-national group), transitional justice and cosmopolitanism. The ethno-national dissociation process which made Croats, Serbs and Bosniaks out of the previous "Yugoslavs" did not significantly concern that circle of individuals. Many went out of their way to defend human rights during talks, seminars and various protests even at the height of the Bosnian war. It became also specific to the Dutch context that the ICTY hired some individuals as legal specialists or interpreters from the Bosnian/Serbian/Croatian languages, and so attracted self-selectively those who believe in the tribunal's mission. These individuals are either very well integrated into Dutch society, with many Dutch friends and family, or associate with other expatriate highly skilled migrants working in the multiple international institutions in The Hague, and having little interest in developing social roots in the Netherlands.

Ad hoc "transnationalism from above" is characteristic for this group. Compared to the more or less organized attempts of other groups to reach out to the EU and lobby for their particular country in southeastern Europe, "Yugoslavs" act in atomized ways through academia or international institutions but are more driven by cosmopolitan values. Some have a clear nostalgia for a country that does not exist, but was governed by the principle of "Brotherhood and Unity" (more on Yugonostalgia see the chapter by Mitja Velikonja). For them the cooperation between peoples is a wonderful artifact of the past, but one that cannot be recreated at present. Many of them, highly educated, acknowledge the existence of new socio-political realities in the Balkans, but do not accept them for themselves. Also, they do not pursue any sustained political activities to instigate domestic change in their countries of origin, but prefer to voice their views on specific occasions and rarely pro-actively. Some may even advocate an approach of "moving on from the past," which could potentially conceal unwillingness to advocate for a better understanding of war-time realities. But one needs to consider also the flip side of the coin, argued one respondent. Although the ICTY is a "big part of [that person's] life," they feel "more stuck in the past than others" in the Balkans, where people are preoccupied with their daily lives and show minimal interest in unravelling recent history (Respondent 11, 2011).

A final note deserves the ad hoc unification function of concerts of well-known singers, who come from the post-Yugoslav space and usually gather different people from the former Yugoslavia living abroad. The function of concerts is in stark contrast to sports matches, which unify on a nationalist basis: football matches are conducted separately within the Bosniak and the Serbian migrants groups, and basketball matches are more pervasive among the Croats. Yet concerts are the venue for sporadic gathering of different people. As Perica demonstrates in this volume, some singers have accrued the image of new heroes for the not-so-dead Yugoslavia. One of my interviewees claimed that the biggest venue in 2012 was in May in The Hague, a Djordje Balašević concert, where "everybody went." "This is our Bob Dilan" (Respondent 1, 2012). During the 1990s Balašević had strong anti-war attitudes, and openly criticized the Milošević regime during his concerts, as well as other nationalisms.

Conclusions

Although in the view of many Dutch the "post-Yugoslav" populations belong to one lump-sum category, this study's empirical evidence problematizes such an attitude as "frozen in time." There is a multitude of ethnonational identities, a multitude of different social and political claims, and a multitude of patterns of political transnationalism. Many respondents of this study associated their origins with more than one country in the former Yugoslavia, with various regions and locations, and even reported that their identities fluctuate depending on context. Some claimed to be "Yugoslavs," but when it came to discussing their political claims, the majority of respondents became clearly associated with Bosniak, Croatian, or Serbian ethno-national categories. Hence, the core of this chapter was dedicated to them, and to capturing their transnationalism patterns.

I followed up on an earlier argument that the failure of Dutch peacekeeping forces to protect the Srebrenica enclave in 1995 created a focal point for the mobilization of Bosniaks in the Netherlands, whether regarding to the Dutch state (on the nation-state level), to Bosnia-Herzegovina through their strong "transnationalism from below" and to European Parliament through their ongoing "transnationalism from above." The absence of such a traumatic event has rendered transnational activism among Croats and Serbs very much related to a pattern of "transnationalism from below," where person-to-person interactions across borders predominate, and are often but not always channeled through diaspora organizations. This chapter captured also a "frozen" Yugoslav identity which does not translate into any specific political projects, but into making ad hoc claims for the pursuit of transitional justice and restoration of cultural cooperation among the peoples of the former Yugoslavia. The Yugoslav identity and cosmopolitan activism also offer a challenge to the existing literature, considering "frozen identities" mostly as detrimental and conducive to conflict-perpetuation. The Yugoslav identity, where preserved, is a cosmopolitan identity that advocates for understanding among the peoples from the former Yugoslav space, and for the creation of new links among the former warring peoples.

This intra-country comparison alludes to the importance of factors other than migration integration regimes that drive diaspora transnationalism. All respondents reported rather quick citizenship integration into the Dutch society, although their social integration was more different. In the eyes of the Dutch majority migrants have acquired the image of the "victim" (Bosniaks), the "criminal" and the "villain" (Serbs), and rather rarely the "criminal" (Croats). Other factors relevant for political transnationalism are a traumatic relationship between host-country and the migrant population in the Bosniak case, and different host-land's foreign policy attitudes in the other cases. Dutch foreign policy was driven by the Srebrenica trauma regarding Bosnia, was adamant that Croatia would not enter the EU unless it cooperates with the ICTY, but became permissive more recently, and continues to be non-supportive of Serbia.

Also, the presence of the ICTY in the Netherlands resulted in the contextualization of a globally conceived UN court into a domestic issue. The ICTY became a venue for ad hoc mobilization for all three groups, often attracting people from the diaspora in the Netherlands, but also from the original homeland and other countries. Hence, this chapter offered also an addition to the statist scholarship on foreign policy analysis: because the ICTY was considered by most of these groups as a political and not only an international legal project, it became a venue for contention where nation states (The Netherlands, Bosnia-Herzegovina, Croatia, Serbia) intersected with the "transnational social field," built on sustained diaspora interactions with ethnic brethren in many different locations.

Notes

1. I would like to express gratitude for funding the research of this paper to the Dutch Institute on Advanced Studies (NIAS) and the European Research Council Starting Grant "Diasporas and Contested Sovereignty" (2012–2017).
2. I discuss at length the relationship between the rise of the ultra-nationalist right and diaspora mobilization in my article "Varieties of Diaspora Mobilization: Comparison of Diasporas from Former Yugoslavia in the Dutch Political Context," 2013, submitted for consideration by an ISI-ranked journal.
3. I express gratitude to Marlies Glasius for this comment.

4. Unless differently noted, the information about organizational structures among Bosniaks, Croats and Serbs stems from Koinova's article "Varieties of Transnationalism" (2013).
5. This argument was first developed in "Varieties of Transnationalism" (2013).

References

Adamson, Fiona (2005). "Globalization, Transnational Political Mobilization, and Networks of Violence", *Cambridge Review of International Studies*, 18 (1), 31–49.

Adamson, Fiona and Madeleine Demetriou (2007). "Remapping the Boundaries of 'State' and 'National Identity,'" *European Journal of International Relations*, 13 (4), 489–526.

Al-Ali, Nadje (2007). "Gender, Diasporas and Post-war Conflict", in Hazel Smith and Paul Stares (eds), *Diasporas in Conflict*, Tokyo: United Nations Press.

Al-Ali, Nadje, Richard Black and Khalid Koser (2001). "Refugees and Transnationalism: The Experience of Bosnians and Eritreans in Europe", *Journal of Ethnic and Migration Studies*, 27 (4), 615–634.

Anderson, Benedict (1998). *The Spectre of Comparisons: Nationalism, Southeast Asia and the World*, London: Verso.

Andreas, Peter. 2008. *Blue Helmets and Black Markets: The Business of Survival in the Siege of Sarajevo*. Cornell University Press, 2008.

Bamyeh, Mohammed (2007). "The Armenian Diaspora and the Karabagh Conflict", in Hazel Smith and Paul Stares (eds.) *Diasporas and Conflict.* Tokyo: UN University Press: 218–238

Basch, Linda, Nina Glick-Schiller and Cristina Szanton-Blanc (1994). *Nations Unbound: Transnational Projects and Deterritorialized Nation-states*, New York: Gordon and Breach.

Baser, Bahar (2012). "Inherited Conflicts: Spaces of Contention between Second Generation Turkish and Kurdish Diasporas in Sweden and Germany", Ph.D. dissertation, *European University Institute*, Florence, Italy.

Bercovitch, Jacob (2007). "A Neglected Relationship", in Hazel Smith and Paul Stares (eds), *Diasporas in Conflict*, Tokyo: United Nations Press.

Boskurt, Emine (2012). "Representative of the Labor Party (NL) in the European Parliament", *Telephone interview with the author*, June 27, 2012.

Brinkerhoff, Jennifer (2008). *Diasporas and Development: Exploring the Potential*, Boulder, CO: Lynne Rienner.

Collier, Paul and Anke Hoeffler (2000). "Greed and Grievances in Civil War", *World Bank Policy Research Working Paper* 2355.

Congress of North American Bosnians (CNAB) (2010). "First Conference of Bosnian Diaspora in the European Parliament", August 30, http://www.bosniak. org/1st-conference-of-bosnian-diaspora-in-the-european-parliament/

Dobbs, Michael (2011). "Srebrenica and the Failures of the UN", *Foreign Policy Blog*, October 20, http://dobbs.foreignpolicy.com/posts/2011/10/20/ srebrenica_and_the_failures_of_the_un

"Enlargement Report for Bosnia-Herzegovina", Debate in the *European Parliament*, Online Video, March 14, 2012, http://www.europarl.europa.eu/ep-live/en/ plenary/video?intervention=1331719488780

EU Framework Contract Commission 2007, Lot 4, Contract 2009, No. 162297, http://stocktaking2009.wbif.eu/docs/Draft%20December%202002009%20-%20 Vol%201%20-%20Main%20report.pdf

Faist, Thomas (2000). "Transnationalization in International Migration", *Ethnic and Racial Studies*, 23 (2), 189–222.

Glick-Schiller, Nina, Linda Basch and Cristina Szanton-Blanc (1992). "Transnationalism. A New Analytic Framework for Understanding Migration", In Nina Glick-Schiller, Linda Basch and Cristina Szanton-Blanc (eds.) *Towards a Transnational Perspective on Migration: Race, Class, Ethnicity and Nationalism Reconsidered*. New York: New York Academy of Sciences.

Glick-Schiller, Nina, Linda Basch and Cristina Szanton-Blanc (1995). "From Immigrant to Transmigrant: Theorizing Transnational Migration", *Anthropological Quarterly*, 68 (1), 48–63.

Guarnizo, Luis Eduado and Michael P. Smith (1998). "The Locations of Transnationalism", in Michael P. Smith and Luis Eduardo Guarnizo (eds), *Transnationalism from Below*, New Brunswick, NJ: Transaction Publishers, 3–31.

Haney, Patrick and Walt Vanderbush (1999). "The Role of Ethnic Interest Groups in US Foreign Policy", *International Studies Quarterly*, 43 (2), 341–361.

Hockenos, Paul (2003). *Homeland Calling: Exile Patriotism and the Balkan Wars*, Ithaca: Cornell University Press.

Hoffman, Bruce et al. (2007). *The Radicalization of Diasporas and Terrorism*, Santa Monica: RAND and Zurich: ETH.

ICTY(2001). "Prosecutor vs. Radislav Krstic. Judgement", Case No. IT-98–33-T, August 2, http://www.icty.org/x/cases/krstic/tjug/en/010802_Krstic_summary_En.pdf

Kantoci, Ivan (2011). "Kroatische Organisaties in Nederland: Doelstellingen en Betekenis" ("Croatian Organizations in the Netherlands: Goals and Meanings"), Lecture delivered (in Dutch) at the symposium "50 Years Croats in the Netherlands", Rotterdam, November 12.

Keck, Kathryn and Margaret Sikkink (1998). *Activists beyond Borders*, Ithaca, NY: Cornell University Press.

Koinova, Maria (2009). "Diasporas and Emerging States: The Mobilization of Conflict-generated Diasporas in the UK Compared", paper presented at the *Explaining Diaspora Politics* workshop, SOAS, University of London, October 30–31.

Koinova, Maria (2010). "Unintended Consequences during Post-conflict Reconstruction", *International Affairs Forum*, 153–158, Arlington, VA: Center for International Relations, Fall, http://dare.uva.nl/document/223157

Koinova, Maria (2011). "Diasporas and Secessionist Conflicts", *Ethnic and Racial Studies*, 34 (2), 333–356.

Koinova, Maria (2012a). "Four Types of Diaspora Mobilization: Albanian Diaspora Activism for Kosovo Independence in the US and the UK", *Foreign Policy Analysis*, online publication on June 12 http://onlinelibrary.wiley.com/doi/10.1111/j.1743–8594.2012.00194.x/abstract

Koinova, Maria (2012b). "Autonomy and Positionality in Diaspora Politics", *International Political Sociology*, 6 (1), 99–102.

Koinova, Maria (2013). "Varieties of Diaspora Mobilization: Comparison of Diasporas from Former Yugoslavia in the Dutch Political Context", Paper submitted to an ISI-ranked Journal, 2013.

Koprivova, Sarka (2011). *The Positioning of Bosnian Muslims in the Netherlands*, Amsterdam: University of Amsterdam, MA thesis.

Kozlowski, Rei (ed.) (2005). *International Migration and the Globalization of Domestic Politics*, London: Routledge.

Levitt, Peggy (2001). *Transnational Villagers*, Berkley: University of California Press.

Levitt, Peggy and Nina Glick-Schiller (2004). "Conceptualizing Simultaneity: A Transnational Social Field Perspective on Society", *International Migration Review*, 38 (3), 1002–1039.

Lyons, Terrence (2006). "Diasporas and Homeland Conflict", in Miles Kahler and Barbara Walter (eds), *Territoriality and Conflict in an Era of Globalization*, Cambridge: Cambridge University Press.

Lyons, Terrence and Peter Mandaville (2010). "Think Locally, Act Globally: Toward a Transnational Comparative Politics", *International Political Sociology*, 4, 124–141.

Maoz, Zeev. 1996. *Domestic Sources of Global Change*. Ann Arbor: University of Michigan.

Milošević.eu (2012) at http://www.Milošević.eu/

Morawska, Eva (2004). "Exploring Diversity in Immigrant Assimilation and Transnationalism: Poles and Russian Jews in Philadelphia", *International Migration Review*, 38 (4): 1372–1412.Mulalic L et al. (2007). Schatting van het aantaal vormalig Joegoslaven naar huiding herkomstgebied, Bevolkingstrends, [Estimates about the numbers of ex-Yugoslav population regarding place of origin, Population trends], Central Bureau of Statistics, 3rd quarter.

Natali, Denise (2007). "Kurdish Interventions in the Iraq War", in Hazel Smith and Paul Stares (eds), *Diasporas in Conflict*, Tokyo: United Nations Press.

OECD (2011). "Review of the Development Co-operation Policies and Programmes of the Netherlands", November 10, http://www.oecd.org/dac/peerreviewsof-dacmembers/thenetherlands2006dacpeerreviewmainfindingsandrecommen-dations.htm

Ostergaard-Nielsen, Eva (2003). "The Politics of Migrants Transnational Political Practices", *International Migration Review*, 37 (3), 670–686.

Portes, Alejandro and Min Zhou (1993). "The New Second Generation: Segmented Assimilation and its Variants", *Annals of the American Academy of Political and Social Sciences*, 350, 74–96.

Ragazzi, Francesco (2009). "The Invention of the Croatian Diaspora", George Mason University series on *Global Migration and Transnational Politics*, Working Paper 10, http://cgs.gmu.edu/publications/gmtpwp/gmtp_wp_10.pdf

Ragazzi, Francesco and Kristina Balalovska. "Diaspora Politics and Post-Territorial Citizenship in Croatia, Serbia and Macedonia", *CITSEE* Working Paper No. 2011/18, http://papers.ssrn.com/sol3/papers.cfm?abstract_id=2388857

Respondent 1 (2012). Cultural Diaspora Entrepreneur of Serbian Background, *Author's Interview*, June 15, Amsterdam.

Respondent 2 (2012). Social Diaspora Entrepreneur of Serbian Background, *Author's Interview*, May 28, Amsterdam.

Respondent 3 (2012). Youth Activist of Bosniak Background, *Author's Interview*, March 22, Amsterdam.

Respondent 4 (2011). Activist of Croatian Background, *Author's Interview*, November 4, The Hague.

Respondent 5 (2012). Public Intellectual of Croatian Background, *Author's Interview*, January 24, Rotterdam.

Respondent 6 (2011). Cultural Diaspora Activist of Croatian Background, *Author's Interview*, December 16, Amsterdam.

Respondent 7 (2012). Cultural Diaspora Entrepreneurs of Croatian/Serbian Background, *Author's Interview*, June 1, Amsterdam.

Respondent 8 (2012). Intellectual of Croatian Origin, *Author's Interview*, January 24, Rotterdam.

Respondent 9 (2012). Intellectual of Serbian Origin, *Author's Interview*, May 28, Amsterdam.

Respondent 10 (2011). Political Activist, *Author's Interview*, November 4, The Hague.

Respondent 11 (2012). Diaspora Intellectual, *Author's Interview*, November 4, The Hague.

Rijsdijk, Erna (2012). *Lost in Srebrenica*, Amsterdam: Free University, Published Ph.D. Thesis.

Risse, Thomas, Stephen Ropp and Kathryn Sikkink (eds) (1999). *The Power of Human Rights*, Cambridge: Cambridge University Press.

Rubenzer, Trevor (2008). "Ethnic Minority Interest group Attributes and US Foreign Policy Influence", *Foreign Policy Analysis*, 4 (2), 169–185.

Shain, Yossi (2002). "The Role of Diasporas in Conflict Perpetuation and Resolution", *SAIS Review*, 22 (2), 115–144.

Škrbić, Zlatko (2007). "The Mobilized Croatian Diaspora", in Hazel Smith and Paul Stares (eds) *Diasporas and Conflict*. Tokyo: UN University Press: 218–238.

Smith, Hazel and Paul Stares (eds) (2007) *Diasporas in Conflict*, Tokyo: United Nations Press.

Srbi u Holandiji (2012). At http://www.servie.nu/srbi%20u%20holandiji.htm

Steigenga, Timothy (2006). "Transnationalism and Collective Mobilization among the Maya of Jupiter: Ambiguities of Transnational Identity and Lived Religion", Paper prepared for the *Transnational Religion in Contemporary Latin America and the United States* Conference, Austin: University of Texas, Jan. 26–27, at http://lanic.utexas.edu/project/rla/papers/Austin.pdf

Subotić, Jelena (2009). *Hijacked Justice: Dealing with the Past in the Balkans*, Ithaca: Cornell University Press.

Tarrow, Sidney (2005). *The New Transnational Activism*, Cambridge: Cambridge University Press.

Traynor, Ian (2008). "Serbia War Crimes: Lukewarm Turnout at Mass Rally for Karadzic", *The Guardian*, July 30, http://www.guardian.co.uk/world/2008/jul/30/radovankaradzic.serbia

Turner, Mandy (2008). "The Discourses on Diasporas and Peace-building", *Paper for WISC 2008*, Ljubljana, July 23–26.

Valenta, Marko and Sabrina Petra Ramet (2011). *The Bosnian Diaspora: Integration in Transnational Communities*, Farnham: Ashgate.

Vertovec, Steven and Susanne Wessendorf (eds) (2010). *The Multiculturalism Backlash*, London: Routledge.

Vogel, Toby (2010). "Croatia Moves Closer to EU Membership", *European Voice*, http://www.europeanvoice.com/article/imported/croatia-moves-closer-to-eu-membership/67170.aspx

Wimmer, Andreas (2011). "How to Study Ethnicity in Immigrant Societies: Herder's Heritage and the Boundary-making Approach", in Marko Valenta and Sabrina Ramet (eds), *The Bosnian Diaspora: Integration in Transnational Communities*, Farnham: Ashgate.

Žarkov, Dubravka (2002). "Srebrenica Trauma: Masculinity, Military, and National Self-Image in Daily Dutch Newspapers", in Cynthia Cockburn and Dubravka Žarkov (eds), *Postwar Moment: Militaries, Masculinities, and International Peacekeeping*, London: Lawrence and Wishart, 183–203.

6
Cinematic Representations of the Bosnian War: *De Enclave* and the Ontologies of Un-Recognizability

Dubravka Žarkov

The wars through which socialist Yugoslavia disintegrated in the early 1990s have generated the production of a number of feature films and TV series, both in the formerly Yugoslav territories and abroad. The war in Bosnia-Herzegovina, in particular, has been in the focus of this production, and the countries whose militaries have contributed to UN peacekeeping forces in Bosnia-Herzegovina seemed to have had a special interest in making movies.[1] In some of the countries, the production was for TV, rather than for the movie theaters.

This is the case with the Dutch TV miniseries *De Enclave*, which based its narrative plots on the Srebrenica genocide.[2] The miniseries was produced in 2002, and in 2005 received a prestigious national award for a screenplay – the LIRA Award – but failed to stir substantial national debates, or to become known internationally. And this is precisely where my interest lies: why a miniseries about Srebrenica – which remains a hugely controversial issue in the Netherlands – did not stir any controversies in the country? What is it that this miniseries did, to receive the highest national award and still receive hardly any public attention? How did the miniseries fit into the socio-political, legal and media contexts surrounding the Srebrenica genocide in the Netherlands?

In trying to answer those questions, I am not interested in the "impact study", that is, in the ways the miniseries may have influenced the Dutch audience. Rather the other way around: I am interested in the ways Dutch politics – and specifically Dutch politics on Srebrenica – may have influenced the miniseries. My main argument is that the miniseries follows the official Dutch position on Srebrenica: denial of responsibility and pointing fingers elsewhere, away from oneself. In this particular case, the ultimate strategy of denial was the production of different, un-reconcilable and un-recognizable ontologies for the main protagonists of the narrative plot, and the places they come from and belong to. This *ontological un-recognizability* was achieved through the use of a number of specific cinematic strategies, characteristic of the feature film as a medium, as well as through narrative strategies, linked to the structure of the narrative plot as written by the screenwriters.

To substantiate my argument I analyze those cinematic and narrative strategies employed in the miniseries, as well as the text of the LIRA Award. I do this by engaging in debate about ontologies and ethics put forward by Judith Butler in her *Precarious Life: The Powers of Mourning and Violence* (2006), and by using the theoretical perspectives that utilize meanings of place and time. Judith Butler's book *Precarious Life* came as a critical response to the torture in Abu Ghraib and a more general critique of the Bush administration's "war on terror." I will not, however, reflect on those two issues, as I have done this elsewhere.[3] Instead I will focus on the central appeal of the *Precarious life*: an appeal to *ethical responsibility* based on fundamental dependency and recognition of primary vulnerability and universality of the human body and human experience of loss, grief and mourning, of the body's mortality, vulnerability and agency. I start from there because it is this appeal to ethics and the universality of human loss and suffering that is crucial for the cinematic and narrative strategies of *De Enclave* – but, in my view, in an utterly unacceptable way; in a way that actually produces (rather than undermines) ontological separation and un-recognizability of the Other, and thus questions the (optimistic, and currently dominant) recourse to universal humanity and ethics in the face of mass atrocities.

Butler actually begins her analysis by stating that there is no human condition that is universally shared (20) and later adds that "there are *radically different* ways in which human physical vulnerability is distributed across the globe" (32; emphases mine). However, those statements seem to bare no theoretical consequences to her further analysis of vulnerability and suffering as *universally* human, and of *ethics* as a ground for ontology of recognition of common humanity. She proceeds to argue that "[l]oss has made a tenuous 'we' of us all" (20) and that "...violence is, always, an exploitation of that *primary* tie, that *primary* way in which we are, as bodies, outside of ourselves and for one another" (27; emphasis mine). In order for the "ethical encounter" of the Western subject and its Other to take place, there must come a perception and recognition of this "primary vulnerability" of the body (42), of suffering and grieving as a fundamental human condition that ties us to each other. Throughout the book Butler returns to this relationships of the "I," "you" and "we" as fundamentally marked by the experience of loss and vulnerability, and calls for this experience to serve as a basis of a mutual recognition of each other's humanity.

There is, of course, no point arguing that the human bodies are not vulnerable or dependent on others. However, one has to ask first: is there a "pure human" condition – or as Butler calls it a *primary* way of being human – uncontaminated by social and geo-political location and history by which this location came into being? If such – ahistorical, essentialized – position does not exist (as I argue), then to what extent is the recognition of the vulnerability, loss and suffering a common human conditions possible? Finally, if this possibility does not exist, and even Butler notes that "there is no guarantee that this [recognition] will happen" (43), what then is the function of ethics as a field of intervention?

While Butler's argument on recognition of life *as life* could be read as an argument on ontology, I would say that her recourse to ethics fails to acknowledge the fundamentally different ontological status that different bodies have acquired in the Western world, through the histories by which that world has become what it is today.

In her later article about torture in Abu Ghraib, "Sexual Politics, Torture, and Secular Time," Butler (2008) has offered one of the best analyzes of the histories that have produced the Western subject. She has argued that histories of colonialism, slavery, imperialism and Christianity have not only produced the West and its Other(s) as ontologically different, but have also produced the history of the West as fundamentally different from the histories of the worlds it conquered and plundered. But in *Precarious Life* she fails to see that those different histories and locations also produce different ontological subjects – and thus, difference in vulnerabilities, suffering and loss. I argue that those differences are currently resulting in a fundamental *ontological un-recognizability* of the Other; that the body, the loss and the vulnerability of the Other belong to different ontological worlds, fundamentally dissimilar to the West. And I take *De Enclave* as a case that shows how such fundamental dissimilarities and un-recognizabilities are reproduced in cinema.

It is my starting assumption that neither the body nor its losses and vulnerabilities exist beyond the historical, social and geo-political *time-space locations* of the embodied subjects. The production of the "symbolic continent" of the Balkans[4] through Orientalist and Balkanist[5] discourses is a case in point. Within "the Balkans," Bosnia exists as a specific, isolated place, whose singular, violent geography is separated from Europe and the West.[6] Such discourses, furthermore, produce people and their bodies, their losses and suffering as inescapably geographically and historically *localized* – that is, existing always only *in situ* – as directly linked only to the fact of inhabiting, and or coming/originating from those "places of violence" and those "violent histories".

In other words, the space/place and its position in time is an essential element in the production of the ontological position of the subjects. Consequently, assuming that the body, its vulnerability and pain can suddenly become a ground for mutual recognition – and in so doing totally erase the relevance of its geo-political location and history – is, in my view, unsustainable. Furthermore, calling for ethics to resolve the problems of ontological un-recognizability carries a danger of building an ethical project of a very specific kind of humanization of those who have been historically dehumanized, by those who have always seen themselves as human, and ethical. I argue that "vulnerability" and "suffering" of the Other in this context, are *not* a ground for "common humanity" but for further ontological differentiation.[7] All the more, we should also remember that in dominant gender narratives of the West, "body in pain" has been an ontological characteristic of the female body. The Western male body is – as a rule – produced through categories of power, not vulnerability. In this context, making vulnerability and suffering of the male body visible often means symbolic emasculation of the vulnerable individual men as well as the community to which they presumably belong.[8] The visibly vulnerable male body is, with few exceptions, the body of the Other, and this visibility is part and parcel of the process of Othering. Thus, calling for the ethics that would change *this* means that, not just the bodies, but also, the very field of ethics itself is abstracted from the social histories and geo-political locations within which they emerged.

As a final point, my argument is *not* that the physical, social and symbolic histories and locations into which we are born are our inescapable destiny. Our choice is not between total essentialization and abstract universalism. Rather I argue that the meanings of the places and times, and the locations of subjectivities associated with them, are neither incidental nor singular; but rather a part of specific geo-political histories, hegemonies and struggles. Consequently, the change of those meanings, locations and subject positions also has to be part of political struggles, rather than of appeals to ethics and the universality of humanity.

De Enclave offers an extraordinarily apt example of the dangers of ignoring historic and geo-political specificities of the processes by which subject positions are produced, and appealing to the universality of human suffering and loss. Before going into the analysis of the miniseries, however, I will reflect first, shortly, on the dynamics of the war, as much as it is needed to contextualize violence in Eastern Bosnia that is now generally referred to under the all-encompassing single word – Srebrenica – and second, on the processes it triggered in the Netherlands.

War crimes in Bosnia and international (non)intervention[9]

The wars of Yugoslav disintegration started in 1991, following decades of growing nationalisms and various processes that led to secession and declaration of independence of (initially) its three republics: Slovenia and Croatia on June 25, 1991, and Bosnia-Herzegovina on October 15, 1991. Bosnia-Herzegovina faced the upheaval of the local population, with Bosnian Serbs and Bosnian Croats scrambling for independent territories towards the end of 1991. In February 1992 Serb leaders within Bosnia-Herzegovina announced an independence of the Bosnian-Serb population and territories, forming the basis of Republika Srpska, which was declared in August 1992.[10]

The secession of territories with predominant Bosnian-Serb and Bosnian-Croat populations was part of a plan designed by the then Serbian President Milosevic and Croatian President Tudjman, who agreed to annex those territories to their respective states. The objective and the driving force of those partitions was a creation of regions with mono-ethnic populations, at a time when ethnic and ethno-religious[11] identities had already became the main – and the only official – mode of being. The tools for achieving this objective were both physical and symbolic violence. Strategies of physical violence included wide-spread destruction, expulsion and massacres of population, sexual violence against women and men, especially within the war camps, and finally, genocide. Strategies of symbolic violence included erasure of all public traces and memories of multi-ethnicity and togetherness, and of the presence of specific groups within specific territories, be it in language, cultural production, school curricula or street names. Equally important were polarized, essentialized, demonizing cultural representations of the Other in literature, film and the media. Physical and symbolic violence often went hand in hand, for example religious buildings and monuments and cultural heritage were deliberately targeted for physical destruction precisely because of their symbolic value.[12]

Those violent strategies have been used in the formation of the Republika Srpska. As the Muslim population was expelled from lands now belonging to the Republika Srpska, two towns were proclaimed by the UN as "save areas."[13] Consequently, a huge number of the Muslim population was gathering in and around them. In the summer of 1995, Bosnian-Serb forces started an offensive to annex some of this territory. In early July 1995, the offensive centered on the town of Srebrenica. At the time, a Dutch battalion was stationed outside the town, in the UN compound housed in an old factory terrain near the village of Potočari.[14]

As the Bosnian-Serb army and their allies led by Ratko Mladić (now tried at the ICTY) advanced towards the town, thousands of Muslim civilians were fleeing towards the UN compound in Potočari, looking for safety.[15] Between July 6–11, 1995 the town fell to Bosnian-Serb forces, with 55 Dutchbat soldiers taken hostage. Seeing Bosnian-Serb forces advancing, Dutchbat asked for UN support, demanding air protection and bombing of the Bosnian-Serb troops. The UN refused however, leaving the Dutchbat to their own strength – which in military terms meant around 450 soldiers with light arms. On July 11, Ratko Mladić and his men entered the UN compound and promised safe passage to the Dutchbat, under the condition of non-interference. With the pretext of making sure Muslim men and boys would not join Muslim forces in the region, a separation of the population begun, women and small children being loaded onto buses and trucks to be "escorted" to other areas, men and boys being taken away in other busloads. Between seven and eight thousand of them were executed, buried and reburied in mass graves, making this the worst crime of genocide in the Yugoslav wars of the 1990s.[16]

Dutch politics of "Srebrenica"

The role of the Dutchbat – what they did and did not do in those few days of July 1995 – has remained an issue ever since, in the Netherlands and Bosnia, albeit in different and sometimes unpredictable ways. It is an established fact that Dutchbat soldiers were involved in the logistics of the separation and loading of the population onto buses, and in so doing, aiding Bosnian-Serb forces.[17] Furthermore, just outside the UN compound, in the nearby warehouses, torture, rape and murder of Muslim civilians, taken from within and outside the UN compound by

Bosnian-Serb forces, was going on. Both the Muslim survivors and the Dutchbat soldiers later testified at ICTY that screams and shots from the warehouses could be heard in the compound, but Dutchbat soldiers did nothing to stop the killing.

Dutchbat left Potočari on July 21, 1995, to Zagreb, where their euphoria of staying alive resulted in a huge party. A few weeks later when the news about massacres appeared in the media Dutch political and military authorities first denied the killing, than denied any knowledge of, or responsibility for it. But as the facts continued to surface, public opinion turned heavily against the Dutch military, and for a while it seemed the story about the responsibility and cover-up would not go away. In a move that Annika Brandstrom and Sanneke Kuipers (2003, 297) called a "brilliant tactical maneuver," the then Prime Minister commissioned "an investigation, by a highly respected institute, so sweeping in scope that it was bound to take many years" (ibid.) thus framing the matter as being of "expert discretion" (294) rather than being a legal, political or military issue.[18] This left the government of the time in place, but in 2002, the Dutch government fell only a week after the seven years awaited report of the Netherlands Institute for War Documentation (NIOD) finally came out.[19] According to Dion van der Berg (2009, 3), "The report distinguishes three main phases: the political decision-making period, the crucial period of July 1995, and the aftermath. NIOD drew fairly hard-hitting conclusions about the first and third phases, but gave a mild and evasive assessment of what occurred in July 1995." The NIOD Report noted political responsibility of the UN and international community, as well as the Dutch political and military top for approving the mission in the first place. However, it largely exonerated the military decision-makers on the ground and Dutchbat soldiers for not engaging in a fight, claiming that the former had to deal with "devilish dilemmas,"[20] and the latter had been outnumbered, not properly armed, and under the mission rules of non-engagement except in self-defense. Reflecting on the NIOD Report, Erna Rijsdijk (2003, 316; 2012, 96) notes that it represents the genocide as a surprise, as an ad-hoc decision of Bosnia-Serb forces and thus an unpredictable event, happening out of the sight of the Dutchbat. She stresses that all those arguments are used in the NIOD report to emphasize that the Dutchbat could not do much about the situation in the town or the enclave and, following this logic, could not be held responsible. Rijsdijk strongly contests this view, and she is not the only one. Van der Berg (2009, 3) notes, for example, quoting the IKV report on Srebrenica and a number of other texts,[21] that the Dutchbat "could have – and should have" done more to protect refugees. The Bakker Report (short for Parliamentary Commission of Inquiry on Srebrenica) that followed in 2003 was more explicit in blaming the Dutch political and military leadership for failures to protect refugees in Srebrenica, noting ambitions and internal quarrels in the government, among other things, but it too refrained from making specific references to the personal responsibilities of politicians and the military.[22]

However, the official Dutch political discourse was pretty much already defined, even before the two reports came out: the finger of blame had long been pointed at the UN and "international community," with vague references to Dutch "political" or "moral" responsibility but no acknowledgement whatsoever of the concrete acts of specific political and military actors in Potočari or The Hague, let alone the fact that the Dutchbat actually aided Serb forces. Quite to the contrary, and to the disbelief of many, the Dutch Ministry of Defense promoted Lieutenant Colonel Karremans, decorated the Dutchbat soldiers and, as Rijsdijk (2012, 113–114) shows, declared a new Dutch vigor and expertise in crisis management.[23]

It is important to note here that Srebrenica has remained a controversial issue in the Netherlands ever since, and that a number of different, often conflicting discourses have co-existed within Dutch public space. Public opinion, media discourses, academics, NGO positions, the official position of the Dutch state and Dutch Army, and personal opinions of individual politicians and Army personnel, as well as individual Dutchbat soldiers, have more often than not been at odds.[24] NGOs, especially those directly involved in work with survivors, such as IKV,[25] have been the most outspoken critics of Dutch official politics on Srebrenica.

Many of those positions have changed through time. Media discourses, especially, have shifted. In 2002, the year *De Enclave* came out, I co-edited with Cynthia Cockburn a book that examined Dutch-Bosnian peacekeeping relationships and practices: *Postwar Moment: Militaries, Masculinities and the International Peacekeeping*. The book analyzed not just what this relationship meant for Bosnia, but also what it meant for the Netherlands and for Dutch national self-understanding and self-image. For that book, I analyzed a selection of five Dutch daily newspapers writing about Srebrenica, in the period between 1995 and 2000 (Žarkov, 2002). I noted that negative media attention directed towards the soldiers was at its strongest in the years immediately after the genocide. But eventually it subsided and by early 2000 Dutch political and military leadership turned to the international peacekeeping scene flatly refusing to look back, claiming excellence in peacekeeping expertise and the right to be an important player in international politics. Nevertheless, Gielt, Elands and Schoeman (2007) show that, compared to the veterans of World War II who were the cherished heroes immediately after the war and ever after, Dutchbat have for a long time remained "bad guys." After the fall of Srebrenica the negative impact on Dutch veterans' image was "immediate and predictable; every insinuation and insult was permitted" (404). Srebrenica became a "bad war" and the media focus shifted from the "Srebrenica tragedy itself" to the national scandal (ibid.).[26] As time passed, however, and media turned to personalized stories of traumas (especially PTSD) of Dutchbat soldiers and other peacekeeping veterans, the image of a veteran-victim appeared (409). This image has not totally replaced, but rather complicated, the negative image of the Dutchbat in the media, where over 60 percent of all negative texts about Dutch peacekeepers in 2000–2004 have still been about Srebrenica. At the same time, the authors show that Dutch public opinion has had a much kinder look at the Dutchbat, when compared to the Dutch media. Using data from Dutch military surveys of public opinion, they show that appreciation of Dutchbat soldiers grew over time, from 59 percent to 67 percent between 2002 and 2004, and that in 2005 Srebrenica Dutchbat soldiers were appreciated as much as those in Iraq and Afghanistan (405). In addressing such high appreciation of Dutchbat soldiers within Dutch society, the authors note two reasons. Firstly, they state "Various studies have shown that the fall of the enclave is to be seen first and foremost as the result of the bankruptcy of the United Nations policy in Bosnia" (406). The footnote in which those "various studies" should be listed, however, lists only the NIOD Report. Secondly, the authors state that "society in general is very well aware of the necessity to dissociate the anger and frustration at the political impotence of the international community from the appreciation for the efforts and sacrifices made by individual soldiers who experienced this impotence firsthand and who, inadvertently, became its personification" (407).[27] In both those statements the authors endorse the official political discourse of the Dutch state that still points fingers at the "international community," refusing to acknowledge its own part in the genocide. But the question here is: are they right? Is this discourse of denial of Dutch responsibility something that is maintained by the Dutch political leadership only, or is it, indeed, present in the wider society? I would argue that the film *De Enclave* and its reception – with the absence of criticism and high praise – is an indication that the discourse of the denial of responsibility has gone far beyond official politics, and has entered the domain of cultural production.

In 2004 and 2007 the ICTY and ICJ respectively declared Srebrenica massacres to constitute genocide. Until now, ICTY indicted and/or prosecuted 21 persons for Srebrenica genocide specifically.[28] However, none of the indicted or prosecuted is from the Dutchbat or Dutch state. Actually, proving that the Dutchbat and Dutch state were criminally responsible has remained difficult.[29] Survivors' associations have tried many different avenues of justice but few have succeeded so far. In May 2011, finally, one of the civil suits that started in 2005 alleging Dutchbat and Dutch state failure to protect specific individuals among the refugees in Potočari, was won on appeal. One of the plaintiffs was Mr. Hasan Nuhanović, former translator for the Dutchbat, whose family was among the massacred civilians taken from the Dutchbat compound.[30] His brother Mohamed and father Ibro were forced to leave the compound and were subsequently murdered by Bosnian-Serb military. This was the first ever admission of Dutch legal responsibility, under any international or national law. It is worth noting, however, that the Dutch state has not accepted this responsibility, as yet, and has appealed the ruling.[31] The civil case by Hasan Nuhanović is important here because *De Enclave* screenplay used a number of facts from the actual life of Mr. Nuhanović, when creating its fictional central character, Ibro. I will come back to this later. First I turn to examine the reception of the *De Enclave* in the Netherlands, taking as a case in point a national screenplay award it received in 2005.

The specific and the universal: *De Enclave* as a moral story

The TV miniseries was produced in 2002 by Dutch TV broadcaster VARA, and aired the same year. Interestingly, the miniseries was first shown in the cinemas, for a while, and only then on TV. The TV premiere was on April 14, 2002, just a few days after the release of the NIOD report (April 10, 2002). The film was directed by the late Willem van der Sande Bakhuyzen, and the scenario was written by Alma Popeyus and Hein Schutz who already had a proven success record in writing movie screens together.[32]

The series, consisting of three episodes, tells the story of a young Bosnian man – Ibro Hadžić – who was a translator for peacekeeping forces in Srebrenica during the fall of the city in 1995. When the Dutchbat evacuated the Potočari enclave, he was allowed to leave with them but his family was not. In the first episode, we see him eight years after the fall of Srebrenica, working as a translator at the ICTY. There he recognizes a member of the Serb military – Darko Bokan – as a person responsible for taking his father and younger brother away, never to be seen again. In the second episode Ibro takes Bokan as a hostage until he admits guilt. In the third episode, some years later again, former Dutch Minister of Defense in the days of Srebrenica – George Terhoef – travels again to Srebrenica with the family, and unexpectedly meets Ibro. After seeing Terhoef, Ibro kidnaps his daughter. The episode ends with Terhoef finding his daughter unharmed, while Ibro kills himself.

In 2005 *De Enclave* won a national LIRA Award, which is given every two years for the best Dutch screenplay. That year's genre was "from docu-drama to political fiction"[33] with a motto "borders between facts and fiction." The text of the Award indicates the interest in how "real events," be they historical or contemporary, are reconstructed into "made-up story lines that have something to say about social and political reality." Criteria for the selection included the demand that "recognizable reality has to play significant role" in the fictional production. There were 19 contenders. The Jury noted that, unlike in England, Germany and Scandinavia, where TV dramas regularly engage with national history and politics, this is hardly so in the Netherlands. Furthermore, all 19 entries were coming from public broadcasters, as "commercial broadcasters literally never engage with such socially relevant work." The text of the Jury's decision states the following:

> The genre that the jury chose is difficult. "True event" is not a guarantee for a good drama, while the unchangeable facts can stand in the way of a dramatic development. Whoever wants to make a careful reconstruction wrestles with an overdoses of explanations and has to firmly hold onto the main plot, in words of subplots. Otherwise, an enjoyable conspiracy theory, if released onto historical events, can deliver a nice thriller – but in this case, while a fan of amusement is served, the one who seeks truth is not. In the center of it all is, thus, a balance between facts and fiction. The jury was most impressed with the screenplays wherein a creative, often made-up story is told, that made it possible for political reality to be empathized with and understood, and in doing so, at the same time, offered a possibility for universal insight that rises above "there and then."

The Jury then announces the three nominees for the award, among which was *De Enclave*:

> De Enclave of Alma Popeyus and Hein Schütz: about Srebrenica and the role of the Netherlands. A brave choice to handle one of

the blackest pages in the recent European and fatherland's history. Fiction that succeeds in making the reality be felt, by pulling the viewer into it, far beyond what TV news or newspaper article would do. Confronting, and because of the topic, inescapably laden.

Finally, statement about the winner:

The jury has proclaimed as winner a screenplay that is both of highest technical level and makes a moral claim. The authors, all those involved in the production and the broadcaster deserve praise for a brave production that is made in the right moment, and can play a role in dealing with the painful past.

How are we to read this praise for *De Enclave* by the LIRA Jury? The text points to several qualities of the screenplay. Firstly, its affective quality – the ability to make reality be felt and understood by the audience, the ability to pull the viewers into the story in a way that does not allow the protective distance that TV or press news offer. Secondly, its moral quality – the courage of addressing a difficult topic, on the one hand, and, on the other hand, doing so in a way that turns a singular, specific event into an universal, ethical story. Finally, its balance between facts and fiction – the way the real event is dramatized. Together, the Jury argues, those qualities allow the film to open up a possibility of "working through the painful past."

It is the painful national past of the Netherlands that is addressed here, again, like in the press, not the past of the survivors and victims of Srebrenica. But the way the Netherlands is imagined in this text is important. The LIRA Jury used the word "fatherland" when noting the "blackest pages" of history. This choice of word is not incidental. As feminist analyzes indicate, the "fatherland" stands for all the qualities that manhood presumably should – and still does – represent in dominant gender hierarchies, even in the countries that claim equality between women and men: strength, courage, steadfastness, protection of the weak, including the ultimate sacrifice in defense of the weak, if needed. Clearly, the Dutchbat failed to exhibit all those qualities when allowing Bosnian-Serb forces to enter their compound in Potočari, to take away and massacre thousands of men and boys, and to rape, torture and murder people just outside the compound. Thus, speaking about "blackest pages of history" the Jury implicitly laments those very specific, military and manly failings of the Dutchbat, and the fatherland whom the Dutchbat symbolizes.

Next to the Dutchbat, there is another representative of the nation in the text of the Jury – the audience. The Jury repeatedly congratulates the screen writers for making a film that can help the audience feel and understand the event, and insists that this is achieved by transforming a story of one event, of a concrete "then and there" into a universal moral drama. It is as such – *universal, moral, affective drama* – and *not* (just) as a drama of a specific, concrete, historical event – that the Jury presents the miniseries to the nation, to feel, to understand, and to work through. As if the failure of the concrete military men and political and military leadership of the Netherlands, in a concrete war event, in a specific place and time, can be felt, understood and worked through *only* if and when this concreteness of Potočari and busses loaded with women and men is erased and replaced by a universal, affective, moral frame; as if the specific political and military failings of Dutch soldiers and leadership can be "worked through" *only* if they are re-classified into the universal, human failings, and thus de-vested of the specific national, military and masculine failures.

The fact that the Jury speaks of (the need to) "work through the painful past" certainly indicates that Srebrenica remains important for Dutch national self-image. As discussed above, the nation has been busy – in many different ways – with the Dutchbat performance in Potočari. But, while Srebrenica itself had an impact on Dutch public opinion, politics and media, it is impossible to say whether *De Enclave* did anything to help "work through the painful past." Establishing the impact of *De Enclave* is, as already mentioned, not my objective here. Rather, I am interested in how the film represents the genocide in Srebrenica and in doing so, how it (re)defines the role of the different protagonists; what "facts" and "fictions" have been used in the process; what histories and worlds have been created thereby. In other words, instead of looking at the impact *De Enclave* had on Dutch society and politics, I now turn to examine the impact of Dutch society and politics on *De Enclave*, or at minimum, their shared discourses on Srebrenica.

De Enclave – narrative plot and cinematic tools

Before starting analysis, a few more words on the narrative plot, and cinematic tools used to tell it. The first episode starts eight years after the fall of Srebrenica. We see a young Bosnian Muslim man – Ibro Hadžić – former Dutchbat translator, whose family was among the murdered civilians in Potocary/Srebrenica. He lives in the Netherlands, is married to a former female Dutchbat soldier with whom he is just about to have a child. He now works as a translator at the ICTY and translates at a trial of a former member of the Bosnian-Serb military – Darko Bokan. Bokan eventually gets released for lack of evidence that he took part in the torture and murders in Potočari. But Ibro remembers seeing him and is sure that Bokan is responsible for the murder of his father and younger brother. Nobody believes him, however, including his wife and Dutchbat friends. So, after a lot of frustration and a few violent outbursts, at the very end of the first episode Ibro takes Bokan as his hostage within the ICTY building. The story is told from Ibro's perspective,[34] with ample use of flashbacks in which he remembers both his childhood and the chaos in Potočari when the Bosnian-Serb military entered the compound.

In the second episode Ibro forces Bokan to confess his participation in the torture and killing of civilians, and his father and brother among them, in a warehouse within the earshot of the UN compound. The episode consists almost entirely of the dialogues between the two men and Bokan's flashbacks, except for a few scenes of the "emergency room" where the Dutch national crisis team (consisting of different political and security figures) is trying to resolve the situation. We see Bokan remembering and confessing the murders. However, throughout the episode he repeats three sets of statements: that he did not want to be a soldier and take part in the war; that there was nothing he could have done to change the situation in Potočari on his own, because even the Dutchbat did nothing, though they knew what was going on; and that he was a victim too, as he too lost family, he too was betrayed by his own and Dutch forces. After the confession, Ibro releases Bokan but in exchange asks for Terhoef – the man who was Minister of Defense during the Srebrenica genocide, and is in the film's present-time a Major of The Hague. In a pretense of accepting such an exchange, in the last moments of the second episode Dutch Special Forces capture Ibro. This story is told from Bokan's perspective,[35] with ample use of flashbacks of his childhood as well as his crimes in Potočari. Through the dialogues between Ibro and Bokan, and Bokan's flashbacks, the audience learns that the two men (and their fathers) met each other, and even played football together, as children.

The third episode takes the audience another four years further into the future. We learn eventually that Ibro was in jail for hostage taking, released and then had gone to Potočari where he works as a physical laborer and searches for the remains of his family. The ex-minister, Major of The Hague, Terhoef is now a member of the European delegation visiting Srebrenica (now part of Republika Srpska) to see the progress of an EU-financed development project. Ibro kidnaps Terhoef's daughter, and the father starts a frantic search for her. He comes across the forensic experts who are still trying to identify bodies from Srebrenica genocide mass graves, as well as mothers still searching for missing family members. He meets Ibro, realizes that Ibro has his daughter, and eventually finds the place where his daughter is kept. After a short conversation with Terfoef, Ibro shoots himself, while the daughter and the father fall into each other's arms.[36]

In terms of narrative and cinematic choices, there are significant difference between the third episode and the other two. The narrative plots of the first two episodes are non-linear, with a substantial amount of the story told through continuous flashbacks starkly marked in different color, light and sound from the real-time story. Besides this similarity in technical characteristics, a number of the flashbacks in the first two episodes are also almost identical in content, or depict exactly the same event but from a different camera angle. Contrary to this, the third episode has a linear structure with one very short flashback different in every respect – content, color, sound, light – from those in the first two episodes. Importantly, many scenes of chaos and violence in Potočari in the first and second episode are "documated," that is, made to look as if original documentary material. This is done within the protagonists' flashbacks as well as within the scenes at the ICTY, where a videotape of killings is used by the prosecution team. This videotape, especially, is made to appear as authentic documentary video material. Here we see one very clear instance of erasure of difference between "facts" and "fiction," for which the LIRA Jury praised the film. The third episode contains just one short scene at the very start – of the Dutchbat partying in Zagreb – made to appear as a documentary material.

Regarding genres, the miniseries is neither a classical war movie nor a classical suspense/action/crime film, nor a clear-cut psychological drama, but a mixture of it all. The third episode is again significantly different from the two others, as it follows some of the classical elements of the suspense story/action movie. The first two – with the documated scenes of war violence and the focus on the personal anguish of the main characters – are a mixture of war genre and psychological drama. In terms of narrative progress of the overall main character – Ibro – we see a change through the three episodes: he is the traumatized war victim in the first; a wronged man seeking justice, albeit by unlawful means of hostage-taking, in the second; and a defeated, broken, but revengeful and cunning man, half crazy from pain and loss, in the third episode.

De Enclave used Dutch actors to play both Ibro and Bokan, and Dutch characters.[37] The actors speak a peculiar mixture of Dutch,

German and Serbo-Croatian[38] language. Despite the invested efforts and claims of great success in using Serbo-Croatian language,[39] Dutch actors often speak it with a bad accent and grammatical and language mistakes. Furthermore, in order to act convincingly as foreigners in the Netherlands, the two actors playing Ibro and Bokan also speak bad Dutch is certain scenes, though not in others. Finally, the use of German – spoken by Bokan at moments when he denies any involvement in Potočari – is supposed to have a symbolic significance, referring to the German denial of knowledge about concentration camps in World War II. All of this has created a rather unfortunate effect for people who speak all three languages and clearly recognize mistakes. Given that many good actors from the former Yugoslav regions work internationally, it seems to me that choosing actors who are native speakers of Serbo-Croatian language would have been a better linguistic choice. However, the choice of actors and language can also be seen as a choice for the audience: this is a Dutch film, for a Dutch audience. It is presumed that this audience will have no idea whatsoever whether the Serbo-Croatian language is spoken properly, but would recognize, and consider normal, the "spoiled Dutch" spoken by the immigrants. Those choices, however, carry an implicit definition of Dutchness, as the use of language indicates that Dutch audience in this case means the "native" Dutch, not the "naturalized" Dutch – and especially not the immigrants from the former Yugoslavia.

Finally, while the actors playing Ibro and Bokan are good actors, neither of them appear as the classical cinematic prototype of a handsome man. Compared to them, Terhoefe is much closer to the cinematic male beauty standards. This may be seen as an irrelevant or even malicious comment. However, if compared to the UK made *Warriors*, it is quite evident that British acting crew consists of young, handsome men, while the actors playing Bosnian-Serb and Bosnian-Croat paramilitaries are a selection of ugly, small, mean-looking men. Make up, costume and acting together help make an actor fit the role, as well as the standards of beauty. Thus I am not arguing here whether the actors are handsome or not. I am arguing about how they are made to look to the audience. Not incidentally, the beauty and the ugliness in the movies have, since the very beginnings of cinema, been used to convey good and evil, have called the audience to identify with, or reject the protagonist. If this is so, then clearly, the Dutch audience is not invited to identify with either Ibro or Bokan, but rather, with Terhoef. In addition, Ibro's masculinity seems to be too unsettled, too violent and too messed up for a proper heterosexual relationship. He almost assaults his wife, furious that she cannot remember Bokan or has even smiled to him. In Bosnia he attaches himself again to a Dutch woman, almost hanging on her shoulders, devastated and in need of consolation. He does not receive it, as both Dutch women appear inapt and inarticulate.

Reflecting on all those narrative and cinematic choices, I turn now to consider first, how are the stories of vulnerability, suffering and loss of the three main protagonists told, in terms of time and space, and "facts" and "fiction"? Second, what are the ensuing representational effects of the narrative and cinematic choices that address time and space, "facts" and "fiction," from a perspective of ontological positions of the protagonists and the possibilities of their mutual recognition as "human subjects."

I will show that the two main representational strategies of *De Enclave* are the equation of experiences of the three main protagonists (the survivor, the perpetrator and the politician) and the erasure of specific, context-bound differences of those experiences. This is done firstly, through the narrative choices – evident in the progress of the film story as well as in dialogues, and in the ways the "facts" and "fiction" are integrated in the narrative. Secondly, this is done through cinematic choices – the use of flashbacks and the positioning of the protagonists in the same or different times and spaces; or rather, positioning them in the past, present and future of Bosnia/Potočari and the Netherlands. Simultaneously, those equations lead to erasures of the specific, time-and-space bound political context of the Srebrenica genocide, trans-ferring the effects of genocide into the realm of the personalized, universalized, ethical dramas of the protagonists, noted in the text of the Jury. Ultimately, I argue that this universalist ethical personaliza-tion exonerates the Dutch state, politicians and the military from any political – let alone legal – responsibility for its part in the genocide. At the same time, those representational strategies lead to the creation of unbridgeable ontological differences.

I turn now to show how those equations and erasures are conduced, by following the representations of the main protagonists and their rela-tionships, and the ways they are positioned in the times and spaces of Bosnia and the Netherlands.

Equations and erasures, or: on ontologies of un-recognizability

The survivor of Srebrenica genocide, Ibro, is, from the start, an outsider to the Dutch society, regarding both the times and the spaces in which he lives. His life in the Netherlands is most often a mere physical, bodily presence, with his mind elsewhere. Cinematically, this is shown by following his mind – the flashbacks of his memory. In his mind, he is in Bosnia: either in Potočari, remembering the sounds and pictures of chaos and despair of separation from his family; or in childhood places, in the sounds and pictures of green grass and bright sun and children running after a football; he is also in the virtual space of the websites where he follows the results of the forensic teams who work on identifying human remains excavated from the mass graves, or those where the belongings of the deceased are displayed, hoping all the time to find a trace of his missing family members; he is also physically at the ICTY, sitting through the court hearings and translating gruesome stories of war crimes, which regularly bring him back again to his own memories of Potočari; finally, even when he is in his own house in the Netherlands, he is someone who observes the life – as when he watches his neighbors at night – rather than someone who is living "here and now." He hardly takes part in the life of his family, for even the rare moments when he looks at his daughter or wife, or makes fun of his mother-in-law, are filled with references to this other life, this other family, lost in different but always present time and space. His body and mind seem to be united only in one single instance when he feels the pain of his birth-giving wife, and screams in agony, at the beginning of the first episode. Never again, after that moment, is there an instance in which the pain of the other body is felt in one's own body. And even if this instance is taken as Butler's hopeful sign of "common humanity," the film narrative goes in a different direction: Ibro leaves his wife and daughter and by the third episode his family by marriage is totally out of sight.[40] The only people he is concerned with at that moment are the dead members of his parental family.

Ibro's time-space is simultaneously "a past-elsewhere" that seems to exist as a consistent, always present, parallel reality. Cinematically, that reality exists through his flashbacks, marked by stark difference in contents, color, light and sound from cinematic present-time reality. Importantly, psychedelic greens, reds and yellows, and blinding, white-bright sun of the open spaces of chaos in Potočari in Ibro's memory are exactly the same as the colors of his childhood memories. This equation of different contexts through the use of the same color and light is important symbolically: it unites the world of peace and the world of war in Bosnia, drawing a direct timeline between the two. Furthermore, those two time-worlds of open spaces and bright daylights in Bosnia are contrasted – especially in the first episode – by the dark shades of the interior spaces in the Netherlands: the dim ICTY offices and rooms of Ibro's family flat, the night shadows of the apartments in the building across Ibro's window.

Discussing the role of landscape in Antonioni's *L'Aventura*, Jazairy (2009, 361) notes that "The landscape comes into being and is sustained not through something inherent within it but through the everyday practices and activities that surround it." If this argument can be used for the understanding of the cinematic places and spaces elsewhere, than the afore-noted differences in light, sound and color that mark Bosnia and the Netherlands are further underscored by the differences in everyday practice: violence as a practice in Potočari, contrasted with simple daily activities of a young mother in the Netherlands, or parallel existences of Ibro who translates through the day and searches the Internet at night. The function of those differences is to create two time-space worlds – the world of Bosnia and the world of the Netherlands, and to show that they are irreconcilable; that Ibro is marked forever by his past-in-Bosnia, that this is where and when he lives his life; that his presence in the Netherlands, all with the wife and daughter, is deceptive; that his mind – locked within spaces of Bosnia – never opened up to life in the Netherlands. His loss, his suffering and vulnerability to the past-place of trauma and violence keep him out and away.

The use of the same cinematic strategy to maintain the distinction between those two worlds is apparent in the second episode as well, when sounds, light and colors are used to establish Bokan's place in relation to the Netherlands and Bosnia, and to Ibro. But something more sinister appears in this episode: Bokan's world is not only separated from the Netherlands, it is brought together with Ibro's world. First and foremost, we see the same scenes of the two boys in the flashbacks of Bokan that we saw in Ibro's: the same content, exactly the same colors and light. As the two men share the same places, activities and memories, cinematically, this means that they belong to the same world. As a cinematic trope this is nothing new – many of the (ex-/post-) Yugoslav films on the war have stressed that the men fighting on opposing sides have once shared the same world. In *Pretty Village, Pretty Flames*,[41] almost identical scenes appear: boys playing football, fathers sitting together at the table, drinking and chatting friendly, looking at their boys playing; those boys as adult men turn against each other in the war, suddenly aware of their different ethnic and religious belonging. However, in *De Enclave*, this positioning of the two men within the same world – who are at the start of the film introduced as a survivor and a possible perpetrator – turns out to be part of the strategies by which the differences between them – including the difference between the survivor and the perpetrator – are systematically erased. Bokan is the Bosnian-Serb sergeant who has directly participated in violence in Potočari. We learn this through yet another type of his flashbacks: memory full of night's darkness, blurred by sounds of human suffering and human cruelty, by Bokan's drunkenness and the refusal to remember and acknowledge his part in the crimes. Eventually, he does remember and admits what he did, as well as how he did it. But in the process, the narrative insists both visually and in the text that Bokan did not want to do what he did – take part in torture and murder. In the flashbacks we see Bokan's meek attempts to resist participating, and in the real-time story we hear him, over and over again, repeating: "I did not want to fight/be soldier/take part in war"; "I am victim, too" ("My family is also killed by Muslims"; "Dutchbat betrayed me, too"); and, "What could I do on my own" ("When Dutchbat did nothing"). Such sentences sometimes stand alone, and sometimes form a long line of laments, accusations and self-pity. What we do *not* hear or see in the film are the rebuttals to those arguments. Consequently, those statements, with the visual effects of the shared time-spaces of the survivor and a perpetrator, have a rather specific effect regarding Bokan: he appears as a victim as much as a perpetrator; he is an individual tormented by his evil deeds, and the audience is invited to sympathize with him.[42]

As a researcher who focuses on social constructions of masculinity in war, and as someone who has actively written against discourses that collectively demonize "the Serbs," and especially "Serb men," I am not against sympathy for reluctant perpetrators of crimes, including war crimes.[43] Showing that an individual is tormented by his crimes has redeeming qualities for his humanity.[44] In this case, showing a reluctant Serb perpetrator comes as a contrast to the strong discourses that have demonized Serbs collectively. However, sympathy for an individual perpetrator and the understanding of the social conditions under which individuals opt to torture and kill, rather than being tortured and killed (if refusing to take part in killing) – cannot, or rather, must not, ever be all that the audience is invited to feel. Individual regrets and torment of the perpetrator must not be used to replace, or to hide, the larger political context within which his crime is perpetrated. For it is this context that gives specific meanings to the war crime that go far beyond the meanings the crime might have for an individual perpetrator, or a victim for that matter. It is also this context that allows for understanding specific social, political and historic responsibilities for the crimes, and towards the victims. Neither responsibilities nor victimhood are just individual or singular. Beyond an individual person who kills or is killed stand very recognizable, very identifiable groups and organizations, institutions and structures, histories and traditions, ideologies and images, economies and politics. This is why ICTY has had prisoners who have not been killers themselves – like for example the late Slobodan Milosevic – but are responsible nevertheless for creating and supporting ideologies and structures that have enabled the killings. This is also why victims' demands are not just about responsibility, guilt and prosecution of an individual perpetrator, but also about specific recognition of injustice of killing and of institutional and political responsibilities. Thus, individual and institutional, personal and social, have to go hand in hand, rather than replace or obscure each other. At the same time, while we can understand an individual's actions in given circumstances, this still does not exonerate this individual of the responsibility for the acts of violence, it does not make him stop being a perpetrator of those acts, nor does it annihilate the need for this individual's recognition/admission of the injustice of his crimes. Finally, what happened in Srebrenica simply cannot be reduced to individual acts of murder or torture, although it was clearly individual men who were killing and torturing. Those individual men were part of social and institutional structures and ideologies that made the killings possible. In discussing the context within which a "local" war crime stops being local and becomes an international issue, Rijsdijk quotes Hannah Arendt stating a qualitative difference between different kinds of murder: when genocide is perpetrated, "an altogether different order is broken and an altogether different community is violated," not just the community of direct victims; thus, "mass murderers must be prosecuted because they violated the order of mankind, and not because they killed millions of people" (Arendt, 1944, 268–269; in Rijsdijk, 2003, 314–315).

Bokan's narrative and visual positioning as a tormented individual who is as much a victim of circumstance as a perpetrator of specific murder extracts him from the context of genocide, and in so doing opens up a possibility to relativize the difference between the perpetrator and the victim. In other words, instead of offering cinematic rebuts to the self-representation of Bokan as a perpetrator-cum-victim, *De Enclave* actually offers two explicit moments that relativize, and directly brings into question, Ibro's position as a survivor-cum-victim. The first is a moment when Ibro breaks an empty bottle and goes towards Bokan, threatening to attack him with it. This scene is important because it was with such a broken bottle that Bokan killed Ibros' father. Although Ibro does not attack Bokan with the bottle (but with bare hands), this scene suggests to the audience that these two men are potentially the same, and it is a kind of mere accident that one of them actually used the weapon (because he was forced to do it), while the other did not. But there is yet another scene making Ibro the guilty party. In the most perfidious sentence of the entire series, Bokan – after admitting that he murdered Ibro's father and brother – ask Ibro: "But what have you done? Have you joined [your deported family]? Have you given your yellow card [that allows passage out of the enclave together with Dutchbat] to your brother? Then he would surely be alive now!"

The "survivor's guilt" is a known psychological phenomenon associated with natural and man-made disasters, including wars. It is also a known feature of Holocaust films (Haggith and Newman, 2005). But never have I seen a film in which such guilt is thrown onto the survivor as an open and direct accusation. Rather, it comes as a self-accusation, regularly rebutted as unjustified. In *De Enclave*, this accusation resonates with force, making Ibro directly responsible for his brother's death, and thus erasing the difference between the mass murderers and their victims.

There is yet another representational effect of Bokan's and Ibro's dialogues in the second episode which concerns the role of the Dutchbat and the Dutch state. Bokan continuously repeats that the Dutchbat "did nothing" to prevent the torture and murder. Visually, we also see the Dutchbat in the Potočari scenes standing and looking around, as if not understanding what is going on. But it is not true that Dutchbat "did nothing." As documents at ICTY show, the Dutchbat actually actively helped Bosnian-Serb forces to separate women and men and load people onto busses, among other things.[43] Thus, making them in *De Enclave* "do nothing" to help the victim, instead of showing how they helped the perpetrator, looks like a narrative choice of a "lesser evil," and a claim of innocence. In the second episode, ex-Minister Terhoef asks, apologetically, at one point: "How could we know that Serbs would be such beasts?" This claim of innocence – while echoing the NIOD report – rests on an assumption of difference between a presumably proper army waging a proper war, properly (i.e., fighting the other army, not civilians), which is of course Dutch; against a presumably "beastly" army of the Other – in this case Bosnian Serbs. The worn-out essentialist, demonizing reference to "beastliness" aside, this claim of innocence is not just a narrative and cinematic choice – it is a political choice. That choice goes along with the continuous refusal of the Dutch government and the military to accept its part of responsibility for the events in Potočari. We see this refusal in the third episode as well. In the first two episodes Ibro and Bokan have been initially positioned as opposites, a victim and a perpetrator, but the differences and distances between them have been systematically erased through the use of both narrative and cinematic strategies, placing the two men within the same onto-logical world of Bosnia in which everybody is both the victim and the perpetrator. In the third episode we see that world firmly separated from the world of the Netherlands. A mixture of strategies of distancing and equations between Ibro and Terhoef is used to achieve such a represen-tational effect.

The distancing first: we meet Terhoef[46] as a former Minister of Defense, present Mayor of The Hague, busy with projects of economic aid to Bosnia. Unlike Ibro and Bokan, whom we see as children, we meet Terhoef only as an adult. His difference from the other two protagonists is stressed through both narrative and cinematic means. He has one short flashback, totally different in contents as well as in color and sound from those of the other two protagonists: he sees the faces and hears the voices of the military and political personnel, discussing assistance to Datchbat in Potočari. He was not at the site of the genocide in 1995, but in the Netherlands. Before the hostage taking events he never met either Ibro or Bokan. So, from the start he is located in a totally different world than the other two protago-nists. Furthermore, Bokan is out of the picture altogether in the third episode, so symbolically, Terhoef remains linked to Ibro only. And this is where equations come into place: their link is defined as a link between two men who have lost their loved ones. More importantly, Ibro is represented as a guilty party here, because he has kidnapped Terhoef's daughter. Terhoef, on the other hand, is at no point depicted as personally responsible for the death of Ibro's family: he is positioned within a larger set of impersonal bureaucracy where stupidity, lack of good will and political ambitions rule.

As mentioned earlier, the story of the third episode is told in a rather linear narrative line, save a short flashback, and all together belongs to a rather different genre than the other two. This leaves Terhoef quite removed from the massacres in Potočari. Interestingly, through the search for his daughter he encounters mothers of the missing persons – in a room whose walls are plastered with photographs of the lost men – and enters the huge hall with endless shelves with the white bags full of human remains that the forensic team is still working on identifying. But he is literally passing through those spaces, in the search for his lost daughter. It is this loss that drives him, and this loss is the only one he understands. Even when in the car with Ibro, he is totally unable to relate to or understand short sentences by which Ibro tells him that he has found his family (remains) and that his work is over. This may be read as a film's criticism of an insensitive politician, unaware of the consequences of his past decisions, or even as insensitivity of the Dutch politics to the enormity of the loss of lives in Srebrenica. However, by the time those scenes come, both protagonists have already been firmly defined as individuals who belong to different worlds and have been linked by an almost incidental moment in time, at a place in which one joined only though distant decision-making powers, while the other lived through it.

This individualization is then what links Ibro and Terhoef – for the film narrative implies that this time and place has defined their human loss: Ibro has lost his family, and this has led him to deprive Terhoef of his daughter and thus also face a loss. And apparently, those losses are the same. In one of the last scenes of *De Enclave*, Ibro explicitly tells Terhoef that he kidnapped his daughter because he always wanted Terhoef, too, to experience the torment of not knowing if someone he loves is alive or not. This equation of loss is also present in the texts by which *De Enclave* is advertised on the Internet, and on the cover of the DVD in sale. Different websites (still) offer a few different versions of text that mainly focuses on the film characters and the three stories, mentioning the "drama around the fall of Srebrenica," as seen "through the eyes of the main characters,"[47] who are described as: a former Bosnian war-time translator whose family members are murdered in Srebrenica, a former sergeant in the Serbian army that occupied Srebrenica, and a former Dutch Minister of Defense of that time.[48] Those descriptions can be found, among others, at a website on which one could see online the programs missed on TV.[49] This website has an introductory paragraph with a general description of the series, where the last sentence describes the link between the three characters:

> *Their powerlessness, their feelings of guilt and their terrible memories are re-lived*, when they are confronted with each other and with the consequences of what happened in Srebrenica. (Emphasis DZ)

The shocking element of this sentence is that it appears to equate the powerlessness, guilt and memories of the three main characters – the survivor, the perpetrator and the politician – apparently without any insight into how monstrous such an equation may seem from the perspective of the Srebrenica survivors. This absence of reflection on the difference in the positioning of the three characters vis-à-vis the events depicted in the film is all the more evident in yet another sentence by which part three of the mini-series is described at a website where A-quality films are introduced:[50]

As his daughter Tara disappears, Terhoef must undergo *the same* agonizing uncertainty as the thousands of victims of the war. (Emphasis, DZ)

Here we see the equation of the "agonizing uncertainty" of those who have gone through the horrors of the Srebrenica genocide with that of a parent whose child is missing. My point here is not to belittle the agony of a parent, but rather, as already stated, to stress how such equations erase the particularity and specificity of the contexts within which each of those agonies would make sense.

That those equations and erasures are not incidental in the film was already obvious in the ways Bokan and Ibro have been made into both a victim and a perpetrator. But the film actually offers many other such instances. For example, in the second episode, while Ibro holds Boakn hostage, his wife is invited into the "crisis bunker" where the emergency team tries to resolve the situation. Asked why she married Ibro, she reacts angrily to the insinuation of this question – that the marriage is bogus. She said: "We survived Srebrenica together." This statement depicts the same erasure of difference between the social locations of those two people, the same erasure of difference in the consequences of those locations for each of the individuals.

What I argue here is that those statements are not there because of screenplay writers' lack of understanding of what happened in Potočari. To the contrary. The screenplay actually offers a very specific understanding of the genocide and its protagonists. In this understanding the Dutch have suffered a loss, the Dutch have been traumatized, and the Dutch have survived – as individual human beings, with or without a sense of guilt or a sense of responsibility. There are two consequences of this individualization. One is the appropriation of the status of the victim for the Dutchbat as well as for Dutch society. Another is the erasure of the political meanings of the genocide. This erasure seems to me to be precisely what the LIRA Jury has referred to – and praised – in *De Enclave* when stressing how a concrete, "there and then" story was transformed into a universal moral story. The fact that recourse to the discourses of "common humanity" of individualized and universalized experiences of loss erases the specific political context of genocide in which a politician, a perpetrator and a survivor have totally different social locations is lost on both the screenwriters and film promoters, as well as on the LIRA Jury.

Towards conclusions

For the end, I wish to go back to the relationship between "facts" and "fiction" in *De Enclave*, and to the ethics as a field of intervention. One of the most disturbing elements of *De Enclave* is the way the life of Hasan Nuhanović is used in the screenplay. The facts of his life and his experiences are used to tell a story that has subverted those experiences and turned the main protagonist into a crazed, criminal person who is an accomplice in the demise of his own family. In *De Enclave*, Ibro kills himself at the end. This fictional element, together with Ibro's cinematic erasure from his family in the Netherlands speaks of the inability of the war survivor to live beyond the war horrors. Contrary to that, Nuhanović, together with another plaintiff, is so far the only person who managed to force the Dutch legal system to recognize that the Dutch state and the Dutchbat have been responsible for the deaths of at least two families in Potočari. Coming to this point in life, 16 years after the genocide, speaks of incredible personal strength and perseverance, not of giving up.

So why was such a man made into a lunatic in *De Enclave*? Why was the character created after him relativized as a victim, while the fictional perpetrator was turned into a victim? I argue that this is in order to establish ontological difference between the Dutch and Bosnians, for this difference is crucial for the discourse of denial. Dutch refusal to acknowledge their responsibility in genocide is easier if the protagonists of the war in Bosnia are all made to look like each other, and different from the peacekeepers. When the victim and the perpetrator are made to inhabit *the same ontological time- space*, it is easier to make the Dutch peacekeepers, and by extension the Dutch nation and nationals, *ontologically different* from both. Dutch politics cannot stomach the fact that it took part in the Srebrenica genocide. The Dutch are certainly not the only ones among the "community of inteveners" (Heathershaw and Lambach, 2008, 270) who are responsible. And their part is certainly not the same as the part of the Bosnian Serb military on the ground who did the actual killing, or those who ordered the killings. But it is there, nevertheless. So, pretending that no part is taken, that the Dutch just stood by, in incomprehension and disbelief about the "bestiality" of others, offers at least some level of consolation in the collective self-deception of the nation. Equating the victim and the perpetrator of genocide by erasing differences between them follows the notorious statement of the Lieutenant Colonel Karremans, that there are no "good guys and bad guys" in the Bosnian war. He meant – among the locals, of course. Dutch politicians still struggle to show that there were some good guys – and that it was them. It is for this reason that the third episode of *De Enclave*, the one where Terhoef is the main protagonist, is not about Srebrenica, even when the episode is located in this very town, on and around the site of the massacres and the hotel where Karramans drank with Mladić. The Srebrenica genocide is erased even when central to the motivation for Ibro's decision to kidnap Terhoef's daughter. Instead, the center stage is given to the craziness and inability of Ibro to cope with life, and to Terhoef as a man who may have some second thoughts about his past work as a politician, but who is first and foremost a father. Interestingly, Ibro is not a father any longer at that point – so a possibility of their humanities to meet through commonality of fatherhood is not used in the narrative. Instead, he is a man who wants vengeance – a desperate, broken, crazy man, symbolically telling the Dutch audience: "Look, this is what the Dutch government has had to deal with when it comes to Srebrenica and survivors." The perfidy of such a representation is not just in erasing the Dutchbat and the Dutch state responsibility for the genocide, but also in erasing the ground for solidarity with the victims and survivors of the genocide. Of course, I do not say that there is no solidarity or that everybody in Dutch society denies Dutch responsibility. This is clearly not so. Nevertheless, *De Enclave* as a movie contributes to those Dutch discourses that have systematically refused to accept responsibility for the part the Dutch political and military leadership played in Srebrenica. The fact that it got a prestigious national award indicates that this discourse is not just about political-military matters. It is about the self-image of the nation. This nation, as Dudink (2002) argues, builds its national self-image on the assumptions of its highest morality. In *De Enclave*, that morality is defined as universalized and individualized experience of loss, vulnerability and suffering. But this universalization still rests on a set of unbridgeable differences: the world of Bosnia is the world of the Other, separate from the beginning to the end from the world of the Netherlands. Ironically, the film appears to invite the Other into the fold of "common humanity" through equating and universalizing human suffering of loss. But I would argue that the film's narrative – instead of embracing a universal human condition – actually shows how dangerous it is to use the language of ethics and "common humanity" in the context of survival and responsibility for mass atrocities. For it seems, such "commonality" rests on the appropriation of the experience of the victim, for the defense of the perpetrators and those who aided them. And ultimately, by erasing politics and the specificity of the context, such language sustains denial and Othering.

Notes

Different people have commented during different stages of my work on this chapter: my NIAS "Balkans" group, as well as a number of NIAS fellows 2011–2012 who joined the viewing of the miniseries in Wassenaar and the subsequent discussion. I have received more substantial comments from Erna Rijsdijk, Rema Hammami, Marlies Glasius and Dino Abazović. I am very grateful to all of them, as well as to NIAS for a chance to work on this project. All the limitations of the chapter remain, of course, mine alone.

1. Such as Spanish *Comanche Territory* (1997, Gerardo Herrero), Polish *Demons of War* (1998, Władysław Pasikowski), Pakistani TV mini-series *Alpha Bravo Charlie* (1998, Shoaib Mansoor), and documentaries about Kenyan and Portugese peacekeepers, respectively: Thomas Balmes', *Bosnia Hotel: Kenyan Warriors in Bosnia* (1997); Joaquim Sapinho's *Bosnia Diaries* (2005).
2. British have also produced a short (two episodes) TV drama series *Warriors* (screened on BBC One in 1999) directed by Peter Kosminsky and written by Leigh Jackson. The series main plot follows massacre of Muslim population by Bosnian-Croat forces in little central-Bosnian village Ahmici. This was a region where British forces were stationed as UN peacekeepers. The miniseries deals with the consequences of the failure of Brits to prevent the massacre. See my analysis of the *Warriors* in Žarkov (2014) 'The Warriors': Cinematic Ontologies of Bosnian War' in *European Journal of Women's Studies*, 21(2): 180-193.
3. See Žarkov (2011), "Exposures and Invisibilities: Media, Masculinities and the Narratives of Wars in an Intersectional Perspective," in H. Lutz et al. (eds), *Celebrating Intersectionality*, Ashgate, 105–120.
4. Bakic-Hayden and Hayden (1992).
5. Maria Todorova (1997) has coined the term *Balkanism* to mark associations of primitivism, violence and masculinity in Western cultural and political representations of the Balkan region, its people, culture and history. For a critique of Balkanism in the representations and self-representations in the regional cinema, see Iordanova (1996, 2001, 2008), Slugan (n.d.), Pavicic (2010) and Marinkova (2010).
6. Literature that analyzes production of difference between the West and its multiple Others, in political and cultural discourses and in media, it is too vast to list here. Clearly, Said's Orientalism (1994, 2004) is a seminal work that inspired many feminist and other critical authors. This analysis, as noted, has received new impetus after the 2001 terror attacks on the United States and the ensuing "war on terror" and then again after revelations of torture of Iraqi prisoners by US prison guards in Abu Ghraib. The work particularly inspiring for this chapter that helped me reflect on symbolic meanings of space-place and space-time is by Shapiro (2007), Butler (2008), Heathershaw and Lambrach (2008), Springer (2011) and for the cinema, Jazairy (2009).

7. This is precisely what we see contemporarily happening in the ways ethics and humanity have become the ground of the "humanitarian interventions" into the "new wars". See for example Helen Dexter (2007), Anne Orford (2011) and Kimberly Hutchings (2011).

8. For invisibility of male victim of sexual violence in Yugoslav war see Žarkov (2007). For the US media on Abu Ghraib and US war casualties literature is too vast to list, so just a few references I found inspiring: Elizabeth Dauphinee (2007), Avery Gordon (2006) and Jared Sexton and Elizabeth Lee (2006).

9. Both mainstream and feminist literature on wars by which socialist Yugoslavia disintegrated is too huge to be listed here. It is also too diverse in the way it explains causes and dynamics of war. I have argued elsewhere that, while ethnicity has been an essential element of identity politics that led to violence, in itself neither ethnicity nor "ethnic hatreds" can be taken as causes of the violence. For some work with similar arguments, see the early studies of Gerrits (1992), Hayden (1996), Sofos (1996) and Cockburn (1998).

10. Supported by Serbia, economically, militarily and politically.

11. While Abazović (in this volume) writes more about the ethno-religious dynamics in producing identities, it is worth noting that within socialist Yugoslavia those two have met in the census category "Muslim", introduced in early 1970s. In the post-1990s war, the category "Muslim" was replaced by (or, sometimes, simultaneously used with) category "Bosniak".

12. See chapter by Abazović in this volume, Hayden (1996) for the relationship between physical and symbolic violence, and Žarkov (2007) for the role of the media.

13. I am grateful to Erna Rijsdijk for pointing out the difference between "safe haven" (which assumes certain level of peace already achieved) and "safe area" which needs consent of the "warring parties."

14. The Dutch Parliament approved the decision of the Cabinet to make Dutch troops available to UN forces engaged in peacekeeping in Bosnia in 1993. The decision was not uncontested: concerns and protests ranged from doubts that Dutch military was ready to take up a peacekeeping task, to questions about the definitions of the UN general mandates for peacekeeping, and specific mandates concerning the "safe areas".

15. Among the military forces led by Mladić, that took Srebrenica, was also the Scorpion paramilitary formation from Serbia. The tape of its members executing Muslim boys and men was broadcasted on Serbian TV in 2005, and was then used for prosecutions in the national war crime courts in Serbia, though as a singular event, not as a part of Srebrenica genocide. See: http://www.isn.ethz.ch/isn/Security-Watch/Articles/Detail/?ots591=4888caa0-b3db-1461–98b9-e20e7b9c13d4&lng=en&id=53124; Scorpions filmed and photographed their actions in other occasions too. See Petrovic (2014).

16. See ICTY "Facts about Srebrenica" http://www.icty.org/x/file/Outreach/view_from_hague/jit_srebrenica_en.pdf

17. For details used in this paragraph see also ICTY "Facts about Srebrenica".

18. The Dutch government was not the only one investigating Srebrenica. The UN Secretary General (1999) and French parliament (2001) requested inquiries too, the former acknowledging a certain level of UN responsibility, the latter lamenting French "failures" but pointing fingers at the UN and Dutch. Republika Srpska also ordered several inquiries and reports in the last

decade, but has been going back and forth in acknowledging the genocide and revising its acknowledgement. Serbia had a Parliamentary inquiry too.

19. NIOD report can be found at: http://www.srebrenica.nl/Pages/OOR/23/375. html

20. The quotation from the NIOD report (in Van der Berg, 2009, 3), refers to moral dilemma (to engage or not with Bosnian-Serb forces) and moral/political commitment to refugees, of the Dutch military and political leadership. This issue has been addressed by others too. Lt. Col P.J. de Vin (2008) writes about moral dilemma of Karremans when weighing whether to fight with the Bosnian-Serb military. Rijsdijk (2012) mentions a number of authors who approach Srebrenica as a moral or instrumentalist issue, and thus – as she rightly argues – essentially *depoliticize* the debate about responsibility.

21. See IKV, Mient Jan Faber, *Srebrenica. De genocide die niet werd voorkomen*, The Hague, March 2002; for other texts see van den Berg (2009; especially footnotes 17 and 18).

22. Bakker report can be found at: http://www.denederlandsegrondwet. nl/9353000/1/j9vvihlf299q0sr/vh8lnhrpmxvc

23. See Rijsdijk (2012) on speeches of Minister of Defense, Henk Kamp, in 2006 (113–114). Especially, his statement that "The Hague has learnt its lessons ...albeit at a high price for Dutchbat" and general referring to Srebrenica as "Dutch trauma" or "open war wound" (116) be it for the country's politics, government, soldiers, Ministry of Defense, or journalism – that is, everybody except the people of Srebrenica.

24. Rijsdijk (2012) gives an excellent critical review of different academic, media and political discourses, and Rijsdijk (2014) of Dutch political discourses on commemorating Srebrenica. See also an extensive review of books on Srebrenica by de Graaff (2006) who analyzes how is "Srebrenica trauma" addressed by different actors (Dutch politicians, academics and journalists, Dutchbat soldiers, survivors, etc).

25. See van den Berg (2009) especially, for a critical discussion on official political discourses as well as diverse attempts at communication and reconciliation between individual Dutchbat soldiers and survivors associations, organized by IKV.

26. This erasure of the actual victims and survivors of Srebrenica from Dutch media through the focus on the national trauma of shattered Dutch self-image was also obvious in my own investigation of Dutch dailies (Žarkov, 2002).

27. I would argue that reference to "impotence" in Gielt, Elands and Schoeman (2007) is not incidental, as my analysis (Žarkov, 2002) shows that it was not just Dutch nationhood, but specifically, Dutch masculinity, and especially military masculinity, that was perceived as failing in Srebrenica.

28. See ICTY "Facts about Srebrenica" http://www.icty.org/x/file/Outreach/view_ from_hague/jit_srebrenica_En.pdf. ICTY has prosecuted over 160 people for all war crimes perpetrated during the war. http://en.wikipedia.org/wiki/ List_of_people_indicted_in_the_International_Criminal_Tribunal_for_the_ former_Yugoslavia

29. The same is true for proving legal responsibility of the UN, as survivors' law suits so far have hit the wall of "UN immunity". See http://www.vandiepen. com/nl/srebrenica/detail/42-srebrenica-survivors-to-appeal-un-ruling.html.

See also Žarkov (2014) for an analysis of the treatment of the international actors within the international humanitarian and criminal legal system.

30. For details of the court case (LJN: BR5388, Gerechtshof's-Gravenhage, 200.020.174/01; English translation) see the following website: http://zoeken.rechtspraak.nl/detailpage.aspx?ljn=BR5388. See also http://www.ejiltalk.org/the-hague-court-of-appeal-on-dutchbat-at-srebrenica-part-1-a-narrow-finding-on-the-responsibilities-of-peacekeepers/

31. I thank Jeff Handmaker for pointing out that, from a legal point of view, this appeal makes sense as an element of regular procedure. But it was criticized nevertheless. See van den Berg (2009) and http://historiek.net/nieuws/algemeen/6602-staat-naar-hoge-raad-in-srebrenica-zaak

32. They wrote several screenplays in recent years about topics related to war and violent conflicts around the world. One is a forthcoming TV movie about Frans van Anraat, Dutch trader in chemicals used by Saddam Hussain against Iraqi Kurdish civilians in 1988. He was tried in the Netherlands and received 15 years of jail in 2005. A book by Arnold Karskens – *No regrets* (*Geen cent spijt*) – published in 2006 should serve as a basis for scenario. Another is a mini TV series *Eileen* (December 12 and 19, 2011; VPRO), about a young Dutch woman – Tanja Nijmeijer – who joined Columbian FARC guerillas (directed by Hanro Smitsman). In 2005 they wrote a scenario for a film about terrorist threat in Europe.

33. All quotations and paraphrasing in this paragraph are from the Jury's text of the Award. This can be found at: http://bulletin.lira.nl/Uitgave-17/Tekst-van-het-juryrapport-Lira-prijs-2005; translation from Dutch is mine, but when in doubt, I benefited from help of Marlies Glasius.

34. Each episode has a different title and indicates whose story is told. The first episode is called "Capital Offence: The Story of Ibro Hadžić".

35. The name of the episode is "Interrogation House: The Story of Darko Bokan". The title refers to both the ICTY where Ibro interrogates Bokan, and the house outside the Potočari compound where the killing and torture of Bosnian Muslim civilians (cynically called 'interrogations' by Bosnian-Serb forces) went on.

36. The episode offers "The Story of Georg Terhoef" with the main title in Dutch being "In de grond". The literal translation in English is "in the soil/ground", could be translated also as "in essence", "basically", but also as "at heart". Thus it could also refer to the bones in the ground of the mass grave site where Ibro looks for the remains of his family.

37. Unlike in UK made *Warriors* (1999), for example, where Bosnian characters are played by actors from the region speaking their mother tongue as well as English.

38. As to the name of the language, I follow in the steps of ex-Yugoslav authors such as Snjezana Kordic (2010) who argue that Serbian, Croatian, Bosniak and Montenegrian languages are actually one and the same – nationally and internationally called Serbo-Croatian – pulled apart by nationalist vigor.

39. See the additions to the DVD on sale – "making of *De Enclave*" – which includes interviews with cast and production team, where the claim of successful use of Serbo-Croatian language by Dutch actors is made.

40. The assumption is that Ibro left his wife and daughter because he went to Bosnia, after completing his jail sentence for hostage-taking, looking for the remains of his parental family. In this way, the narrative makes Ibro "choose"

the family that matters to him, and by default, the country that matters to him. This choice is yet another way in which Ibro is depicted as not belonging to the Dutch society. I suggest that the relationship between Ibro and his Dutch wife and daughter be read also in the context of Dutch debates about both "mixed marriages" and "bogus marriages". Given the inaptness of the female Dutch characters, it is not clear whether the film actually insinuates that only *such* Dutch women go out with foreigners, and whether only *such* Dutch women are then abandoned by their foreign husbands. But the warning is there anyway: marry a foreign man – a Balkan/Bosnian man? – and you and your children will be abandoned.

41. *Pretty Village, Pretty Flame* (1996; *Lepa sela lepo gore*; original title), Director: Srdjan Dragojević, Writers: Vanja Bulic (story), Srdjan Dragojević (dialogue); http://www.imdb.com/title/tt0116860/
42. This was certainly happening in a discussion at NIAS. The first reaction of some NIAS fellows who came to the "movie evening" when *De Encaleve* was shown was that of understanding and empathizing with the human torment of a reluctant perpetrator.
43. See also the text by Meulenbelt (1999).
44. Reflecting on "facts" and "fiction", it is possible that the character of Darko Bokan is modeled after Drazen Erdemovic, a member of Bosnian-Serb army who took part in Srebrenica genocide and was tried at ICTY. He openly expressed regrets for his role. See http://www.icty.org/sid/7686. However, in *De Enclave* we actually never hear Bokan expressing regrets for the crimes he did. Instead, we hear him crying over his own plight.
45. There are other accusations, too. Bakker Report (2003) mentions that, next to separating women and men, the Dutchbat drove in panic over refuges with military vehicles, and refused medical assistance to wounded local population (210–211). The role with photos taken by Dutchbat soldiers that documented some of the events in Potočari has been submitted to the Ministry of Defense, but has apparently disappeared. See among others de Graaff (2006).
46. Going back to "facts" and "fiction" the name Terhoef plays with the name of Joris Voorhoefe, who was Dutch Minister of Defense in 1995.
47. The same text appears at http://www.filmfestival.nl/nl/films/de-enclave and http://www.moviemeter.nl/film/33299
48. See for example: http://www.uitzendinggemist.nl/programmas/5343-de-enclave; http://www.filmfestival.nl/nl/films/de-enclave; and http://www.moviemeter.nl/film/33299
49. At: http://www.uitzendinggemist.nl/programmas/5343-de-enclave
50. At: http://www.a-film.nl/dvd/00008726/De-Enclave. Exactly the same text is also to be found at another quality films website: http://www.qualityfilmcollection.nl/film/00009181/1/enclave_de.html

References

Alexander, J. (1994). "Not Just (Any) *Body* Can be a Citizen: The Politics of Law, Sexuality and Postcoloniality in Trinidad and Tobago and the Bahamas", *Feminist Review*, 48, 5–23.

Arendt, H. (1963). *Eichmann in Jerusalem: The Banality of Evil*, New York: Viking Press.

Bakic-Hayden, Milica and Robert Hayden (1992). "Orientalist Variations on the Theme 'Balkans': Symbolic Geography in Recent Yugoslav Cultural Politics", *Slavic Review*, 51 (1), 1–16.

Bay, Lisa (2008). Changing Nationhood and Masculinity: Dutch Veterans of Peace Operations, MA Thesis, International Institute of Social Studies, The Hague.

Bourke, J. (1996). "Fragmentation, Fetishization and Men's Bodies in Britain", *Women, a Cultural Review*, 7 (3), 240–250.

Brandstrom, Annika and Sanneke Kuipers (2003). "From 'Normal Incidents' to Policy Crises: Understanding the selective Politicization of Policy Failures", *Government and Opposition*, 38 (3), 279–305.

Butler, Judith (2008). "Sexual Politics, Torture, and Secular Time", *The British Journal of Sociology*, 59 (1), 1–23.

Butler, Judith. (2006). *Precarious Life: The Power of Mourning and Violence*, London, New York: Verso.

Cockburn, C. (1998). *The Space between Us: Negotiating Gender and National Identities in Conflict*, London: Zed Books.

Cockburn, Cynthia and Dubravka Žarkov (eds) (2002). *The Postwar Moment: Militaries, Masculinities and International Peacekeeping*, London: Lawrence and Wishart.

Dauphinee, Elizabeth (2007). "The Politics of the Body in Pain: Reading the Ethics of Imagery", *Security Dialogues, Special Issue on Securitization, Militarization and Visual Culture in the Worlds of Post 9/11*, 38 (2), 139–155.

De Graaff, B.G.J. (2006). "Enclaves van leed en werkelijkheid; wiens trauma is 'Srebrenica' eigenlijk?" *BMGN Low Countries Historical Review*, 121 (1), 42–54.

De Leeuw, Mark (2002). "A Gentlemen's Agreement: Srebrenica in the Context of Dutch War History", in Cockburn and Žarkov, 162–182.

De Vin, J.P. (2008). *Srebrenica: The Impossible Choice of a Commander*, MA Thesis, US Marine Corps, Command and Staff College, Marine Corps University, Quantico, Virginia.

Dexter, Helen (2007). "The 'New War' on Terror, Cosmopolitanism and the 'Just War' Revival", *Government and Opposition*, 43 (1), 55–78.

Dudink, Stefan (2002). "The Unheroic Men of a Moral Nation: Masculinity and Nation in Modern Dutch History", in Cockburn & Žarkov, 146–161.

Gerrits, A.W.M. (1992). "Some Comments on the Civil War in Yugoslavia", *Helsinki Monitor*, 3 (1), 54–56.

Gielt, Algra, Martin Elands and Jan Rene Schoeman (2007). "The Media and the Public Image of Dutch Veterans from World War II to Srebrenica", *Armed Forces & Society*, 33, 397– 413.

Gordon, Avery, F. (2006). "Abu Ghraib: Imprisonment and the War on Terror", *Race & Class*, 48 (1), 42–59.

Haggith, Toby and Joanna Newman (2005). *Holocaust and the Moving Image: Representations in Film and Television since 1993*, London, New York: Wallflower Press.

Hayden, R. (1996). "Imagined Communities and Real Victims: Self-determination and Ethnic Cleansing in Yugoslavia", *American Ethnologist*, 23 (4), 1–19.

Heathershaw, John and Daniel Lambach (2008). "Introduction: Post-Conflict Spaces and Approaches to Statebuilding", *Journal of Intervention and Statebuilding*, 2 (3), 269–289.

Hutchings, Kimberly (2011). "Gendered Humanitarianism: Reconsidering the Ethics of War", in Christine Sylvester (ed.), *Experiencing War*, London & New York: Routledge, 28–41.

Iordanova, Dina (1996). "Conceptualizing the Balkans in the Film", *Slavic Review*, 55 (4), 882–890.

Iordanova, Dina (2001). *Cinema of Flames: Balkan Film, Culture, and the Media*, British Film Institute.

Iordanova, Dina (2008). "Intercultural Cinema and Balkan Hushed Histories", *New Review of Film and Television Studies*, 6 (1), 5–18.

Jazairy, El Hadi (2009). "Cinematic landscapes in Antonioni's *L'Avventura*", *Journal of Cultural Geography*, 26(3), 349–367,

Kordic, Snjezana (2010). *Jezik i nacionalizam*, Zagreb: Durieux.

Marinkova, Milena (2010). "Po-co-co Balkans: Dancing Bears and Lovesick Donkeys, Bouncing Mines and Ethnic Conflict in Two Films from the Region", *Third Text*, 24 (4), 457–469.

Messerschmidt, J. (1998) "Men Victimizing Men: The Case of Lynching, 1865–1900", in Bowker, Lee (ed.), *Masculinities and Violence*, ILL (IBL) copy Thousand Oaks, London, New Delhi: Sage, 125–149.

Meulenbelt, Anja (1999). "Sympathy for the Devil: Thinking about Victims and Perpetrators after Working in Serbia", in S. Sharratt and E. Kaschak (eds), *Assault on the Soul: Women in the Former Yugoslavia*, New York: Haworth Press, 153–160.

Orford, Anne (2011). "The Passions of Protection: Sovereign Authority and Humanitarian War", in Christine Sylvester (ed.), *Experiencing War*, London & New York: Routledge, 8–27.

Pavicic, Jurica (2010). "'Cinema of Normalization': Changes of Stylistic Model in Post-Yugoslav Cinema after the 1990", *Studies in Eastern European Cinema*, 1 (1), 43–55.

Petchesky, Rosalind (2005). "Rights of the Body and Perversions of War: Sexual Rights and Wrongs Ten Years Past Beijing", *International Social Science Journal*, 57 (2), 301–318.

Peteet, J. (2000). "Male Gender and Rituals of Resistance in the Palestinian Intifada: A Cultural Politics of Violence", in Ghoussoub & Sinclair-Webb (eds), *Imagined Masculinities. Male Identity and Culture in the Modern Middle East*, London: Al Saqi Books, 103–126.

Petrovic, Vladimir (2014). "A Crack in the Wall of Denial. The *Scorpions* Video in and out of the Serbian Courtrooms", in Žarkov, Dubravka and Marlies Glasius (eds), *Narratives of Justice in and out of the Courtroom. Former Yugoslavia and Beyond*, Cham: Springer, 89–109.

Razack, Sherene (2004). *Dark Threats and White Knights: The Somalia Affair, Peacekeeping and the New Imperialism*. University of Toronto Press.

Rijsdijk, Erna (2003). "Srebrenica, genocide en de reterritorialisering van international verantwoordelijkheid", in *Vrede en Veiligheid*, 32 (3), 303–320.

Rijsdijk, Erna (2012). *Lost in Srebrenica, Responsibility and Subjectivity in the Reconstructions of a Failed Peacekeeping mission*, PhD Thesis, Vrije Universiteit Amsterdam.

Rijsdijk, Erna (2014). "'Forever connected': State narratives and the Dutch memory of Srebrenica", in Žarkov, Dubravka and Marlies Glasius (eds)

Narratives of Justice in and out of the Courtroom. Former Yugoslavia and Beyond, Cham: Springer, 131–146

Said, Edward (1994). *Orientalism*, New York: Vintage Books.

Said, Edward (2004). "Orientalism Once More", *Development and Change*, 35(5), 869–879.

Schiebinger, L. (1999). "Theories of Gender and Race", in Price Janet and Margrit Shildrick (eds) *Feminist Theory and the Body: A Reader*, Edinburgh University Press, 21–31.

Sexton, Jared and Elizabeth, Lee (2006). "Figuring the Prison: Prerequisites of Torture at Abu Ghraib", *Antipode*, 1005–1022.

Shapiro, M.J. (2007). "The New Violent Cartography", *Security Dialogue*, 38 (3), 291–313.

Sion, Liora (2006) "'Too Sweet and Innocent for War?': Dutch Peacekeepers and the Use of Violence", *Armed Forces & Society*, 32, 454–474.

Sion, Liora (2008) "Dutch Peacekeepers and Host Environments in the Balkans: An Ethnographic Perspective", *International Peacekeeping*, 15 (2), 201–213.

Slugan, Mario, "Some Methodological Concerns Regarding the Study of Balkanism in Cinema", at http://lucian.uchicago.edu/blogs/theslavicforum/files/2011/12/SLAVICFORUM_2011_SLUGAN_PUBLICATION.pdf

Sofos, S. (1996) "Inter-Ethnic Violence and Gendered Constructions of Ethnicity in FormerYugoslavia", *Social Identities*, 2 (1), 73–92.

Springer, Simon (2011). "Violence Sits in Places? Cultural Practice, Neoliberal Rationalizatism, and Virulent Imaginative Geographies", *Political Geography*, 30, 90–98.

Thanouli Elaftheria (2006) "Post-Classical Narration: A New Paradigm in Contemporary Cinema", *New Review of Film and Television Studies*, 4 (3), 183–196.

Todorova, Maria (1997) *Imagining the Balkans*, Oxford University Press.

Van der Berg, Dion (2009) "Rekindling the National Debate: How Public and Private Recognition Can Shift the Dutch Discourse on Srebrenica", article based on opening address at the "Transforming Images of the Enemy", Seminar in Utrecht, the Netherlands, October 8–9, 2009; forthcoming in Lucien van Liere and Klaas Spronk (eds), *Between Reconciliation and Enmity: Texts, Transformations, Best Practices*, Münster: Vit Verlag.

Žarkov, D. (2002) "'Srebrenica Trauma': Masculinity, Military and National Self-image in Dutch Daily Newspapers", in Cockbrun and Žarkov (eds), 183–203.

Žarkov, D. (2007). *The Body of War: Media, Ethnicity and Gender in the Break-up of Yugoslavia*, Durham and London: Duke University Press.

Žarkov, D. (2011). "Exposures and Invisibilities: Media, Masculinities and the Narratives of Wars in an Intersectional Perspective", in H. Lutz et al. (eds), *Celebrating Intersectionality*, Ashgate, 105–120.

Žarkov, D. (2014). "Ontologies of International Humanitarian and Criminal Law: 'Locals' and 'Internationals' in Discourses and Practices of Justice", in Žarkov, Dubravka and Marlies Glasius (eds), *Narratives of Justice in and out of the Courtroom. Former Yugoslavia and Beyond*, Cham: Springer, 3–21

Žarkov, D. (2014) "*The Warriors*: Cinematic Ontologies of Bosnian War", *European Journal of Women's Studies*, 21 (2), 180–193.

Documents

Bakker Report (2003) Tweede Kamer der Staten-Generaal, *Missie zonder Vrede* . *Parlementaire Enquête Srebrenica, rapport,* The Hague. Tweede Kamerstuk 28 506, nr. 3; at http://www.parlement.com/9291000/d/tk28506_3.pdf

French Government Report (2001). Assemblée National, *Srebrenica: rapport sur un massacre,* Paris.

NIOD Report (2002). *Srebrenica. Een 'veilig' gebied. Reconstructie, achtergronden, gevolgen en analyses van de val van een Safe Area,* Amsterdam.

United Nations Report (1999) *Srebrenica Report. Report of the Secretary-General Pursuant to General Assembly resolution 53/35 (1998).*

Filmography

De Enclave (2002) Screen-play by Alma Popeyus and Hein Schütz, directed by Willem van de Sande Bakhuyzen, Aired by Netherlands Public Broadcasting/ VARA.

Conclusions: Building on Regional Trends to Develop New Mechanisms for Political Change

Maria Koinova

This book steps out of the beaten path of a much discussed topic on how states in the Western Balkans can advance on the path to EU integration, despite a stalled political development and deep Euro crisis. It serves as a litmus test for the old patterns of political and social behavior in the Western Balkans and for the new patterns of change that emerge from within the region because of and despite the existing local and international institutions. The book attests to the need to look at the region beyond formal institutional arrangements, and to understand trends that are entrenched or organically emerge from within populations. It would be exaggerated to say that this book is about people's power, since the populations discussed here have not been captured in vigorous action, despite some protests more recently in Bosnia-Herzegovina. The book deploys its strengths by detecting the ideational, political, social and cultural signs of long-term healing from the wounds of the 1990s Yugoslavia wars, embedded in enduring political realities and seeking their ways to be channeled better into everyday life.

The first chapter by Marlies Glasius and Francesco Colona – "The Yugoslavia Tribunal: The Moving Targets of a Legal Theatre" – discusses the trajectory of the formation and functioning of the ICTY from the prism of perceptions and expectation of people who have worked in it, been close to it or have analyzed it academically. From its inception the tribunal was vested with high expectations to contribute to restoration of justice and peace, was believed by some to deliver on such expectations, but by others to possibly flounder, and was opposed by the Serbian public. While over time legal and policy experts exerted much effort to adjust the tribunal to local and international criteria, such criteria were often mutually exclusive and unbridgeable. Tribunal proceedings started being used to convey political messages to different publics. Beyond the legal function, the ICTY acquired a new one: to engage different publics through an unofficial script of a "theatre." Local and international agents acquired specific "roles," endowed with specific political and social meanings and expectations for performance. Prosecutors, judges, and defendants seem to not have been lacking self-awareness as "actors" in this process. Since the post-conflict publics continue to be polarized, and the ICTY is already having controversial but long-lasting effects on the region, its assessment – prompted by anticipation of a coming closure – needs to take place through the interpretation and understanding of these performativities.

The second chapter by Dino Abazović – "Reconciliation, Ethnopolitics, and Religion in Bosnia-Herzegovina" – speaks of other contradictions that need adequate bridging. From the outset of its existence since 1995 Bosnia-Herzegovina was constitutionally built as a unified state, but two entities were defined to constitute it – the Bosniak/Croat Federation and Republika Srpska – which are often antagonistic against each other. Democracy was supposed to be the new political regime where individual rights are affirmed, but de facto ethnic majoritarianism was legitimized through institutional structures. People developed a widespread belief that "reconciliation-as-forgiveness" is unacceptable, because perpetrators are left unpunished and the victims' needs are not met. The need to rebuild society is pressing, but the ways are not clear. Alternative pathways to reconciliation exist, most notably reconciliation as a political value and a political community. The author sees a special role for religious leaders, who have remained "eloquently silent" on controversial occasions, but who could step out of their silence, and launch a public dialogue. This could help affected individuals within their communities to publicly experience their own subjectivity and the internal empowerment they deserve.

The third chapter by Mitja Velikonja – "New Yugoslavism in Contemporary Popular Music in Slovenia" – is an analytical celebration of musical genres in Slovenia, mostly rock 'n' roll and pop music, through their messages about Yugoslavism. In Slovenia, a state that emerged out of socialist Yugoslavia in 1991 but made its way quickly into the European Union in 2004, the antipode of the self-image of "Slovenia" has been "Yugoslavia." The author worked through hundreds of musical entries and showed that despite deliberate attempts to dissociate from

Yugoslavia, Slovenian musical production gives life to its image. There is an interesting list of juxtaposed messages between the "Self" (Slovenia) and the "Other" (Yugoslavia). In this list Slovenia is considered in the present, in Europe and international organizations, where neoliberal capitalism reigns, where individualism, nationalism, and historical relativism are key, and where one needs to work hard and to conform. By contrast, Yugoslavia is all about the past, in the Balkans and related to non-aligned countries, where economic self-management reigns, where communitarianism, multi-cultural living (brotherhood and unity) and anti-Fascism are key, and where one does not need to work hard because of easy living in a welfare state, but needs to rebel. There is an appeal in this chapter that after more than 20 years of independent statehood, it is high time for Slovenia to integrate its Yugoslav past, which anyway already lives in the popular imagination as cool retro, rather than as old-fashioned nostalgia.

The fourth chapter by Vjekoslav Perica – "Heroes of a New Kind: Commemorations and Appropriations of Yugoslavia's Sporting and Pop-Cultural Heritage" – continues the discussion about legacies of former Yugoslavia over the selection, appropriation and redistribution of cultural property. Especially after the wars of disintegration of socialist Yugoslavia, the notion of heroism has been constructed around archetypal images of the warrior, the bandit, the guerilla-fighter and the martyr. Archetypes introduced by modernity – such as the scientist, sport and rock star, writer or film maker which emerged in socialist Yugoslavia – were pushed away by the nationalist elites during the past two decades. Yet currently the pantheon of heroes started to be depleted. Regular people start looking back into the Yugoslav past to claim sport, music and film stars as their current heroes. Such claims do not emerge alone from people of an "old generation" that remember socialist Yugoslavia, but by younger people making comments on Internet blogs, and by some diaspora as well. The author goes through the personal histories of eight people, whose star reputation whether when living or posthumously became a subject of this newly (re)constructed heroism: Mate Parlov (boxing), Mirza Delibašić (basketball), Dražen Petrović (basketball), Milan Mladenović (rock music), Margita "Magi" Stefanović (rock music), Branimir "Johnny" Štulić (rock music), Djordje Balašević (pop music), Emir Kusturica (film). The narrative discusses their different faiths, and among them the agreements of post-Yugoslav nations about personalities who did not buy into nationalism, and disagreements over others. Most notably, this chapter captures a sign of healing societies, the search for a discussion about the common hero that did not get credentials through nationalism, but through other worthy pursuits.

The fifth chapter by Maria Koinova – "Diasporas and Contextualized Transnationalism" – turns the attention to the ways in which the Dutch political context has influenced different transnational mobilization patterns among the migrants from the former Yugoslavia. Although the Dutch majority continues to view the "post-Yugoslav population" in monolithic terms, the author argues against such qualifications. Many migrants who identified as "Yugoslavs" when they arrived in the Netherlands as guest-workers in the 1970s or as refugees in the 1990s, have dissociated themselves from this overarching identity, and have become Bosniaks, Croats and Serbs during the wars of Yugoslavia's disintegration, when already on Dutch territory. During the 2000s the Dutch political context, and the presence of the ICTY in the Netherlands, provided different stimuli for transnational mobilization. A focal point for the mobilization of Bosniaks has been the failure of Dutch peacekeeping forces to protect the Srebrenica enclave in 1995, a theme that does not allow for healing of conflict-generated identities of both Dutch and foreigners. It fosters Bosniak's transnational mobilization through multiple channels, namely international institutions, the nation state, and through people-to-people connections. Such an underlying theme does not exist for the Croats and Serbs, where conflict-generated identities have subsided after the war's end, and have become politically less relevant. The author identifies a fourth group, who consider themselves "Yugoslavs," and who mobilize on an individual basis and primarily through international organizations. Against the findings of scholarly accounts arguing that "frozen" diaspora identities can be detrimental to conflict resolution, the author finds – much in agreement with Velikonja and Perica – that the frozen Yugoslav identity in the Netherlands is weak, is not very influential in transnational politics, but is good for reconciliation.

The final chapter by Dubravka Žarkov – "Cinematic Representations of the Bosnian War: *De Enclave* and the Ontologies of Unrecognizability" – focuses on the analysis of the Dutch TV miniseries "The Enclave," featuring the controversial Dutch peacekeeping involvement in Srebrenica. Consisting of three episodes, the series tells a story of a young Bosnian man – Ibro Hadzic – who was a translator for the peacekeeping forces when the city fell. The first episode presents him after eight years, working as a translator at the ICTY, where he recognizes a member of the Serbian military – Darko Bokan – responsible for taking his father and younger brother away. In the following episode Ibro takes Bokan as a hostage until he admits guilt. In the last episode, former Dutch Minister of Defense in the days of Srebrenica – George Terhoef – travels to Srebrenica with his family, and unexpectedly meets Ibro. Ibro sees

Terhoef and kidnaps his daughter. The series end with Terhoef finding his daughter unharmed, while Ibro kills himself. It is puzzling why the miniseries received a prestigious national award for a screenplay, but stirred little to no controversy in the Netherlands. The author finds the answer through the media analysis, pointing out that the film followed the official Dutch position on Srebrenica, and its denial of responsibility about the peace-keepers' failure to protect the enclave. Denial was cinematically introduced through the production of unreconcilable and unrecognizable ontologies for the main protagonists and for the places they come from and belong to. For example, Ibro was presented as violent, with unsettled masculinity, unable to cope with realities and seeking revenge. Cinematic "flashbacks" introduced disturbing chaotic pictures about the Balkans, and colorful tranquil pictures about the Netherlands. Dutch actors were invited to play Ibro and Darko, despite their linguistic inadequacies with Bosnian/Serbian/Croatian. The TV audience was not invited to identify with them, but with Terhoef, his professional and moral dilemmas and suffering as a father. In short, this chapter closes the book by showing that trauma and denial of responsibility take place in different political and social contexts, and that post-conflict reconciliation needs to be also a subject of conscious choices by foreign governments.

While the European Union and other international institutions – apart from the ICTY – have not been central to this discussion, this book speaks to policy makers dealing with such institutions, and extends three lines of suggestions for change.

So far, the ICTY proceedings have been largely incorporated into the EU enlargement policy for the Western Balkans, but both domestic and diaspora populations have questioned the legitimacy of the processes, and the excessive length of trials, as Glasius and Colona's contribution demonstrated. Some verdicts have even empowered current national leaders with questionable war record to acquire a veneer of heroes in their countries of origin, as Perica and Koinova mentioned. While further assessment of the ICTY will require more research and analysis especially after its closing, it is worthwhile for EU policy makers at this stage to think of the political implications of ICTY's verdicts on a case-by-case basis, and to avoid cookie-cutter approaches to further policy development based on "compliance with the ICTY." Ticking the box of "compliance" does not mean that a country has increased its democratic record. It could have increased its nationalist record by empowering nationalist leaders as well. In this vein, and with regard to other criminal tribunals and other world regions, it is worth thinking as to whether their legal proceedings need not be clearly separated from processes aspiring to foster political change.

The second major suggestion is to seek new actors and themes that strike a positive cord in the Western Balkans, but have been beyond the radar screen of policy makers. Abazović suggested thinking of engaging religious leaders more actively in reconciliation processes, since they often command more authority than other local or international elites. Working with diasporas to transform their conflict-generated identities and foster political and social development across borders would be another venue, a suggestion flowing from Koinova's contribution. Velikonja and Perica pointed to the new interpretation of "Yugoslavia" in cultural production and symbol creation, organically developing from within the countries of the former Yugoslavia. Instead of viewing cultural production about "Yugoslavia" only as nostalgia for the past, policy makers could seek to foster the appropriation and re-appropriation of common symbols belonging to Yugoslavia, hence fostering a reconciled post-Yugoslav space, even if initially in symbolic terms.

The third major implication of this book for policy makers is to look beyond the dichotomy between "us" in the EU and "them" in the Western Balkans, in order to understand how issues are intertwined and to seek new approaches to tackle them effectively. Koinova and Žarkov pointed out that political reconciliation is not simply to be demanded from vulnerable populations, but needs to be addressed in Western capitals as well. Beyond the radar screen of policy makers zooming into EU enlargement are some war-related traumas and contentious political issues taking place in the Netherlands and possibly in other Western European countries, which bind them with traumatized populations whether in the Balkans or far beyond their territories. Hence, a natural conclusion is that new mechanisms need to be developed to address issues that are clearly intertwined.

Index

Printed and bound by CPI Group (UK) Ltd, Croydon, CR0 4YY